THE OLMECS

RICHARD A. DIEHL

THE OLMECS
America's First Civilization

With 152 illustrations, 20 in color

THIS IS VOLUME ONE HUNDRED AND TWELVE IN THE SERIES
Ancient Peoples and Places
FOUNDING EDITOR: GLYN DANIEL

This book is dedicated to Michael D. Coe and to the memory of
Sophie Dobzhansky Coe, my guides down the Olmec Road.

Frontispiece Jade Olmec maskette. This small ornament was at least 2,000
years old when Aztecs reverentially included it in a buried offering at the
principal temple at their capital Tenochtitlán, AD 1470. Ht 10.2 cm (4 in).

First published in the United Kingdom in 2004 by
Thames & Hudson Ltd, 181A High Holborn, London WC1V 7QX

www.thamesandhudson.com

British Library Cataloguing-in-Publication Data
A catalogue record for this book is available from the British Library

ISBN 0-500-28503-9

Printed and bound in China by Midas Publishing (HK) Ltd

Contents

Preface

The Olmecs are one of antiquity's most mysterious, fascinating, poorly understood, and controversial civilizations. In this book I attempt to clear up some of the mysteries, convey the fascinations, correct the misunderstandings, and describe the controversies. With regard to the controversies, I must warn the reader that I am not an impartial judge and I have strong opinions concerning many of them. I hope I have presented the data and every reasonable interpretation of them in sufficient detail for the interested reader to trace the arguments back to their sources and draw his or her own conclusions. I also realize that tomorrow's research may overturn many of my interpretations and conclusions.

The origins of this book go back to 1964 when Michael D. Coe invited me to participate in his Yale University Río Chiquito Archaeological-Ecological Project. At the time I was a graduate student pursuing my Ph.D. degree in anthropology and Mexican archaeology at Pennsylvania State University. Coe planned to excavate the virtually unknown Olmec center of San Lorenzo and ultimately answer some of the great questions about the origins of Mesoamerican civilization. I still marvel at the truly incredible opportunity that somehow fell into my lap. I had just finished four seasons of field training and research at the giant ancient metropolis of Teotihuacan outside Mexico City and longed to gain experience in another region and ancient culture. My move from the arid Mexican highlands to the lush, sweltering lowlands on the banks of the Coatzacoalcos river provided the framework for my doctoral dissertation and also sparked a life-long love of things Olmec. My career has led me down some wonderful if unpredictable paths in the past forty years but I always return to the Gulf coast lowlands and the Olmecs. This book is a distillation of what I have learned since then. I hope it instructs and entertains.

Since I began working on the manuscript ten years ago I have discussed its contents with many people. They all gave freely of their knowledge and advice. They include Philip J. Arnold III, Elizabeth P. Benson, Francisco "Paco" Beverido, Beatriz de la Fuente, David Freidel, Susan Gillespie, Rebecca González Lauck, Gillett Griffin, David C. Grove, Barbara Kerr, Justin Kerr, G. Ray Krotser, Robert P. Kruger, Sara Ladrón de Guevara, Roberto Lunagómez, Christine Niederberger, Ponciano Ortíz C., John

Pohl, Mary E. D. Pohl, María del Carmen Rodríguez, Robert S. Santley, Barbara L. Stark, Stacey Symonds, Karl Taube, and Sergio Vásquez Zárate. Portions of the manuscript were read by John E. Clark, Robert Cobean, Ann Cyphers, Peter D. Joralemon, Thomas W. Killion, Mary Pohl, Christopher A. Pool, Kevin O. Pope, F. Kent Reilly III, Javier Urcid, and Marcus Winter. My friend and mentor Michael D. Coe read the entire manuscript. I thank all of them and ask their forbearance if I failed to follow their advice on occasion. I owe very special debts of gratitude to my wife Sue Scott and to the staff of Thames & Hudson. Without their support and understanding I would never have completed the manuscript.

If Aztec sages knew about their Olmec predecessors, they never passed that information on to the Spaniards who recorded their legends and myths. Furthermore, although we now know the Olmecs had a writing system, no complete texts, historical or otherwise, have survived. Thus everything we know about them comes from investigations by archaeologists, art historians, linguists, and other scholars. The Olmec story told in this book is an "undocumented history," an account of people who left no recorded history, constructed on the basis of what scholars have learned in the past sixty-five years.

Archaeologists divide Mesoamerica's pre-Columbian past into five major epochs: the Paleo-Indian, Archaic, Formative (or Preclassic), Classic, and Postclassic periods. Radiocarbon dating and cross-dating with sites in other parts of Mesoamerica firmly anchor Olmec culture to the Early and Middle Formative periods (1800–300 BC). At one time scholars believed the Formative period was an era of village farmers living in egalitarian societies following what Old World prehistorians call a "Neolithic" way of life. Today we realize that the Olmecs and some of their contemporaries lived in societies too large and complex to be considered simple village farmer folk. Nevertheless, intellectual traditions are hard to break and names even harder to change, thus the terms Formative and Preclassic continue in use today. In one sense Formative is really quite appropriate because, as we shall see, the Olmecs truly were a formative phenomenon, the Mother Culture that underlay later civilizations.

Olmec civilization itself can be subdivided into four stages, pre-, Early, Late, and Epi-Olmec. The last three stages are defined by the rise and fall of three great Olmec centers, San Lorenzo, La Venta, and Tres Zapotes. Of course, Olmec history was much more complex than any simplified scheme like this might suggest. For example, early La Venta overlapped with San Lorenzo and although San Lorenzo was abandoned for a time during La Venta's prominence, it reemerged as a minor local center during the latter stages of La Venta's florescence. Even the history of Tres Zapotes turns out to be much more complicated than previously realized. Finally, and perhaps most seriously of all, many large Olmec archaeological sites lie undisturbed beneath cattle pastures and jungles. A few of these sites are mentioned in Chapters 2 and 3, but others remain completely unknown to modern

CHRONOLOGICAL TABLE

	Olmec stages	OLMEC HEARTLAND			Chalcat-zingo	Basin of Mexico	Oaxaca Valley	Pacific Coast SE	Chal-chuapa	Copán
		San Lorenzo	La Venta	Tres Zapotes						
AD 400	Epi-Olmec						Monte Albán II			
BC–AD										
400 BC							Monte Albán I			
500	Late Olmec	Palangana	Late La Venta	Hueyapan	Late Cantera			Escalón	Kal	Bosque
600			Middle La Venta	Tres Zapotes	Early Cantera	Zacatenco	Rosario	Late Conchas	Colos	Uir
700		Nacaste			Late Barranca	Tetelpan	Guadalupe	Early Conchas		
800			Early La Venta					Jocotal		
900	Early Olmec	San Lorenzo		Early Formative	Middle Barranca	Manantial	San José	Cuadros	Tok	Gordon
1000					Early Barranca	Ayotla		Cherla		Plata
1100								Ocós		
1200		Chichárras			Late Amate		Tierras Largas			Rayo
1300		Bajío	Barí		Early Amate	Nevada		Locona		
1400		Ojochí								
1500	Pre-Olmec							Barra		
1600							Espiridión	?		
1700										
1800										
1900										
2000							Martinez	Chantuto B		
						Zohapilco				
2500							Blanca			

9

archaeology. Thus Olmec history resembles a story for which we have only a few chapter headings and text fragments. Future investigations will surely reveal a vastly richer and more dynamic story than that related in this book.

Olmec chronology is based entirely upon radiocarbon determinations. Olmec scholars do not normally calibrate their radiocarbon readings to correct for deviations from true calendar dates as is the custom in many other parts of the world, and this book continues that convention. I justify this flouting of modern archaeological practice by observing that we have so few radiocarbon determinations for the critical points in Olmec history that to calibrate them would appear to lend them more validity than they merit. I prefer to continue to use our "old-fashioned" three-century blocks of time, periods that are supported by the existing radiocarbon dates, until we are better equipped to inject fine nuances into our history.

1 · Introduction

To most people the term "Olmec" evokes visions of gigantic stone heads that are both startlingly realistic and awe-inspiring, symbols of an ancient culture staring into the twenty-first century across a chasm of 3,000 years. However, thanks to the efforts of a small cadre of Mexican and North American archaeologists, the creators of these sculptures are no longer the mysterious race that baffled both scientists and the public even sixty years ago. Recent efforts have revealed the broad outlines of the Olmec culture that flourished in southeastern Mexico's Gulf lowlands between 1500 and 400 BC as well as many details of life during this pivotal period of American Indian history. Today we know that Olmec culture was the earliest civilization in Mesoamerica (central and southern Mexico and northern Central America), and one of only six pristine civilizations in human history.

1, 2

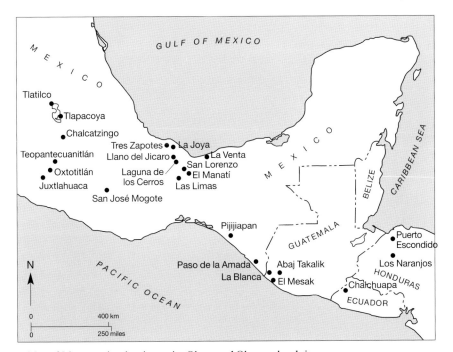

1 Map of Mesoamerica showing major Olmec and Olmec-related sites.

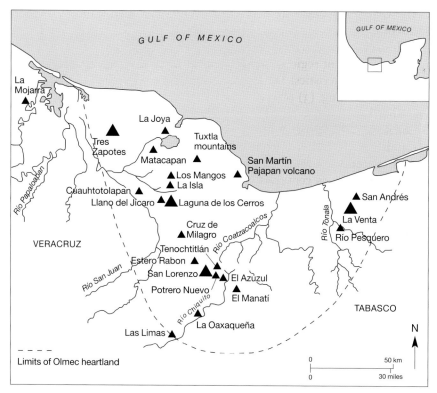

2 Map of the Olmec heartland (Olman) showing archaeological sites discussed in the text.

Pristine civilizations were the earliest civilizations in their respective regions, cultures that developed *sui generis* without any older models to guide their development. They include Egyptian and Sumerian cultures in the Near East, Indus civilization in modern India and Pakistan, China's Shang culture, and Chavin culture in Peru. The fact that the Olmecs were the only one that evolved in a lowland tropical forest environment makes them an important case study in the evolution of civilization.

Today the Olmecs are best known for their accomplishments in the sculptural arts, particularly their spectacular large stone monuments and exquisite small objects carved from jadeite and other semi-precious stones. In addition to being master artisans, Olmecs were the first Native Americans to erect large architectural complexes, live in nucleated towns and cities, and develop a sophisticated art style executed in stone and other imperishable media. These traits reflect the complex social, political, economic, and religious institutions that led archaeologist Michael D. Coe to proclaim the Olmecs America's First Civilization and Mesoamerica's Mother Culture, the template for all later civilizations in Mexico and Central America.[1] While not every archaeologist agrees with Coe, as we shall see, the mounting evidence in favor of it has convinced almost everyone but the most die-hard opponents.

By what criteria may we consider the Olmecs a "civilization"? French archaeologist Christine Niederberger maintains that civilizations, including the Mesoamerican variants, came into existence with the rise of cities that served as centers of regional integration.[2] According to Niederberger, cities share six characteristics: (1) elaborated political and religious power, (2) clear social ranking, (3) planned public architecture, (4) a group of highly specialized craftspersons, (5) control and active participation in inter-regional trade networks, and (6) complex intellectual achievements such as a sophisticated, codified iconography for the permanent recording of certain concepts or events. San Lorenzo, the earliest Olmec city, exhibited these characteristics centuries before they appeared anywhere else in the Americas.

Who were these Olmecs? Although archaeologists have debated the finer points of this question for sixty years, for our purposes we will simply define them as the inhabitants of Mexico's south Gulf coast lowlands during the period 1500–400 BC. While many distinct Olmec societies existed in the region during that era, all shared certain cultural practices and a distinctive art style we call Olmec.

Virtually no Olmec skeletons survive in the acid tropical soils of Olman, the portion of southern Veracruz and Tabasco occupied by the Olmecs, thus their physical appearance remains a mystery. However, Olmec artists occasionally created realistic depictions of their fellow citizens in art. These renderings depict people similar in appearance to modern indigenous inhabitants of Olman, with short, squat muscular bodies, short wide noses, epicanthic folds that give the eyes an oriental cast, fleshy mouths with thick, at times down-turned, lips, short necks, and straight black hair. We cannot identify their language or languages with certainty. Linguists Lyle Campbell and Terrence Kaufman believe the Olmecs spoke proto-Mixe-Zoquean languages related to modern Popoluca dialects still heard in the region today. Other authorities question this attribution, suggesting that the Olmecs spoke proto-Mayan or some other language.[3] In any case, it is unlikely that all of Olman's inhabitants spoke the same dialect or even the same language. Mesoamerica has always been a linguistic mosaic where speakers of mutually unintelligible tongues lived cheek by jowl in the same region, and the same surely was true of the Olmecs.

The origins of Olmec culture have intrigued scholars and lay people alike since Tres Zapotes Colossal Head 1, a gigantic stone human head with vaguely Negroid features, was discovered in Veracruz 140 years ago.[4] Since that time, Olmec culture and art have been attributed to seafaring Africans, Egyptians, Nubians, Phoenicians, Atlanteans, Japanese, Chinese, and other ancient wanderers. As often happens, the truth is infinitely more logical, if less romantic: the Olmecs were Native Americans who created a unique culture in southeastern Mexico's Isthmus of Tehuantepec. Archaeologists now trace Olmec origins back to pre-Olmec cultures in the region and there is no credible evidence for major intrusions from the outside. Furthermore,

3

not a single *bona fide* artifact of Old World origin has ever appeared in an Olmec archaeological site, or for that matter anywhere else in Mesoamerica.

We do not know what these people called themselves, or if they even had a term that encompassed all the inhabitants of Olman. There is no evidence that they formed a single unified ethnic group, and almost certainly no Olmec considered people living more than a few hours' walk away as members of his or her own group. Nevertheless, the numerous independent local cultures were so similar to one another that modern scientists consider them a single generic culture. When the Spaniards arrived in Mexico, the Nahuatl-speaking Aztecs called the inhabitants of Olman the *Olmeca-Huixtotin* (Olmeca: inhabitant of the Rubber Country; Huixtotin: People of the Saltwater). Although the Olmeca-Huixtotin lacked any direct connection with their Formative-period predecessors, early archaeologists mistakenly applied the term Olmec to the remains of both cultures. Today it remains the accepted name of choice for the Formative-period cultures, despite occasional attempts to replace it with one that is less confusing.

3 Matthew W. Stirling measuring Tres Zapotes Colossal Head 1 (ht 147 cm/ 57 in, estimated weight 7.8 tons) after clearing it in 1939. This photograph and others like it in the *National Geographic* magazine brought Olmec culture and its achievements to the attention of the modern world in the 1940s.

Olmec studies: a short history

When Olmec objects first appeared in European and Mexican antiquities collections in the nineteenth century, they were incorrectly attributed to the Aztecs, the Maya, or even the Chinese.[5] It was not until 1932 that George C. Vaillant of the American Museum of Natural History correctly identified their great age and their connection with southern Mexico's Gulf lowlands. Seven years later Matthew W. Stirling initiated a seven-year campaign of pioneering investigations on Olmec and related sites in Veracruz, Tabasco, and Chiapas designed to reveal Olmec civilization and locate it in time and space. His approach was to investigate systematically every archaeological site known to contain Colossal Heads or other Olmec-style stone sculptures. With the support of the Smithsonian Institution and the National Geographic Society, Stirling, his wife Marion, photographer Richard Stewart, and archaeologist Philip Drucker conducted excavations at Tres Zapotes, Cerro de las Mesas, La Venta, Izapa, and San Lorenzo.

Cerro de las Mesas and Izapa proved to post-date Olmec times, but Tres Zapotes, La Venta, and San Lorenzo yielded scores of Olmec sculptures and spectacular small offerings placed beneath plazas and buildings. Stirling and his colleagues defined the geographical limits of Olmec culture as we know them today, but had no way to determine accurately the age of Olmec culture. Stirling believed the Olmecs preceded the great Classic-period civilizations of Teotihuacan and the Maya, while Drucker argued that all three were contemporaries. Most archaeologists agreed with Drucker, arguing that such sophisticated architecture, sculpture, and art could not have existed prior to the Classic period. The famous Mayanist J. E. S. Thompson even relegated Olmec culture to the Postclassic period after the Classic centers had collapsed!

The true age of Olmec civilization was finally resolved when University of California-Berkeley archaeologists Robert Heizer, Philip Drucker, and Robert Squier returned to La Venta in 1955. The Berkeley team focused on the architectural history of Complex A, the ceremonial precinct north of La Venta's Great Pyramid where Stirling and his colleagues had uncovered unusual buried earth constructions and spectacular offerings of jade and other exotic goods. Their careful excavations revealed four construction phases containing charcoal fragments that allowed them to date the occupations using the newly perfected technique of radiocarbon dating. Many archaeologists were shocked when the radiocarbon determinations revealed that Stirling had been correct all along and that La Venta emerged as a thriving community by 800 BC and was abandoned in the fifth century BC, 700 years before the Classic period even began.

The focus of Olmec studies shifted to San Lorenzo and the Río Chiquito, an arm of the Coatzacoalcos river, when Michael D. Coe and his colleagues began work in the region in 1966. San Lorenzo had attracted the attention of Stirling and his wife Marion in 1945 when they heard rumors about a giant stone eye peering out of the ground near the recently established village of

4

4 Michael D. Coe excavating San Lorenzo Monument 34 on the Group D Ridge in 1967. The head and arms were never located.

pl. VI Tenochtitlán. A quick trip to the site verified that the eye belonged to an Olmec Colossal Head. The Stirlings returned the next year along with Philip Drucker and Richard Stewart and in a period of a few months uncovered more than twenty stone monuments, including the five largest and best-preserved Colossal Heads known.

Stirling's inability to date the San Lorenzo sculptures and the Olmec culture that created them was a problem that had intrigued Coe ever since his student days at Harvard. He suspected that the San Lorenzo heads were older than those of La Venta and Tres Zapotes, even though they were better carved and more sophisticated. But, how could he prove it? He organized the Yale University Río Chiquito Archaeological-Ecological Project to test his ideas and shed light on the origins of Olmec culture. The excavations, surveys, and mapping projects carried out between 1966 and 1968 established the first firmly dated Olmec ceramic sequence and first complete map for any ancient Olmec center, and revealed numerous stone monuments in contexts that allowed us to date their abandonment. It also yielded important information on San Lorenzo's architectural history and detailed studies of every major class of artifact recovered in the excavations. In the realm of ethnography and ethnoarchaeology it produced the only comprehensive study of a modern Jarocho Veracruz farming community, documenting modern rural life and land use as an aid to understanding ancient lifeways.

At the end of the Yale project San Lorenzo was left untouched (except for the occasional looter) until 1991 when Ann Cyphers opened a new round of investigations under the auspices of Mexico's National Autonomous University (UNAM). The final publications of her project are just beginning to appear in print and the first two have already relegated some of my most cherished beliefs to the realm of "what I once thought I knew," and future volumes probably will do the same. On the other hand, I am not convinced that every claim made by the UNAM project will be substantiated without renewed field investigations in the years to come.

La Venta's modern history is interwoven with the story of Petroleos Mexicanos (PEMEX), Mexico's national oil company. The La Venta ridge caps an upward-pushing salt dome, a sure indication of buried oil deposits. Foreign oil company geologists were already exploring the region when Frans Blom and Oliver La Farge, the first modern scientists to visit La Venta, arrived in 1926. By the time Stirling and Drucker began their pioneering excavations fourteen years later, the pace of exploration had increased, culminating with construction of a PEMEX refinery on the edge of the ridge in the late 1950s. That facility and the town that grew up around it inflicted tremendous damage on the archaeological site. Mounds were destroyed to create an aircraft landing field, while bulldozers leveled the summit of the Great Pyramid to create a park complete with an aviation windsock and a thriving red light district at its base. Tabasco's renowned poet Carlos Pellicer managed to rescue the largest and most spectacular sculptures by moving them to an open-air sculpture garden in the state capital at Villahermosa.

In the late 1960s Heizer and Drucker returned to La Venta with Berkeley students to conduct limited investigations that clarified many problems and provided important new information on that site. They also alerted the archaeological world to the ongoing destruction of the site. Unfortunately, the Yale and Berkeley projects marked the end of major fieldwork in Olmec country for nearly twenty years. A few small excavations were carried out at Tres Zapotes and La Venta in the 1970s, but in general looters were much more active in the region than professional archaeologists. As the national and international markets for Olmec pottery, figurines, sculptures, and jades grew rapidly, local farmers and professional treasure hunters responded by ransacking Olmec sites for objects to sell. The clandestine digging continues largely unabated today, destroying archaeological sites while feeding the growing body of unprovenanced Olmec objects that fill museums and private collections, stripped of their historical value.

Protests from both archaeologists and the public failed to halt the destruction of La Venta until the Instituto de Cultura de Tabasco and INAH ('Instituto Nacional de Antropología e Historia') managed to create a protected archaeological zone in 1986. The state of Tabasco purchased the 100+ ha (250-acre) core of the site, fenced it in, removed the houses, created walking paths, and placed replicas of stone monuments on the original find spots. Honky-tonks where refinery workers and visiting archaeologists once drank cold beer with hardworking young ladies gave way to a museum and visitor center. These efforts saved an irreplaceable piece of the world's cultural heritage from certain oblivion.

After Stirling and his crew left Tres Zapotes in 1941, it lay untouched for thirty years until a young Mexican student named Ponciano Ortíz C. excavated a few small test pits. He hoped to establish a reliable chronology for the site, something that Stirling's investigations had failed to do for reasons too complex to go into here. Suffice it to say that Ortíz succeeded in creating a ceramic chronology based on changes in pottery designs, forms, and pastes through time. After his work at Tres Zapotes, Ortíz went on to study other sites in the region, including El Manatí, of which we will have more to say below.

While archaeologists were delving into Olmec sites, art historians and anthropologists turned their attention to Olmec art and iconography. Miguel Covarrubias, a Mexican artist and *aficionado* of pre-Columbian art, laid the foundation for this field in the 1940s. His exquisite descriptions and illustrations of many small Olmec objects, including many that he purchased for his outstanding personal collection and today may be seen in Mexico's National Museum of Anthropology, brought Olmec art to the attention of both archaeologists and connoisseurs. His early insights into the nature of the Olmec style and its antiquity remain as valid today as they were sixty years ago. Beatriz de la Fuente and Elizabeth Benson carried forward the Covarrubias tradition after his early death in 1957, and continue to provide leadership in the field of Olmec art into the new millennium. Meanwhile Michael D. Coe and his students, especially Peter D. Joralemon and Karl Taube, have led the way in deciphering Olmec religion as reflected in the art, as major figures in what has been called the Yale School of Olmec Iconography.

The Olmec world

The Olmec world consisted of three environments: a physical realm of plants, animals, land, and water; a human environment of villages and towns scattered across Olman and the rest of Mesoamerica; and a spiritual world that controlled the other two. The spirit world, shadowy and "unreal" as it may seem to us, was as real as maize seeds, jaguars, and human enemies were for the Olmecs. Here we will examine the physical setting for Olmec culture, leaving the human and supernatural environments for subsequent chapters.

Fray Bernardino de Sahagún, the great Spanish chronicler of sixteenth-century Mexico, queried his Aztec informants about the lands and people of southern Veracruz and Tabasco. They responded that it was called *Olman*, "The Rubber Country" or *Tlalocan*, "Place of Wealth," and that "These [Olmeca-Huixtotin, the inhabitants] were rich; their home, their land, was really a land of riches, a land of flowers, a land of wealth, a land of abundance."[6] The more nautical-minded Spaniards christened it the *Sotavento* ("Leeward Coast"), a term still heard today in the region. The actual area included in Aztec Olman is unclear, but probably encompassed 10,000 sq. km (3,860 sq. miles), including the Papaloapan, Coatzacoalcos, and Tonalá river basins as well as the volcanic Tuxtla mountains that loom over them like a gigantic Mesoamerican temple base surrounded by lowland river valleys.

Although most archaeologists equate the ancient Olmec territory with Aztec Olman, some believe that the Formative-period inhabitants of the Tuxtla mountains did not participate fully in Olmec culture. Recent investigations here have failed to reveal evidence for large settlements, complex

5 The Tuxtla mountains provided the Olmecs with basalt and special clays for ceramics.

societies, monumental sculpture and art, and regular contact with the greater Mesoamerican world. Although Olmec sculptors employed basalt that originated in the mountains, their raw material may have been boulders that washed down to the piedmont below the volcanoes. Even Tres Zapotes, long considered a first-line Olmec center located on the western slopes of the Tuxtlas, was only a minor village prior to the demise of Olmec culture at 400 BC. Thus the true Olmec core zone was restricted to the Coatzacoalcos and Tonalá river basins and the adjacent foothills south and east of the Tuxtlas.

This heartland extended from the Gulf of Mexico to the crests of the sierras (mountains) of Oaxaca and Chiapas, and the Isthmus of Tehuantepec on the south. The sierras have always posed formidable barriers to human travel, channeling it into steep canyons filled with fast-running, unnavigable rivers, while the low hills of the Isthmus could be traversed as easily in antiquity as they are by highways and railroads today. The environment varies from one part of Olman to another, but the entire region is hot, humid, and blessed with plentiful plant and animal life. Elevations are so low that crop-damaging frosts are unknown. Temperatures rarely fall below 20° C (68° F) or exceed 30° C (86° F). These relatively high values, combined with almost constant high relative humidity and low evaporation rates, lead to frequent complaints about the heat by locals as well as visitors from the temperate zones. Rainfall is abundant and both standing and running water appears everywhere. The mountains facing the Gulf of Mexico receive extraordinary quantities of rainfall. Most precipitation falls between May and November, the traditional wet months of Mesoamerica's lowlands, but *nortes*, storms that blow in from the Gulf during the "dry season," are so common that March and April are the only truly dry months of the year.

6   The Coatzacoalcos and Tonalá basins are complex mosaics of large streams, tributaries, natural levees, swamps, upland ridges, and plateaus. Today, as in the past, seasonal changes in river levels dominate life in the region. Summer rains swell their currents until they spill over their banks and inundate the surrounding countryside. By September the cattle pastures of May are vast lakes better suited to fishing than ranching. By
7   November the rivers return to their established courses as the floodwaters recede. Water levels continue to drop until the next rainy season, when the cycle begins once again.

Rivers, streams, and lagoons influence every aspect of life in the region. Until highways and bridges were constructed in the 1980s, riverboats and dugout canoes were the main means of transport in much of the region. Rivers were also significant sources of fish, turtles, caimans, manatees, mollusks, river shrimp, and other high-quality protein foods before the 1970s, when pollution and over-exploitation decimated the stocks. Finally, the region's most productive farmlands have always been the natural levees that receive fertility-restoring silt after each flood. Today, as in the past, elevated plateaus, ridges, and levees overlooking the rivers are favored spots for

6 The Coatzacoalcos river from the air. The river's width varies tremendously over the course of the annual rainy season/dry season cycle.

7 Harvesting fish in the Laguna Platanal, an oxbow lake near San Lorenzo. During the dry season fish stranded in oxbow lakes grow as the lake surface shrinks, creating a protein-rich paradise.

human settlement. In addition to being safe from flooding, they provide fertile agricultural land, hunting territories, wood for house construction and cooking fires, and natural raw materials for all sorts of manufactures. Originally dense forests of tall perennial tropical trees covered the uplands; today they are covered with *acahual*, low shrubs and trees that result from generations of slash-and-burn agriculture.

Olman's tropical lowlands are a very dynamic environment, constantly changing in response to natural and human-induced causes. Deeply buried salt domes thrust the earth's surface upward, rising sea levels flood coastal margins, rivers change their courses, and humans clear the jungle for farmland. These processes affect modern inhabitants as much as they affected their Olmec predecessors. Although the Tuxtla mountains lacked dense Formative populations and true Olmec centers, they were an important presence in the Olmec world and visible from every major Olmec center. Four volcanoes dominate the landscape: San Martín Tuxtla, San Martín Pajapan, Santa Martha, and Pelon. Santa Martha, the tallest, appears to be extinct, but so did neighboring San Martín prior to its last major eruption in AD 1793. Lake Catemaco, a jewel-like crater lake at the center of the Tuxtlas, was an attractive spot for Formative-period farmers and may even have been invested with sacred qualities by them and their lowland Olmec neighbors.

Archaeological investigations near the lake reveal that volcanic ashfalls disrupted human occupation on many occasions in the past, and one episode in the seventh century BC deposited a thick ash mantle that forced humans to abandon much of the region for centuries. Nevertheless, Olmecs managed to acquire basalt from Cerro Cintepec as well as fine white kaolin clay and volcanic ash temper for pottery manufacture. The mountains also played an important role in Olmec cosmology and worldview. Mountains were believed to be the abode of gods who controlled human affairs and the volcanoes may have provided the inspiration for the manmade mountains we call "temple pyramids" at La Venta. Olmecs, probably from La Venta, even constructed a shrine at the top of San Martín Pajapan focused on an outstanding stone sculpture depicting a young lord in the act of creating the world.

Olman in the eyes of the Aztecs

By AD 1519 the Aztecs had incorporated the western part of Olman into their empire and established commercial ties with groups living to the east. We are fortunate to have sixteenth-century documents that record Aztec impressions of the region's inhabitants and resources, particularly the *Codex Mendoza* and Fray Bernardino de Sahagún's *Florentine Codex*. The *Mendoza* is an Early Colonial copy of a pre-Columbian codex that lists every province in the Aztec empire along with the tribute paid by each.[7] In it, Tochtepec, a province that included the Papaloapan basin and a portion of the Tuxtla mountains, is described as one of the wealthiest and most heavily taxed regions in the Aztec domain. Every six months Tochtepec's leaders were obligated to send their Aztec overlords 1,600 richly decorated *mantas* (pieces of cloth), 800 striped *mantas*, and 400 women's tunics and skirts. An additional annual tribute included: 1 fancy warrior costume; 2 shields richly decorated with feathers; 2 necklaces, a headband, and a diadem, all of gold; 7 necklaces and 3 large beads of precious green stones; 20 lip plugs of crystal and 20 of clear amber; 4 bunches of rich green feathers trimmed with yellow feathers; 80 handfuls of rich green Quetzal feathers; 8,000 handfuls of green feathers, red feathers, and blue feathers; 100 pots of fine liquid amber; 200 loads of cacao beans; and an astounding 16,000 balls of rubber.

The substantial cloth tribute reflects Olman's importance as a producer of cotton goods. Gold and rock crystal were probably extracted from the streams in the nearby Sierra de Oaxaca, a likely source of the green stones as well. Amber and green feathers, especially the highly prized long iridescent Quetzal bird tail feathers, must have been imported from somewhere outside Tochtepec, perhaps the highlands of Chiapas and Guatemala.

Fray Sahagún queried elderly Aztecs about the lands and peoples of their former empire.[8] His informants considered Olman a rich land endowed with cacao (chocolate) beans, the "divine ear" spice, wild cacao, rubber, beautiful flowers, precious feathers, green stones, fine turquoise, gold, and silver.

"The old people gave it the name of Tlalocan, which is to say, 'place of wealth.'" The inhabitants of this paradise were richly dressed in fine sleeve-less jackets and bark paper breechcloths. Sahagún's sources praised Olman's women as great embroiderers, skilled in work with cotton thread, and commented favorably on the arm bands of green stones, plaited necklaces decorated with pendants, and sandals, even some made from rubber, worn by the locals.

Olman in the eyes of the Spanish conquistadors

Even though European concepts of wealth differed greatly from those of the Aztecs, the Spaniards initially had high hopes for this wealthy land. Feathers, rubber balls, cacao, and green stones did not interest them, but the promise of gold and native labor quickly attracted their attention. Cortés sent explorers to search out Tochtepec's gold sources in 1520 even before he completed the conquest of the Aztecs. Shortly thereafter he laid personal claim to the Marquesado del Valle, a vast territory stretching from the Pacific Ocean to the Papaloapan basin, and immediately established New Spain's first sugar plantation in the Tuxtlas. He imported African slaves to operate the plantation, opening the long, ignoble episode of African slavery in North America. At about the same time, Gonzalo de Sandoval and a few companions founded the Spanish settlement of Villa de Espíritu Santo near the mouth of the Coatzacoalcos river. Bernal Diaz del Castillo, the major eyewitness chronicler of the Conquest of Mexico and an original settler at Villa de Espíritu Santo, later lamented that he and his colleagues had been deceived by Olman's apparent wealth.[9] Significant gold deposits were never found and the Indians who were supposed to support the Spaniards with labor and taxes died off rapidly from disease and mistreatment. The Spanish settlers soon began to drift away to more attractive places and in 1541 Diaz moved on to present-day Antigua, Guatemala. By 1580, Villa de Espíritu Santo had only twenty Spanish residents, and the Indian population of the entire province was estimated to be 3,000, down from at least 50,000 only sixty years before.

Olman's pre-Olmec inhabitants

Although humans surely inhabited Olman in Paleo-Indian times, the oldest known archaeological remains date to 5100 BC. At about that time farmers occupied the edge of a former lagoon at San Andrés, Tabasco, 15 km (10 miles) south of the current shore of the Gulf of Mexico and 5 km (3 miles) northeast of La Venta. San Andrés is unusual in that its waterlogged soils contain many well-preserved plant fragments and other organic materials. William F. Rust identified pre-Olmec occupations at the site in 1986. Recent investigations by Kevin O. Pope, Mary E. D. Pohl, and their multi-disciplinary team of archaeologists, geoarchaeologists, botanists, and palynologists revealed important new information on the predecessors of the La Venta Olmec.[10] Using deep-soil coring, flotation, water screening and other advanced paleoenvironmental and archaeological techniques not previously employed in Olmec research, they recovered pollen of an early form of maize, together with evidence for initial clearing of the natural forest. Maize was imported from mid-latitude west Mexico (most likely modern Guerrero state) where DNA research indicates its wild ancestor *teosinte* is native, and quickly adapted to Olman's moist, warm environment. The San Andrés core also contained manioc pollen, most likely from a domesticated plant, dated to 4600 BC. Later peoples in the American tropics consumed calorie-rich manioc tubers as a daily staple, and some archaeologists suspect the plant played an important role in lowland Mesoamerican diets prior to 800 BC.

By 2500 BC farmers at San Andrés and their neighbors were living around an estuary bordered by channels of the Grijalva river delta and practicing a mixed economy of foraging and farming. In addition to domesticated maize, they cultivated sunflower for its nutritious, oil-rich seeds, and cotton for fiber. They also utilized the abundant wild resources of the area such as plants of the squash family. Rust maintains that they used pottery vessels for cooking and storage but later investigators suggest that his sherds may be intrusions from more recent occupations higher up in the excavation. The early inhabitants of San Andrés must have used canoes, weapons, digging sticks, net baskets, and ritual objects fabricated from wood and other organic materials. Someday examples of such perishable objects may be recovered from sealed, waterlogged deposits at San Andrés and other habitation sites like those found at the El Manatí water shrine, discussed below.

Paleobotanist Barbara Leyden was able to identify the carbonized maize kernels, cupules, and pollen from San Andrés as a small popcorn variety with 10 to 14 rows of kernels similar to contemporaneous maize found at Real Alto, Ecuador, and to modern Argentine popcorn.[11] Argentine popcorn, a relatively small plant with tiny ears and kernels, is well adapted to wet soils and high humidity but produces less food per plant or cultivated land unit than other modern varieties. Farmers in Olman would have certainly appreciated its ability to thrive in their humid, rainy environment.

8 Maize cobs some 5,000 years old uncovered at San Andrés, Tabasco. While these small ears yielded relatively little food, they were the harbingers of a major Mesoamerican food revolution.

The origins of Olmec culture: the Ojochí, Bajío, and Chichárras phase (1500–1200 BC)

Until recently archaeologists believed that Olmec culture did not emerge as an identifiable entity until 1200 BC, but today they can trace its origins probably to at least 1600–1500 BC. During that century true Olmec remains were ritually deposited at El Manatí, a sacred shrine near San Lorenzo in the lower Coatzacoalcos basin. There is good reason to believe that the worshipers came from San Lorenzo, the first large Olmec center and possibly the original hearth of Olmec culture and art. The identity of these first Olmecs remains a mystery. Some scholars believe they were Mokaya migrants from the Pacific coast of Chiapas who brought improved maize strains and incipient social stratification with them. Others propose that Olmec culture evolved among local indigenous populations without significant external stimulus. I prefer the latter position, but freely admit that we lack sufficient information on the period before 1500 BC to resolve the issue.

Cerro Manatí is a prominent hill that rises out of the lowland swamps and lagoons 17 km (9 miles) southeast of San Lorenzo. Ponciano Ortiz C., María del Carmen Rodríguez, and their colleagues have revealed a rich record of early Olmec ritual life and culture hardly imagined when they began their investigations in 1989.[12] El Manatí was an isolated Olmec shrine at the place   9

9 Excavations in the El Manatí bog, Veracruz, where Olmec celebrants deposited sacred objects.

where permanent freshwater springs come to the surface at the base of the hill. The Olmecs believed that water and mountains were both imbued with sacred qualities, which made this spot a natural shrine site. Although other isolated Olmec shrines are known, El Manatí is the only one that has received careful study and detailed publication. Painstaking excavations in the muck revealed three ritual episodes during which celebrants deposited sacred objects in an open pond below the spring. During the first episode (Manatí A phase: 1600–1500 BC), worshipers prepared an artificial bed of sandstone rocks, including some with man-made grooves on their surfaces, on the floor of the shallow pond. Next they placed pottery vessels, stone bowls, fire-cracked hearthstones, high-quality jadeite celts and beads, and nine rubber balls on the sandstone floor.

All these objects, including the pots and hearthstones, are perfectly expectable occurrences in a ritual context. The jadeite and rubber surprised many archaeologists who did not expect to find either substance in use at such an early date. Jadeite, or more technically jadeitite, is a tough, dense bluish-green rock highly valued by Mesoamericans of all times, probably because its color served as a metaphor for maize, the staff of life, and fertility in general. Later Olmecs avidly searched out this rare stone and carved it into exquisite celts, figurines, beads, masks, and other precious objects known collectively as "jades," but until the El Manatí find, most scholars believed that jadeite only came into use after 800 BC. The source of Olmec jadeite was a mystery until 2001 when geologists and archaeologists positively identified natural outcrops and workshops in eastern Guatemala's Motagua valley, 1,000 km (580 miles) from Olman. Clearly the El Manatí worshipers participated in highly developed trade routes even at this early date.

10 Green stone celts buried as offerings at El Manatí. Their abundance indicates extensive commercial ties with the Sierra de las Minas source zone in eastern Guatemala at a much earlier date than once believed.

The rubber balls likewise created a stir in archaeological circles, for although Olman means "Land of Rubber," this substance had never been successfully identified in Formative-period Mesoamerican archaeological sites. Ortiz and Rodríguez recovered nine examples, clear evidence of the great antiquity of the ball game (described in detail in Chapter 4), and the fact that it had sacred and ritual aspects from its very inception.

A mat of peat-like organic material that naturally accumulated over the first set of offerings sealed them into a tight archaeological context. A century later during the Manatí B phase (1500–1200 BC), pilgrims deposited beautiful, highly polished jadeite axes and other stones in carefully laid-out patterns on the floor of the spring. Some axes were arranged in circular, flower-petal arrangements with their bits pointing upward. Eleven were carefully laid horizontally as a set, while other sets were oriented to the cardinal directions. Celebrants continued to deposit rubber balls, but pottery vessels and other utilitarian objects were no longer included in the ritual deposits. The final episode of ritual activity occurred during the San Lorenzo phase and will be discussed in Chapter 2.

El Manatí was an isolated, secluded shrine, far from any major settlement. The small hamlet of Macayal was located 1 km (0.62 miles) away but was far too insignificant to amass the wealth left in the spring at El Manatí. Where then did the worshipers live? I believe they were residents of San Lorenzo, the largest settlement in the region at this time.

Excavations at San Lorenzo have revealed three phases of occupation prior to its emergence as a full-blown city at 1200 BC: Ojochí (1500–1350 BC), Bajío (1350–1250 BC), and Chichárras (1250–1150 BC).[13] Remains of these occupations lie deeply buried under later debris but even so, recent excavations suggest that San Lorenzo covered at least 20 ha (49 acres) by 1250 BC.[14] Surveys in the 400-sq. km (155-sq. mile) region around San Lorenzo identified more than 100 Bajío and Chichárras-phase sites that formed a complex three-tiered settlement hierarchy with the village of San Lorenzo at its apex. The subsidiary communities included nine small villages and scores of small hamlets and farmsteads. Most settlements were located on high ground that did not flood, but yet provided access to fresh water and fluvial transport. San Lorenzo was the largest village in the region and seems to have dominated the entire zone even at this early time, perhaps receiving food and other tribute from its subordinates.

Ojochí-phase pottery includes utilitarian wares used in daily life as well as finely made vessels suitable for ceremonial feasting. Vessel forms included bowls, thin-walled *tecomates* (restricted-mouth jars that resemble gourds), and jars with out-flaring necks. Red slips and a variety of surface modifications such as gadrooning, grooving, punctation, and contrasting polished and roughened areas all added to the attractiveness of the vessels. Ojochí-phase pottery is virtually identical to Manatí A-phase ceramics, as well as more distant Pellicer-phase materials in Tabasco, and Barra-phase pottery found in coastal Chiapas across the Isthmus of Tehuantepec.

Bajío-phase pottery (1350–1250 BC) emerged directly out of Ojochí antecedents during a period of marked population growth. *Tecomates* continued to be popular but occur alongside flat-bottomed bowls with constricted upper walls and greatly out-flared rims and a large assortment of bottles that probably served as drinking or serving vessels in festival or ceremonial contexts. Similar bottles appear in Tabasco to the east and further afield in central and west Mexico. Differentially fired pottery with contrasting black-and-white surface areas, an unusual ceramic decoration technique that remained popular for centuries, appeared for the first time in the Bajío phase. Large hollow figurines depicting human babies, a later hallmark of Olmec ceramic art and ritual paraphernalia, appear for the first time. Bajío-phase Olmecs at San Lorenzo moved large quantities of earth for the construction of earth platforms. We do not know how large these platforms were or what functions they had, but their presence alone indicates the existence of Olmec leaders who controlled sufficient labor to create these public works at their behest.

The Chichárras phase (1250–1150 BC) was a critical juncture in San Lorenzo's history that presaged the full emergence of Olmec culture. The population continued to grow dramatically while the pottery assemblage underwent dramatic changes. Michael D. Coe and I originally attributed these changes to immigrants from elsewhere in the Olmec region, but I am less convinced of this hypothesis today than I was in 1980. Differentially fired black-and-white pottery increased in popularity while many old pottery types disappeared. White pottery and a black type called Mojonera Black appeared for the first time, both continuing on into the succeeding San Lorenzo phase, the pinnacle of Olmec culture at San Lorenzo.

Chichárras-phase deposits contain several defining characteristics of Olmec culture, including Olmec-style hollow and solid-clay figurines and stone sculpture. One solid figurine portrays a pregnant seated woman with slightly outspread legs, wearing a short skirt covered with red paint. The single securely dated Chichárras-phase fragment of stone sculpture depicts two parallel ropes painted with red hematite. Ropes often appear on later Olmec sculptures where they occur in the headgear shown on Colossal Heads or tied around stone blocks that appear to be in transit. Both settings seem to signify rulership and power, expressed as control over precious basalt, a likely meaning for the Chichárras piece as well. Its fragmented condition also suggests the existence of the later practice of destroying monuments and reusing the stone.

By 1200 BC the Olmec world was experiencing cultural ferment as processes that had begun three or four centuries earlier coalesced into a new rich and flamboyant civilization of a sort that never existed before in Mesoamerica. All of Niederberger's six characteristics of civilization already existed in at least incipient form as emerging social, political, economic, religious, and artistic realities began to transform local cultures as well as those in other parts of Mesoamerica. San Lorenzo was the primary hearth of this new civilization.

2 · San Lorenzo's Realm

San Lorenzo emerged as Mesoamerica's first city, and perhaps the oldest urban center anywhere in the Americas, by 900 BC. By then it covered 500 ha (1,235 acres), had several thousand permanent residents, and exhibited the full range of urban characteristics outlined by Christine Niederberger (see 11, 12 previous chapter): political and religious power, social ranking, planned public architecture, highly skilled craftspeople, control of interregional trade networks, and complex intellectual achievements. Today it is clear that the Olmec capitals at San Lorenzo and La Venta were what William T. Sanders and David Webster define as Regal-Ritual Cities: urban centers that have highly developed ritual functions but fairly modest populations, relatively weak, decentralized rulership, and limited economic functions.[1] Regal-Ritual Cities were common in later Mesoamerican societies, where only Teotihuacan, Tula, and Tenochtitlán and a few other mega-centers advanced beyond this state.

San Lorenzo occupies a long ridge that rises above the surrounding riverine lowlands 60 km (37.5 miles) from the Gulf of Mexico. Today the Chiquito branch of the Coatzacoalcos river flows east of the ridge, but 3,000 years ago a riverine network surrounded the ridge on all sides, creating a giant island at the head of the lower Coatzacoalcos basin. San Lorenzo occupied the ridge at the center of the island while subordinate secondary centers at El Remolino and Loma del Zapotes controlled the river junctures at its northern and southern edges. Location was as critical to success in Early Formative times as it is today and the San Lorenzo ridge was one of the best pieces of real estate in the Olmec world. High enough to remain dry during even the worst floods, yet close to fertile river levee farmlands and aquatic resources, it was also easily defended. Freshwater springs at the summit yielded the best drinking water in the region while asphalt, hematite, sandstone, limestone, and other prized natural resources occurred nearby. Finally, control of the river junctures at the base of the island gave San Lorenzo's rulers control over every important fluvial and terrestrial transportation route in the Coatzacoalcos drainage. Little wonder then that the site emerged as the first Olmec political and economic power.

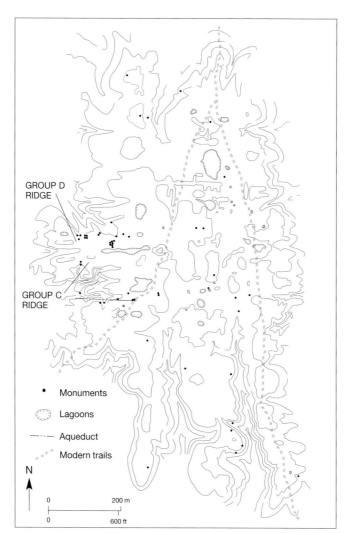

11 Site plan of the San Lorenzo plateau surface, showing monuments, lagoons, and modern trails. This core of the ancient settlement accounts for less than 20 percent of the entire San Lorenzo-phase community.

GROUP D
RIDGE

GROUP C
RIDGE

• Monuments

◌ Lagoons

—·—· Aqueduct

- - - Modern trails

N

0   200 m
0   600 ft

12 The boundaries of San Lorenzo at its height. The inner core is the plateau surface once mistakenly thought to be the entire site, the outer limit was recently defined by archaeologists Stacey Symonds, Roberto Lunagómez and Ann Cyphers.

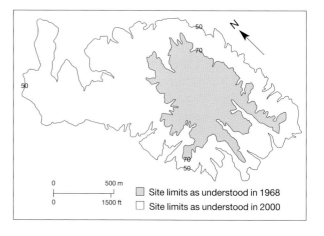

0   500 m
0   1500 ft

▨ Site limits as understood in 1968
☐ Site limits as understood in 2000

San Lorenzo's Olmec occupation

The history of San Lorenzo is written in the broken pottery and charcoal that fill its thick stratified soil layers.[2] Pre-San Lorenzo-phase remains were described in Chapter 1; here we pick up the story at 1150 BC. Three phases of substantial Olmec occupation have been identified: San Lorenzo (1150–900/800 BC), Nacaste (900/800–700 BC), and Palangana (600–400 BC). The plateau, along with much of San Lorenzo's hinterland, was then abandoned until Late Classic Villa Alta-phase (AD 700–900) settlers reoccupied it 1,100 years later. Excavations at El Remolino, a rich refuse zone exposed in the riverbank near Tenochtitlán village, recovered thousands of potsherds and numerous charcoal samples that served to define and date the San Lorenzo phase. San Lorenzo-phase pottery fills the upper levels of the entire San Lorenzo plateau, blanketing deeply buried Ojochí-, Bajío- and Chichárras-phase refuse. Subtle changes in pottery styles and frequencies allow definition of two sub-phases, San Lorenzo A and B, but the precise duration of each is not known.

San Lorenzo-phase ceramics are found throughout the Coatzacoalcos basin and other parts of Olman, indicating substantial populations at this time. While the pottery is broadly similar to the Chichárras-phase wares that preceded it, two important new decorated wares, called "Calzadas Carved" and "Xochiltepec White," appeared for the first time. Calzadas Carved is a gray-to-black ware with deep designs cut into the exterior walls of bowls after the vessel had been allowed to dry to leather hardness. The boldly carved designs, often colored with red hematite, include crossed bands, the paw-wing motif, cross-hatching, opposed lines, flame eyebrows, and other Olmec symbols. Xochiltepec White has a fine clear ivory-to-white paste made from kaolin clay found locally in the Coatzacoalcos basin as well as in the Tuxtla mountains. Vessel forms include collared jars with restricted orifices and lower bodies modeled like squashes, thin-walled *tecomates*, and deep bowls. All three forms probably functioned as elite food-serving vessels reserved for feasts, rituals, and other special occasions. Calzadas Carved vessels appear at many sites in other parts of Mesoamerica, often side by side with locally made imitations, while Xochiltepec White pots manufactured at San Lorenzo have been identified in Oaxaca and the Basin of Mexico. "Limón Carved-Incised," a type similar to Calzadas Carved but only found at San Lorenzo, was often differentially fired to produce contrasting black-and-white zones on the surface, and features incised rather than carved curvilinear designs.

The Nacaste phase post-dates the collapse of San Lorenzo as an Olmec capital. Nacaste-phase materials lay directly on top of San Lorenzo-phase layers at various places on the plateau. New vessel forms and modes of decoration replaced most of the older San Lorenzo-phase hallmark ceramics. Such changes may signal the arrival of immigrants who displaced or overwhelmed the local population, but it is also possible that the Nacaste population were descendants of locals who remained in the area after San

Lorenzo's fall. Regardless of who they were, the Nacaste people did not create any known monuments or architecture and after a few generations they abandoned the site.

The Palangana phase was a time of continued decline at San Lorenzo and its hinterland. Immigrants who settled the ridge erected several small mounds placed around plazas, including one of Mesoamerica's oldest-known ballcourts. Recent surveys show the site only covered 20 ha (49.5 acres), down from the 500 ha (1,235 acres) of a few centuries earlier. The relationships between the new San Lorenzo and the thriving Olmec capital at La Venta are unclear, but the village was so small and the entire region so under-populated that they may not even have been of concern to La Venta's rulers. The last Olmecs left the plateau by 400 BC. When Villa Alta-phase pioneers settled there a millennium later, what marvelous stories they must have made up about the creators of the majestic stone sculptures they encountered in their cornfields and houselots!

San Lorenzo in the tenth century BC

San Lorenzo is a great disappointment for modern visitors accustomed to the impressive pre-Columbian architectural remains of central Mexico, Oaxaca, and the Maya lowlands. There are no soaring temples or lavishly decorated building facades, and the finest sculptures have been removed to museums in far-off Mexico City and Xalapa. A new site museum on the grounds of the former Yale Project field camp in Tenochtitlán village contains recently discovered sculptures, including the latest Colossal Head. A hike across the plateau reveals modest Palangana- and Villa Alta-phase earth mounds and occasional fragments of basalt broken off some monument or drain stone, but San Lorenzo's Olmec story lies deeply buried beneath the modern cattle pasture and soy bean fields.

Modern visitors approach San Lorenzo from the north. Thirty years ago they disembarked from their boat at Tenochtitlán village, but today most drive in on the recently constructed all-weather road from Acayucan. Ancient visitors entered the city from several directions, depending on their point of origin. Some approached it through a port complex at the southernmost extension of the plateau, near modern Loma del Zapote; similar formal entrances may have existed at El Remolino to the north of the plateau and elsewhere. We can imagine one such ancient traveler, perhaps an Olmec merchant returning home from a successful trading mission, as he landed his dugout canoe at Loma del Zapote and proceeded to the top of the plateau to pay homage to his ruler, the king.

Loma del Zapote straddled the fork of the ancient river system 3 km (1.9 miles) from the plateau summit.[3] Different parts of it have been assigned distinct names in the archaeological literature, including Potrero Nuevo, Rancho El Azuzul, and Las Treinta. Upon landing on firm ground, our visitor would have surveyed Loma del Zapote's most prominent features, including a terraced acropolis adorned with stone monuments, two low, broad earth causeways or dikes, and an extensive residential zone strung out along the causeways. The causeways each measured at least 500 m long by 60 m wide and 2 m high (1637 x 196 x 6.5 ft), and provided all-weather connections between the ancient riverbank and high ground while serving as dikes that protected the lands to the north from seasonal floods.

Ann Cyphers' investigations at Loma del Zapote revealed houses on leveled spaces, together with ceremonial zones where stone sculptures were displayed in multi-monument settings or tableaus visible from the river. One apparently *in-situ* setting contained a sculpture of a seated or kneeling human, now mutilated and decapitated, resting on a bentonite (consolidated volcanic ash) pavement while facing the setting sun. Bones of a possible human sacrificial victim were carefully placed beneath the pavement along with pottery vessels and other objects. A second ritual setting included another badly destroyed statue depicting a seated human with one raised arm and one leg crossed while the other leg hangs down. This unusual posture also appears in an Olmec cave painting in far-away Oxtotitlán, Guerrero, where the man sits on top of a throne. Cyphers suspects the Loma del Zapote sculpture may also have sat on a throne.

Loma del Zapote's most intriguing sculptural setting is found at Rancho El Azuzul where four sculptures were uncovered in an undisturbed tableau 13 resting on a bentonite floor. Two virtually identical kneeling human twins face the rising sun. Both are perfectly preserved except for the deliberate obliteration of the insignia in their headdresses. They confront two seated snarling jaguars that were recarved from older monuments. The entire tableau recalls the ancient Mesoamerican myth of the Hero Twins and their epic struggles with the forces of the Underworld on the behalf of humanity (see Chapter 4). The tableau was visible from the river, suggesting it served to remind visitors of the power and sanctity of San Lorenzo's rulers, presumed descendants from the Hero Twins.

Four sculptures long identified as coming from Potrero Nuevo can now be attributed to Loma del Zapote. One shows a seated person grasping a snake draped around his body while another is a curious serpent carved in the round. Potrero Nuevo Monument 3 is a very puzzling sculpture that shows a jaguar seated atop a human. Matthew Stirling suggested the jaguar is copulating with a woman, but a less lurid and more likely interpretation has the jaguar attacking a human of unknown gender. It may even be a metaphor for human sacrifice carried out by a supernatural feline. The final Potrero Nuevo monument is a small tabletop throne supported by two chubby 14 Atlantean dwarfs who grimace as they sustain the seat and the undoubtedly corpulent ruler who sat on it in real life. All four sculptures reflect themes of Olmec rulership while emphasizing connections with the supernatural world, appropriate topics to display at the entrance to the great capital.

When our visitor left the causeway and began to ascend to the plateau surface, he passed through a densely settled residential zone where houses and workshops sat on leveled terraces carved into the plateau sides. The existence of these terraces was not suspected until ranchers removed the dense jungle cover hiding them in the 1980s. Roberto Lunagómez's surveys on the recently cleared slopes revealed terraces extending down to the 30-m (98-ft) contour line on all sides of the plateau.[4]

Subsequent excavations revealed closely packed houses, some quite large (one measured 9 x 12 m [29 x 39 ft]), on the hillside. Some were constructed much like modern rural homes with walls of poles, thatched roofs, and simple earth floors, but many others were built using the *terre à pisé*, or compacted earth, technique. Many hillside dwellers were craftsmen and artisans who probably enjoyed an intermediate social status between that of villagers in the hinterland and the nobility who occupied the plateau surface.

One of San Lorenzo's great mysteries is the actual appearance of the plateau surface during the city's zenith. The earth mounds visible today were constructed after 600 BC and do not contain buried earlier structures. Very limited excavations down to the San Lorenzo floors beneath the mounds failed to reveal any San Lorenzo-phase structures, although perishable wattle-and-daub structures may have existed. However, enough research has been done to allow us to speculate on what our visitor would have seen when he reached "the heights of San Lorenzo," as they are called today. The evidence suggests he entered a vast open plaza paved with red

13 The El Azuzul twins. These youths face a pair of carved stone jaguars in a tableau thought to portray an Olmec creation story.

14 Potrero Nuevo Monument 2 is the most perfectly preserved small throne known (see p. 113 for more details). The chubby dwarfs support the upper jaw of the Olmec Dragon. Ht 94 cm (37 in).

sand and yellow gravel floors dotted with clusters of stone sculptures, many protected by "ramada"-style thatched roofs or shelters of perishable materials, extending along a north-south axis. At least ten Colossal Heads and several thrones form various lines that extend roughly north-south across the plateau surface. Contrary to earlier interpretations, these large sculptures may lie close to their original San Lorenzo-phase settings and were buried by subsequent erosion. Archaeologists agree that these sculptures served as "rulership monuments," the heads as portraits of living or recently deceased rulers, and the thrones as their royal seats. Thus the identification of individual sets of heads and thrones along the north-south axis of the plateau is highly significant.[5] The most likely explanation is that they formed a ritual processional way created to honor the living ruler and his real or fictitious ancestors. This gigantic display of dynastic history would have served to justify the power of the rulers and probably functioned until the San Lorenzo polity collapsed. If this interpretation is correct, the entire plateau surface was given over to royal ritual and state affairs. It is important to note that San Lorenzo did not employ the later Mesoamerican architectural arrangement of mounds and courtyards forming plaza groups. Early Formative public architecture here and elsewhere in Mesoamerica emphasized large flat platforms rather than high mounds. In fact, the entire San Lorenzo plateau was the largest platform of all.

G. Ray Krotser's topographic map of the San Lorenzo plateau documents a very unusual outline to the plateau perimeter, one most easily viewed from the aerial perspective of a bird, a helicopter, or a celestial deity.[6] Numerous large ridges extend out from the core of the plateau on its north, south, and west sides. How would the plateau have appeared from such an Olympian view 3,000 years ago? Michael D. Coe has proposed that the ridges are eroded remnants of enormous artificial platforms constructed by the Olmecs in an attempt to turn San Lorenzo into a gigantic bird effigy.[7] Small excavations in the 500-m (1637-ft) long Group D Ridge in 1967 penetrated 7 m (23 ft) of fill before reaching undisturbed subsoil. Coe and I believe that the 67,000 cu. m (2.36 million cu. ft) of this soil was construction fill deposited one basket-load at a time. If the Group D ridge was an artificial platform, what about the other ridges that extend out from the plateau? Are they also artificial constructions? Were they all conceived as a single, coordinated construction project designed to create the gigantic bird effigy Coe proposes? He argues that the natural plateau formed the bird's body, the north and south ridges its wings, and the two ridges on the west the tail, and that the head, originally planned for the east, was never completed. Although this effigy would only have been visible from above, humans on its surface would have understood its shape as well as its symbolic meaning, and may even have enacted complex ritual peregrinations on its surface. Coe's interpretation has been rejected by most archaeologists, including Ann Cyphers, who believes that the soil accumulated gradually as earth buildings and platforms were erected and demolished over the centuries.[8] I was once quite skeptical of the "Giant Bird Flying East" scenario, but am much more comfortable with it today than before.

San Lorenzo's Royal Compound

The west side of the San Lorenzo plateau has been a known "hot spot" for monuments since Stirling's day, with more than fifty sculptures and fragments recovered in the area of Groups C, D, and E alone.[9] Cyphers' recent excavations in the area have revealed the reason for such wealth of sculpture:

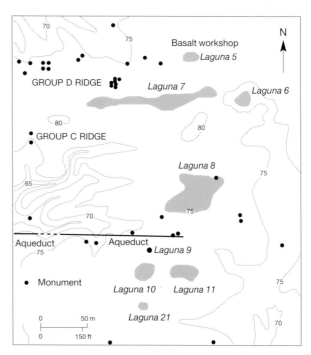

15 Plan of San Lorenzo Group C and Group D ridges. The many monuments, basalt workshops, aqueduct, and elaborate architecture concentrated in this area suggest it was San Lorenzo's Royal Compound.

15

this was San Lorenzo's "Royal Compound," home to its rulers. It included a residence dubbed the "Red Palace," a workshop where artisans carved sculptures and utilitarian tools from basalt and several ritual settings that included monuments and an aqueduct.[10] The Red Palace is a large structure with red gravel floors and mud walls plastered with red sand. Limestone, bentonite, and basalt were used as architectural accents. Basalt elements included a huge columnar roof support, bench-shaped stair tread covers, and a carefully constructed curved drain system that wound its way beneath the front of the building. While this drain probably served a utilitarian purpose, it undoubtedly had ritual functions as well.

Many of the sculptures found in or near the Royal Compound were either being recarved or stockpiled for future recycling when the area was abandoned. When the Yale team discovered some of these battered monuments in 1967, Coe and I concluded that rebels or invaders deliberately defaced them in a cataclysm that brought the San Lorenzo dynasty to a close. Now it appears we uncovered portions of a pre-Columbian sculptural junkyard where sculptors stored obsolete monuments, carved new ones from both "virgin" stone and existing monuments, and manufactured maize grinding implements known as *manos* and *metates* from the smaller fragments. Several recarved monuments have been identified at San Lorenzo, including the El Azuzul jaguars and two Colossal Heads made from older thrones, but it is impossible to know whether they came out of this specific workshop. The reuse of existing sculptures, especially those belonging to a predecessor, may have been an attractive alternative to the Herculean effort needed to bring virgin stone from distant quarries, especially in unsettled times when enemies may have blocked the transport route. The workshop's proximity to the Red Palace suggests that sculptors were members of the ruling family, just as Classic Maya scribes and sculptors often were lesser nobles. Occasional offerings of pottery, sacrificed animals and human infants placed underneath the monuments vividly highlight the sanctity of the undertaking.

The Group E Setting, a giant stage for public rituals focused on water, a superabundant but unpredictable feature of the Olmec environment, occupied the area southeast of the C and D ridges. It included a stone-lined 16 aqueduct that extended at least 171 m (560 ft) and a suite of thematically related stone monuments. In 1946 Matthew Stirling discovered scattered U-shaped basalt troughs on the sides of the barranca south of the Group C Ridge, and perceptively suggested they were water drain conduits. Twenty years later the Yale team discovered an *in-situ* trough emerging from the barranca wall. G. Ray Krotser, the team topographer and a retired civil engineer, excavated the intact aqueduct that lay buried beneath later overburden. Krotser's lifetime of engineering experience convinced him that, like many other Olmec construction enterprises, the aqueduct required considerable practical knowledge of engineering principles. The builders laid the troughs end to end along a carefully graded ground surface with an average 2 percent grade or rate of fall. Junctions for three branch lines were

16 Portion of a San Lorenzo aqueduct exposed in 1967. Constructed of hundreds of carefully carved basalt troughs and covers weighing many tons, this impressive system revealed the Olmecs' considerable practical engineering knowledge and skills.

17 (*below*) This duck-shaped font (San Lorenzo Monument 9) originally capped the end of a stone aqueduct. Ducks played an important role in Olmec religion and water lore. Ht 41 cm (16 in).

constructed, but the branches were either never finished or were removed at a later date. Carefully carved troughs and covers adhered to a standard design of uniform measurements and one cover even had an inspection hole through which the water flow could be monitored.

The drain system appears to terminate at Monument 9, a hollowed-out boulder carved in the likeness of a duck. The upper portion of the duck is missing but its wings, breast, and feet remain visible. The chest is adorned with two tripartite designs believed to represent blood or precious water and a profile rendering of a playful-looking duck with outstretched wings. This duck on a duck may have much deeper meaning than mere whimsy; even today local farmers believe that ducks flap their wings in the dust to

17

18 San Lorenzo
Monument 14
probably functioned
as a throne for an
Olmec ruler whose
image may occupy the
central niche.
Ht 183 cm (72 in).

announce impending rain. A square opening the size of a trough stone occupies one side of the boulder, suggesting that the aqueduct emptied into the duck's hollow body where a small hole in the bottom served as a drain for the basin. Might this unusual monument have functioned on occasion as a bathing tank where an Olmec ruler ritually acted out his role as rainmaker and Lord of the Waters?

Monuments 14, 61, and 52 lay near the upper (east) end of the drain line. Monument 14, a large tabletop throne, rested in a patio next to an earth platform while Monument 61, one of the most beautiful and best-preserved Olmec Colossal Heads, was found tipped over on its side on the yellow/red sand plaza floor directly south of the throne. Both sculptures are symbols of Olmec rulership. Monument 52, a seated dwarf-like creature with his hands crossing his drawn-up legs, lay adjacent to the east edge of the drain. He has an archetypal Olmec were-jaguar face with a cleft head and his headdress is embellished with tripartite designs and wavy streamers thought to symbolize water. His back is hollowed out in a way that resembles a trough stone, although the original spatial relationship between the monument and the drain is not known.

What can we make of this assemblage of sculptures and aqueduct and the lavish expenditure of rare basalt and human labor that it represented? Ann Cyphers believes that San Lorenzo's last ruler created the entire ensemble to carry fresh water from a spring located in or near the royal compound to the edge of the plateau, and that it was abandoned when his reign ended. She points out that potable water is a critical commodity in any hilltop settlement, and suggests that water channeled through the aqueduct served the daily needs of the inhabitants while figuring prominently in periodic rituals. Any Olmec ruler who controlled such an important resource would have wielded considerable power over the general populace, while forcefully demonstrating his unique relationship with the supernaturals that controlled rainfall and the annual river-level fluctuations. The rituals he sponsored would have united the entire community in the common purpose of ensuring the wellbeing of the realm and its inhabitants.

18

19

Remnants of other aqueducts have been identified in various parts of the plateau. Did they all function at the same time? I suspect not. Cyphers speculated that San Lorenzo's water table dropped gradually during the San Lorenzo phase. Such changes would have rendered older systems connected to higher springs useless, and perhaps even forced rulers to relocate their Royal Compound from one part of the plateau to another over the decades.

Twenty or more artificial pits known locally as *lagunas* dot the plateau. Their role in ancient water management is another disputed issue.[11] Coe and I suggested that some were borrow pits that provided soil for platform construction while others functioned as San Lorenzo-phase water tanks or cisterns. We proposed that Laguna 8, a large pit at the edge of the Group E Setting, served as an artificial reservoir or ritual bathing tank connected to the aqueduct. However, Cyphers maintains that her excavations into Laguna 8 failed to establish its antiquity and she considers it a twentieth-century pond excavated by local ranchers. This interpretation seems to ignore the fact that Laguna 8 existed when Stirling excavated Monument 14 in 1946, long before modern ranchers began to utilize the plateau. The controversy may be resolved when her final excavation report appears.

19 San Lorenzo Monument 52. Wavy ear ornaments, a V-shaped depression in the top of the head and the triple drop elements identify this creature as the Olmec Water or Rain deity. Ht 93 cm (36 in).

San Lorenzo sculpture

An Olmec deity gazing down on San Lorenzo would have marveled at the multitude of stone sculptures displayed in the Royal Compound and elsewhere around the site. Some monuments depicted supernaturals, others their flesh-and-blood embodiments on earth. The details of Olmec sculpture are discussed in Chapter 6, but a few observations about the San Lorenzo corpus are relevant here. To date, 124 stone sculptures have been recovered in the San Lorenzo area and archaeologists suspect that many more remain buried.[12] They range from small pieces weighing a few hundred kilograms to gigantic Colossal Heads and a tabletop throne (Monument 14) estimated to weigh a massive 28 tons. We have no way of knowing how many were ever displayed at one time, or installed permanently, perhaps in visual displays of the dynastic legacy, as opposed to those brought out only on special occasions. All the basalt used at San Lorenzo can be traced to Cerro Cintepec volcano in the Tuxtla mountains. Petrographic analyses have defined three distinct classes of Cerro Cintepec basalt at San Lorenzo, one (Type A), a fine-grained porphyritic basalt, was the sculptor's raw material of choice for monuments and drain stones, while the others were reserved for *manos*, *metates* and other utilitarian tools.[13]

Archaeologists and art historians have tended to view Olmec sculptures as isolated works of art, objects to be interpreted solely on the basis of what is seen on each individual specimen. Cyphers' recent discovery of group scenes or tableaus suggests that monuments frequently formed part of larger contexts or settings. Such tableaus may have stood in front of architectural backdrops. There may have been permanent displays of Colossal Heads, thrones and other large sculptures, accompanied from time to time by smaller monuments that were added or taken away as needed. The contents of a tableau may even have changed during a given ritual as the story progressed over the hours or days. Monument 34, a robust kneeling man, apparently even had movable wooden arms that could have been manipulated at will! Settings like that at Loma del Zapote may have been "permanent installations" in modern museum parlance, while others were more akin to changing exhibits designed to draw crowds back to the same spot time after time.

These carvings were not simply art for art's sake or handsome embellishments of a great capital, but forceful, awe-inspiring expressions of the ways Olmecs perceived their deities, deified ancestors, and the cosmos. At the same time they symbolized the power of rulers to direct the creation of these works. Successful delivery of a stone or finished monument involved complex organization and the ability to command prodigious amounts of labor. A ruler had to oversee the quarrying and transport of the stone 80 km (50 miles) over treacherous waterways and rough jungle-covered terrain, negotiate passage through potentially hostile territory, ensure the feeding and housing of workers for periods of months, and anticipate unpredictable weather and river conditions.

Two basic themes pervade San Lorenzo sculptures: realistic portrayals of humans, at times engaged in ritual acts, and animals. The latter range from naturalistic denizens of the forest to phantasmagoric congeries that never existed in the real world. While these themes are also found at La Venta and elsewhere, San Lorenzo's corpus has its own unique patterns and features. One such specialty focuses on felines and depictions of humans transforming into jaguars or other felines; humans wearing jaguar pelts are also common. The modern distribution of monuments strongly suggests they were stored and displayed in elite zones at the peripheries of the plateau. Only a few remain intact. Most were either mutilated or already in the recycling process. Crisp lines and un-weathered surfaces are common enough to suggest that many monuments were protected from the elements, perhaps inside buildings or under protective roofs. Remnants of stucco and purplish paint on La Venta Colossal Head 4 suggest that at least some Olmec sculptures were painted in bold color schemes, another form of protection for the underlying surface.

San Lorenzo's Realm

Olmec civilization cannot be understood without considering the rural settlements that supported the urban capitals. Traditional archaeological emphasis on these capitals with their impressive architecture and stone monuments has greatly skewed our picture of Olmec life and culture by ignoring the villages where most Olmecs lived out their daily lives. Recent surveys of San Lorenzo's hinterland have helped to correct this imbalance.[14] They reveal a densely populated hinterland at the core of the San Lorenzo Realm. The physical extent of that Realm is still unclear, but must have included the entire Coatzacoalcos basin at the least. Two zones of settlement surrounded the capital, an Inner Hinterland filled with densely packed communities, and a more distant and lightly populated Outer Hinterland.

20   Communities in both zones varied widely in size and complexity, but formed a well-defined hierarchy. San Lorenzo occupied the apex of the hierarchy. Beneath it were four nearby secondary centers situated at the confluence of rivers or other transport control points. Loma del Zapote and neighboring Las Camelias controlled passage from the south, while El Remolino served the same function to the north. El Remolino and neighboring El Bajío formed a large village that straddled the Río Chiquito. Excavations in the well-stratified midden deposits exposed in the riverbank at El Remolino yielded quantities of San Lorenzo pottery and, in 1946, Philip Drucker discovered a large basalt column similar to the Red Palace roof support in the river bottom. Unfortunately he could not determine its stratigraphic association, and the river reclaimed it shortly after the excavation closed. Estero Rabon controlled access to San Lorenzo from the west. Several fragmentary Olmec sculptures are known from the site, including a detached head that probably belongs to a seated human and a possible

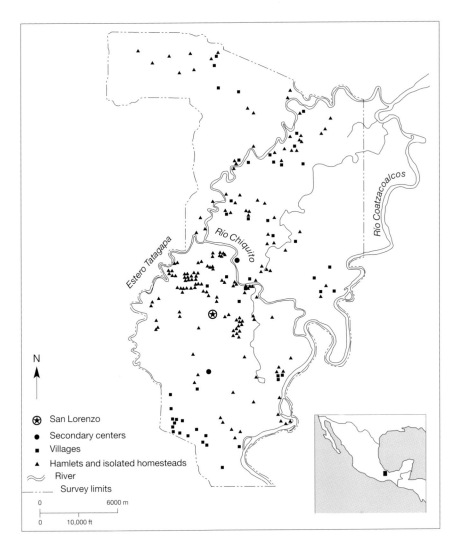

20 The distribution of San Lorenzo settlements revealed by archaeological surveys in the hinterland of the Early Formative capital. Note the population clustering close to the city.

throne. A fourth second-tier community may remain to be discovered east of San Lorenzo.

Olmec farmers occupied virtually every high spot near San Lorenzo, even going to the trouble of creating "islotes," small artificial islands high enough to avoid the annual floods. Stacey Symonds and Roberto Lunagómez identify six community types in addition to those in the top two tiers: large, medium and small villages, large and small hamlets, and the household-sized islotes. Special-purpose settlements such as shrines and seasonal fishing camps existed alongside more numerous permanent communities.

All were socially and politically subordinate to San Lorenzo in some fashion, and almost all disappeared at the end of the San Lorenzo phase.

El Manatí continued to function as a shrine during the Macayal A phase (1200–1000 BC), the local equivalent of the San Lorenzo phase.[15] On one notable occasion, worshipers deposited a massive offering of objects carved from wood and other perishable materials that miraculously survived in the anaerobic submerged environment of the bog. The most spectacular offer-

21, 22, pl. XIV   ings were forty life-sized human busts carved from the wood of a local tropical cedar tree. They were accompanied by wooden scepters, sacrificial stone knives hafted into wood handles with tar adhesive, rubber balls, lumps of hematite, knotted cords, woven mats, plant leaves, nuts, fruit pits, and hematite-impregnated animal bones. On a more macabre note, bones of human neonates, infants and children, likely sacrificial victims, were deposited amongst the offerings. Ortíz and Rodríguez speculate that the Olmecs realized that these objects would resist decay in the protective waters of the bog, perhaps an added benefit to the rituals, but could they have imagined they would endure more than 3,000 years?

El Manatí was not the only shrine where Olmecs buried ritual offerings. At least three separate offerings were placed in standing or slowly moving water at nearby La Merced, including one that contained more than 600 roughly carved limestone celts in an area 30 m (98 ft) on a side. Although not as finely made as the El Manatí celts, they were accompanied by hematite and pyrite mirrors, a beautifully carved 72-cm (30-in) high stela-like stone with a classic Olmec face, and a carved greenstone celt depicting a squalling infant nicknamed "El Bebé."

San Lorenzo's contemporaries

While San Lorenzo apparently was Olman's dominant Early Formative polity, contemporaneous centers existed at La Venta, Tres Zapotes, Las Limas, Ojo de Agua, and La Oaxaqueña, and perhaps Laguna de los Cerros. A now-outdated line of thought once held that San Lorenzo, La Venta, and Tres Zapotes formed a great triumvirate of Olmec centers that rose and fell in succession. The reality is not quite so simple and neat. The latter two did achieve their greatest prominence after San Lorenzo's demise, but both contain poorly known Early Formative occupations. La Venta was a consid-erable presence in its region after 1000 BC and numerous of its sculptures share specific traits and motifs with San Lorenzo examples. Archaeologists have not yet identified pre-1000 BC layers at La Venta, but nearby Isla Alor dates to this time. I suspect that La Venta emerged as an important regional center after 1200 BC and ultimately played a major role in San Lorenzo's demise, or at least benefited tremendously from it.

23   The history of Tres Zapotes and its relationships to other Olmec centers was one of the great enigmas of Olmec archaeology until Christopher Pool and his colleagues at the University of Kentucky began investigations at the

21 Ponciano Ortiz C. (*left*) clearing the muck from a wooden bust at El Manatí. The anaerobic environment preserved the organic wood for 3,000 years, providing a unique window on Olmec sculptural achievements and ritual.

22 Three of the more than forty wooden busts uncovered in the El Manatí bog near San Lorenzo. Their variable expressions suggest they depict actual persons rather than abstract deities.

23 Tres Zapotes. The archaeological site occupies the rolling piedmont in the foreground, with Cerro Vigía, one of the major Tuxtla mountain volcanoes, behind it.

site in 1995.[16] Their surveys confirmed the existence of three small Early Formative settlements within the limits of the later and much larger Epi-Olmec center founded in 400 or 300 BC. *Bona fide* Olmec remains at the site include two Colossal Heads, San Lorenzo-like pottery, jadeite celts, perforated iron-ore cubes, Olmec-style pottery figurines, and a stone column tomb enclosure similar to that found at La Venta. The Colossal Heads and the tomb signal the presence of local rulers, but not all authorities consider the heads truly Olmec. Art historian Beatriz de la Fuente argues that they differ so much from other Colossal Heads in style and workmanship that they may represent the very latest survivals of the Olmec sculptural tradition. Other scholars consider them regional variants of that tradition, the sort of thing expectable at an Olmec frontier settlement. Whether the heads are Olmec or not, the jadeite celts, perforated ilmenite cubes, ceramic and figurine styles, and a basalt column tomb clearly indicate an Olmec presence, albeit one with a simpler, less hierarchical sociopolitical organization than those of contemporary communities to the east.

Laguna de los Cerros

Laguna de los Cerros is a large archaeological site spread across the low rolling foothills south of the Tuxtla mountains. It includes at least ninety-five mounds, some reaching 30 m (98 ft) in height, clustered in a 40-ha (99-acre) area.[17] Most probably date to the Late Classic period, but the pres-

ence of forty stone monuments at the site
and nearby settlements suggests a substantial Formative population. Laguna de los
Cerros has long been a source of considerable and unwarranted confusion.
When Alfonso Medellín Zenil's brief
investigations in 1960 recovered Classic-
period pottery everywhere, even beneath
Olmec sculptures, he assigned the major
occupation and the sculptures to AD
600–900. Today we realize that Late
Classic inhabitants probably moved and
perhaps even venerated the Formative-
period monuments.

Laguna de los Cerros lacks realistic
Colossal Heads but does have two smallish
and, some would say, ugly heads depicting fantastic
creatures with curly hair, fanged were-jaguar mouths, and
square eye plaques. Monument 19, a beautifully executed standing male
wearing a cape and carved in the round, is hauntingly reminiscent of ancient
eastern Mediterranean sculpture. Unfortunately, this masterpiece is
missing its head.

25

25 (*above*) Laguna de los
Cerros Monument 1 appears
to portray a curly-haired
individual whose face is
covered with a mask carved
in the likeness of a
supernatural. Ht 75 cm (29
in), estimated weight 0.81
tons.

24 This Colossal Head,
one of two uncovered at
Tres Zapotes, suggests
the community had at
least two powerful Early
Formative rulers. The
large ornaments that pass
through his ear lobes
were presumably made of
a lightweight wood or
other organic material.
Ht 147 cm (57 in).

47

Monument 9 is one of the most curious and informative sculptures at Laguna de los Cerros. It depicts a large rectangular block trussed up with ropes. A human rider, now almost completely destroyed, originally sat on top of the block with his left leg hanging over one side and hands resting in his lap. The ropes are so detailed that we can discern the form of the knots. Like San Lorenzo Monument 15, this sculpture seems to depict the act of moving a large stone over land. Even the most clinically dispassionate scientist totally lacking in imagination can visualize an obese Olmec ruler seated on the block destined to become his throne, exhorting long lines of sweating men to pull harder on the last leg of the ascent up the hill into his royal workshop.

The transport of stone is an especially appropriate theme at Laguna de los Cerros since Medellín Zenil identified an actual monument workshop at nearby Llano del Jícaro. Susan Gillespie's recent investigations at Llano del Jícaro identified unworked boulders native to the spot, unfinished monuments, stone tools, and carving debris.[18] Laguna de los Cerros and subordinate workshops like Llano del Jícaro may have provided San Lorenzo and other Olmec centers with raw material or even finished sculptures on at least some occasions.

Individual Olmec sculptures have appeared at La Isla, El Cardonal, Loma de la Piedra, Cuatotolapan, Cruz del Milagro, and other places near Laguna de los Cerros. Unfortunately none of them have been investigated so we do not know if they were independent Olmec centers, subsidiary communities analogous to Loma del Zapote and Estero Rabon, or sculpture workshops.

26 Cruz del Milagro Monument 1, the "Prince of Cruz del Milagro." The seated posture and forward lean of this man occur in both large sculpture and small ceramic figurines, suggesting some special significance. Ht 130 cm (51 in), estimated weight 7 tons.

I Aerial view of La Venta Pyramid C, a 30-m (98-ft) high construction that dominates the entire region. The ridges and depressions may be intentional or simply the result of erosion during the 2,500 years since it was abandoned.

II Aerial view of Laguna de los Cerros. The mounds have become rounded through erosion; dimples on their summits probably signal pits excavated by looters searching for saleable antiquities.

III Reconstruction of a ritual burial of a Mosaic Mask in La Venta's Complex A. A priest or ruler deposits a bundle of quetzal feathers and three jade celts as richly attired companions ceremonially dump the first loads of specially selected soils on the Mask. Nobles observe the proceedings from above while workers carry basket loads of earth and raise basalt columns with ropes and levers.

IV In this reconstruction Olmec workers use log rafts to transport two roughed-out sculptures from the quarry to their final destination. The Olmecs must have taken advantage of water transport whenever possible for moving multi-ton monuments. Dugout canoes were such an indispensable part of Olmec life that artisans carved small ritual canoes from jade.

V La Venta Monument 1, a Colossal Head, may be the portrait of La Venta's last ruler. It was found in the plaza south of Pyramid C.

VI Marion Stirling and two unidentified colleagues admire San Lorenzo Monument 1 (El Rey [the king]) after it was excavated in 1946. The appearance of its eye in an eroded trail led to the Stirlings' discovery of the then-unknown San Lorenzo, the first Olmec capital.

VII San Lorenzo Monument 61 (Colossal Head 8): its outstanding preservation, sensitivity of carving and carefully executed proportions make it one of the finest Colossal Heads known. Jaguar claws or eagle talons decorate the headband.

VIII This warrior or priest, carved on the native rock face of a cliff, is one of three that dominate a fourth individual on Chalcatzingo Monument 2 (see ill. 126, p. 178).

IX A saurian monster grasps a helpless human in its jaws in Chalcatzingo Monument 5. While such creatures were commonly depicted in Olmec art and beliefs, as one might expect with the ubiquity of alligators and crocodiles in Olman, at Chalcatzingo their living analogs never existed.

27 Artist's sketch of Las Limas with modern houses scattered amongst the archaeological remains.

Las Limas

Las Limas was a major Olmec center situated in the heart of the Isthmus of Tehuantepec 40 km (25 miles) south of San Lorenzo. In his recent survey of the site, Hernando Gómez Rueda recorded more than 800 densely clustered mounds, all assumed to date to the Early Formative period in a 100-ha (247-acre) area.[19] The only monument discovered so far, a magnificent greenstone sculpture known as the "Lord of Las Limas," depicts a seated young man holding an inert were-jaguar baby on his lap. The baby, together with four lightly incised faces on the young man's shoulders and knees, provided the inspiration for the Las Limas Hypothesis, a major insight into the Olmec pantheon discussed in Chapter 6.

27

pl. XX

The modern history of the Lord of Las Limas is as fascinating as the sculpture itself.[20] Two children discovered it while searching for a stone they could use to crack palm nuts. After excavating the statue, their parents brought it into the house and, along with the neighbors, began to venerate it as a miraculous apparition of the Virgin Mary. Residents of a nearby village borrowed it for the festival of the Virgin del Carmen, adorning it with paper flowers and a silk cape and giving it the place of honor on an improvised altar for nine days. They even moved the Virgin of Guadalupe, Mexico's patron saint, to one side of the altar because the Matron of Las Limas, as villagers now called her, was deemed "more important because she is older."

Word of this unusual sculpture soon reached Xalapa, the state capital, where archaeologists decided to bring it in to the museum. The villagers agreed to part with their newfound Saint only after state officials resolved a long-standing land dispute, constructed a school, and ensured that the monument would be displayed on public view in the museum. The Matron, now changed into Lord, was installed in a place of honor in the museum where it quickly became the talk of Xalapa. Shortly thereafter the young discoverers visited the museum where they received an ovation from local schoolchildren that happened to be viewing the sculpture.

Most fairy tales, be they true or false, would end at this point, but the true-life story was far from over. Several years later thieves removed the sculpture from the museum in the middle of the night. Many archaeologists believed a private collector was keeping it hidden to avoid prosecution. However, it appears the thieves were unable to sell such a high-profile object, for police later found it in a motel room in San Antonio, Texas. It was returned to Xalapa, where it has remained except for occasional legal trips abroad as a featured participant in international exhibitions of Olmec art.

La Oaxaqueña

La Oaxaqueña lies nestled in a bend of the Coatzacoalcos river 27 km (17 miles) south of San Lorenzo and 14 km (8.75 miles) from Las Limas. Robert Cobean's recent investigations encountered numerous large mounds and ample Early Formative pottery. A 10-m-deep-by-15-m-wide (39 x 49-ft) manmade ditch encircles the core of the ancient community.[21] The ditch probably functioned as a fortification, making it Mesoamerica's oldest known military construction and a powerful testament to the warfare that many archaeologists have long suspected was an integral part of Olmec life. Although no sculptures have been reported at La Oaxaqueña, nearby Ojo de Agua boasts a rounded basalt monument marked with the curious concave depressions so common on San Lorenzo carvings and many sherds of Calzadas Carved pottery.

San Lorenzo's demise

The specter of military conflict brings us to San Lorenzo's decline and fall. The only thing we know for certain is that it happened sometime during the tenth century BC. What actually happened and why are questions that remain unanswered. Coe and I once argued for internal revolt or external conquest based on our belief that all the stone monuments were deliberately destroyed in one gigantic cataclysm. Today it seems more likely that instead monuments were frequently recarved and reused prior to San Lorenzo's collapse and that our "mutilated" monuments were merely in the recarving process when the city was abandoned. But why was the work suspended? Why did San Lorenzo's last ruler, whoever he was, not have a successor? Warfare, invasions, economic decline, environmental changes and the emergence of rival centers have all been suggested as causes or factors that contributed to San Lorenzo's downfall, and all may indeed have played a role. Some authorities suggest that populations abandoned the lowland river valleys for the adjacent Tuxtla piedmont, but that seems to be an effect rather than a cause.

Whatever else happened, we know that the region experienced important physical and environmental changes. Geomorphologist Mario Arturo Ortiz Pérez has shown that the rivers around San Lorenzo were shifting their courses at this time.[22] That change alone would have severely impacted upon San Lorenzo's commercial and political fortunes, compounding whatever other problems it was experiencing. The causes of these changes in river courses are unknown but tectonic uplift, fluctuations in sea levels and coastlines, and silt build-up resulting from extensive land clearing for agriculture are all possible culprits. This environmental explanation obviously does not rule out revolt, external conquest, or other socio-cultural factors; in fact, such changes in the natural world may have even triggered them. Whatever the explanation, Mesoamerica's first city faded into the background of history and myth and was replaced by La Venta, a rising star to the east.

3 · La Venta's Realm

La Venta stands as one of ancient America's greatest paradoxes. How could this city, the capital of a realm that extended from the Tuxtla mountains to the Grijalva river and Middle Formative Mesoamerica's most influential community, have flourished in the heart of a vast wetland zone? Why did its rulers import hundreds of tons of basalt, serpentine, and jadeite into a riverine floodplain where none occurred naturally? Finally, why did La Venta emerge as the most advanced society in Mexico and Central America and manage to maintain that eminence for centuries? We address these questions in the following pages, but much more information is needed before archaeologists can reconstruct the full story.

La Venta's Olmec history

La Venta occupies a ridge overlooking the ancient course of the Palma river, 15 km (9.3 miles) from the Gulf of Mexico, embedded in a complex network of rivers, streams, elevated ridges and oxbow lakes that provided excellent transportation routes, rich river levee farmland and abundant aquatic foods. Humans first exploited these resources more than 7,000 years ago when incipient farmers settled at nearby San Andrés (Chapter 1). The earliest known occupation at La Venta itself dates to 1200 BC, but older remains almost certainly lie buried somewhere on the ridge. Regardless of whatever local importance La Venta may have enjoyed in the second millennium, it rapidly emerged as the dominant Olmec capital after 900 BC, and maintained that eminence for the next four centuries.

Our best information on La Venta's history comes from the Complex A precinct of earth mounds and plazas located immediately north of the Great Pyramid, where excavations in 1955 revealed four construction phases dated to 1000–600 BC by radiocarbon.[1] The lack of a ceramic chronology makes it impossible to trace the details of historical developments at La Venta, but recent investigations at the nearby San Andrés village site identified a ceramic sequence that probably holds for the main center as well.[2]

Charcoal resting on the outermost face of the Great Pyramid radiocarbon-dated to 394 ± 36 years BC suggests that the mound and probably the entire city were abandoned shortly after 400 BC.[3] Squatters camped in the ruins after the city was abandoned and a small Late-Classic period settlement occupied the northern edge of the abandoned Olmec center. Over the centuries countless visitors must have passed by the pyramid that even today is the largest eminence on the coast east of the Tuxtla mountains. What stories they must have told about the builders of this fabled city with its silent mounds and stone sculptures lying amidst the jungle!

The lack of significant post-Olmec occupation minimized the opportunities for significant later disturbance and looting, thus preserving La Venta's sculptures and buried caches in their original contexts. This happy circumstance has led to important insights about the organization and functional aspects of the ancient city.

La Venta at its height

La Venta's urbanized zone may originally have covered as much as 200 ha (494 acres), much of it given over to elite activities.[4] González's site map of the "downtown" core shows numerous large earth mounds and courtyards that form "plaza groups" extending north–south along a carefully delineated centerline oriented eight degrees west of modern magnetic north.[5] This centerline bisected the community into east and west segments that frequently appear to be mirror images. The "Great Pyramid" (designated Complex C by archaeologists) occupies the center point of the city, while lower mounds to the north and south created independent but interconnected architectural units. Thus La Venta, like San Lorenzo, was a Regal-Ritual City where ritual and ideology dominated the lives of the inhabitants. F. Kent Reilly III has argued that its mounded architecture formed a three-dimensional cosmic model that served as a "backdrop, a ritual stage, and a sanctified location for world renewal ceremonies and ritual reenactments of creation events." [6]

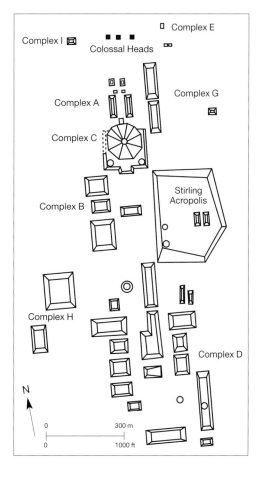

28

28 La Venta site plan showing the major mounds visible in 1980.

La Venta's status as a Regal-Ritual City was not apparent until publication of Rebecca González Lauck's detailed topographic map allowed archaeologists to visualize the distribution of mounds, sculptures, and buried offerings as an integrated entity. The main elements of this constructed environment include formally marked entrances at the north and south, 40 earth mounds forming 9 architectural complexes, 90 known stone sculptures, and scores of buried offerings and caches. Mounds probably served as substructures for houses and other buildings, but excavation is needed to verify this assumption.

While La Venta's elite and ceremonial character is indisputable, we must not forget the presence of farmers, artisans, and other people of all social ranks. They are not visible on the map because their unassuming homes, constructed of perishable materials directly on the ground, have left no visible traces. It is also important to remember that most Olmecs lived in villages and hamlets strung along the river levees in the nearby hinterland rather than the urban center.

La Venta's formal entrances: Complexes D and I

Architectural Complexes D and I mark La Venta's southern and northern edges. Each Complex includes three stone monuments placed in ways that suggest they signified formal entrances to the city. Group D contains twenty mounds separated by long linear plazas or avenues. David Grove considers it a possible royal residential zone, but Complex B to the north appears better suited to that purpose. Archaeologists generally assume the mounds supported houses or other structures, but excavation is needed to determine their actual uses. I suspect many functioned as flat open-air stages where rulers and priests enacted rituals viewed by crowds standing in the plazas below, or viewing stands from which onlookers observed rituals carried out in the plazas. Mounds D-11 and D-12 appear to form a ballcourt directly south of the Stirling Acropolis. Excavations into D-7, a small mound located near the southern edge of the complex, revealed a U-shaped building surrounding a sunken patio.[7] Three large sandstone monuments originally rested on the mound summit. These sculptures, now badly eroded, appear to depict squatting human figures holding helmets in their outstretched arms. González believes Mound D-7 may have served as a formal entryway for visitors entering La Venta from the south.

Complex I may have served a similar function at the north end of the city. Most of the mounds were destroyed when an airstrip was built, and two groups of sculptures may be the only remnants of a formal entrance for visitors arriving from the Gulf of Mexico. One group, composed of Monuments 19, 20, and 21, appears to rest directly on the site center-line, but may have been moved there during construction of the airstrip. Monument 19, one of La Venta's finest low relief sculptures, depicts a human male with a bag in his hand nestled in the body of a rattlesnake. The serpent's head appears to be crowned with plumes, making it the oldest known depiction of a feathered serpent in Mesoamerican art. Monument 20 is an amorphous sculpture thought to portray a stylized whale or manatee, and Monument 21 is a mutilated and headless human figure shown seated behind a rectangular block. Not even my most audacious colleagues have dared suggest a functional explanation for this trio of figures.

The second set of sculptures contains three Colossal Heads placed in a line oriented east to west. David Grove believes they proclaimed La Venta's divine nature personified in its deified rulers, a very appropriate theme for the entrance to the dynastic center.[8] Ivan van Sertima and other "Afrocentric" writers have recently tried to "prove" that the Olmecs were migrants from Africa with the false claim that Matthew W. Stirling found the heads gazing eastwards towards their African homeland.[9] In reality, Stirling clearly stated that all three faced north.

La Venta's Royal Compound

La Venta's largest mounds form four architectural units, designated Complexes A, B, and C and the Stirling Acropolis, at the center of the ridge. I believe they functioned as an integrated Royal Compound that included the ruler's residence and the primary settings for both public and private ritual performances that connected the ruler and his subjects to the supernatural world. The precise extent of the Royal Compound is not well defined and indeed in some respects La Venta's entire urban core probably functioned as a Royal Compound in the minds of most Olmecs. However, these four complexes surely formed the heart of La Venta's Royal Compound and the focus of elite life and culture for the entire La Venta Realm.

Complex C (Mounds C-1 through C-5, known collectively as the Great   pl. 1
Pyramid) dominated La Venta's landscape 2,500 years ago just as it does today. In its day no known structure anywhere in Mesoamerica rivaled it in size or architectural sophistication. Even after more than 2,000 years of erosion, it measures 128 m (422 ft) north–south, 114 m (376 ft) east–west, over 30 m (100 ft) high, and contains 99,100 cu. m (3.5 million cu. ft) of earth fill. An earth apron (C-3) covered the east, west, and south sides while a projecting ramp or stair descended from the apron to Plaza B.

The original shape of this massive construction is a matter of consider-   29
able controversy. When it was still shrouded in tropical forest, archaeologists assumed it to be rectangular like later Mesoamerican buildings. Robert Heizer and his University of California-Berkeley team laid this misconception to rest in 1967 when they prepared a detailed topographic map shortly after the vegetation had been removed.[10] Today it has the form of a fluted cone with a round base and 10 troughs and 10 ridges extending up the sides rather like an upside-down paper cupcake mold. Is that what the Olmecs intended, or is it the product of 3,000 years of erosion? Heizer argued that the Olmecs deliberately created it in imitation of a prominent volcano in the

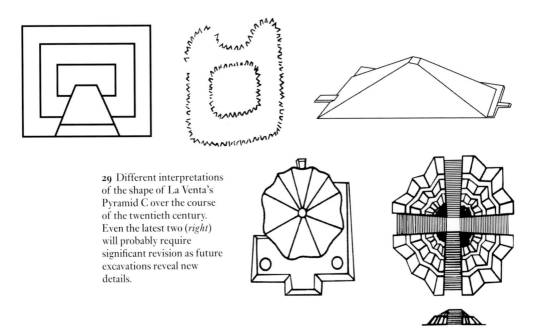

29 Different interpretations of the shape of La Venta's Pyramid C over the course of the twentieth century. Even the latest two (*right*) will probably require significant revision as future excavations reveal new details.

Tuxtla mountains. The issue remained unresolved until González carried out controlled excavations on the mound's south face where it joins the apron. These excavations exposed intact fragments of the original sandy clay surface held together with slabs of white limestone. She believes Complex C was "a pyramidal structure with a series of stepped taluses and inset corners that recede from the sides of the central access," rather than a true fluted cone, and observes that "the sophistication of the shape and construction methods indicate a pre-established and long architectural tradition."[11] Future excavations may reveal earlier stages of this long architectural tradition in the form of older buildings beneath the outer shell. Unfortunately the meter or two of soil bulldozed from the mound summit in the 1960s makes it unlikely that archaeologists will ever know if any buildings ever stood there or what their functions may have been.

A magnetometer survey in 1967 revealed a strong magnetic anomaly high on the south side of the pyramid.[12] The source of the anomaly has never been investigated. It may be nothing more than a patch of burned clay, but it may also instead be a cache of buried monuments or even the tomb of an Olmec ruler, perhaps the founder of the La Venta dynasty. Only excavation can resolve this mystery.

The apron around the south, east, and west sides of the Great Pyramid greatly enhanced the visual impact of the towering earth mound as viewed from Plaza B while providing an elevated stage for public rituals. Much like modern theater designers, Olmec architects employed scenery backdrops composed of two small earth mounds (C-4 and C-5) at the southeast and southwest corners of the apron and large stone sculptures. The mounds may have supported small shrines or served as open-air ritual settings. Six large stone slabs with carvings on one face (stelae) were firmly embedded in the apron floor at the foot of the Great Pyramid, while two multi-ton thrones rested on the south edge of the ramp. The stelae formed two sets of three, each forming a linear sculptural tableau that faced the plaza to the south. Monuments 87, 88, and 89, all carved from volcanic stone, formed the set placed southwest of the Great Pyramid's centerline, while Monuments 25/26, 27, and Stela 5 located east of the line were made from greenstone. What might the obviously deliberate choice of materials have meant? Did the colors refer to different parts of the Olmec universe, or did they replicate the original sources of the raw materials? The designs are equally puzzling. Monument 87 is smooth but may once have had a painted design. Four sculptures (88, 89, 25/26, and 27) depict the supernatural or mythological creature identified by Karl Taube as the Olmec Maize God. Stela 5 shows three standing people being observed by a fourth placed in a register above them. This scene may depict an actual or imagined historical incident in which a ruler and other dignitaries were being watched over by a supernatural patron or ancestor.

The thrones (designated as Altars 2 and 3) are two large flat-topped monoliths that sat on the ramp in front of the apron. Both depict seated human adults emerging from niches; that on Altar 2 holds a baby in his hands while his companion on Altar 3 does not. Both probably served as thrones where rulers sat during public ceremonies, but what might the presence of a baby on one and its absence on the other signify? Whatever specific meanings Olmecs read into the depictions, the entire sculptural setting framed by the Great Pyramid looming behind it must have been charged with symbolic meaning for both the actors on this outdoor stage and the multitudes who observed them from the plaza below. F. Kent Reilly III

30 Five stelae located on the south side of Pyramid C at La Venta. They formed a sculptural tableau that included two basalt "altars" or thrones, and perhaps other sculptures. A Stela 5, B Monument 89, C Monument 88, D Monument 25/26, E Monument 27.

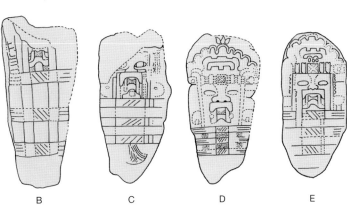

A   B   C   D   E

31 La Venta Monument (Altar) 5. Although badly mutilated in ancient times, this throne preserves the frontal scene of a personage emerging from a niche or cave holding an infant in a pose that suggests presentation of a precious cargo. Scenes in which two adults attempt to control lively were-jaguar babies cover the two lateral sides. Ht 154 cm (60 in).

believes the Great Pyramid served as a surrogate Mountain of Creation while the monuments depict water, fertility, the Olmec Maize God, and rulership, the essential elements of Olmec life.[13] We may never understand all the subtleties encoded in these remains, but careful archaeological excavations could shed considerable light on this gigantic tableau of earth and stone.

Complex B, located south of the Great Pyramid, includes Plaza B with Mound B-4 at its center, and Mounds B-1, B-2, and B-3 on the east. Plaza B is a large open area covering 42,000 sq. m (452,000 sq. ft) that would have provided ample space for thousands of spectators attending public rituals on the Great Pyramid or its apron. The many sculptures placed around the plaza included a Colossal Head, three thrones, Stela 2, and a large basalt column. Fragments of six other sculptures were found at or near Mound B-4, a small altar-like platform in the plaza center. All these stones seem to lie at or very near their ancient locations, and all served to bring the concept of divine rulership into the public plaza.

The Stirling Acropolis, an immense (324 x 260-m by 7-m high [1069 x 858-ft by 23-ft high]) irregularly shaped platform, looks down over Complex B from the east. On its upper surface we find remains of two circular mounds and a pair of small parallel mounds that may someday prove to be a ballcourt. Exploratory excavations on the summit revealed numerous

31, pl. V

basalt columns, four drain lines constructed of basalt troughs, and a buried cache of badly battered monument fragments, remains consistent with the idea that the Acropolis served as La Venta's Royal Palace, the actual residence of the ruler and his family.

La Venta's hidden sanctuary: Complex A

A small group of earth mounds and plazas directly north of the Great Pyramid form one of the most unusual architectural complexes in the Olmec world. Known as Complex A, the buildings visible on the surface, 32 together with richly stocked human burials, and caches and offerings, formed a three-dimensional replica of the Olmec cosmos. This was a very private space enclosed by a fence constructed of stone columns, a secluded retreat where La Venta's royalty gathered to commune with their deceased and deified ancestors.

Complex A included two open-air courts surrounded by earth mounds. The South Court formed a corridor that led to the North or Enclosed Court, connecting Mound C-2, a small platform at the foot of the Great Pyramid, to the Enclosed Court. Both courts contained surface buildings and buried features placed equidistant from the La Venta site centerline, extending the community's bilateral symmetry to the subterranean world as well as its visible surface. Indeed, the bilateral symmetry may have extended beyond Complex A to include the mounds of Complex G to the east and a corresponding set of mounds, unfortunately destroyed before they could be mapped, to the west.

Construction history
Even though Complex A has been more intensively studied than any other Olmec architectural unit,[14] many questions remain about its history of construction and functions.

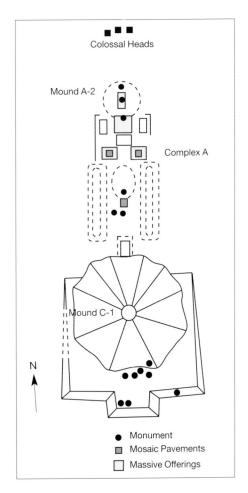

32 Ground plan of Pyramid C and Complex A at La Venta showing locations of mounds, monuments, and buried architectural features. See ill. 28, p. 61, for wider context.

Colossal Heads

Mound A-2

Complex A

Mound C-1

N

● Monument
■ Mosaic Pavements
□ Massive Offerings

The most commonly accepted scenario has it being constructed in four major episodes or phases (I–IV), each lasting approximately 100 years. Phases I–III appear to have grown out of each other in an orderly fashion without drastic changes of the basic plan, however Phase IV saw major innovations that resulted in a truly unique set of buildings.

Olmec builders began Phase I by leveling the terrain, laying out the orientation line, and erecting a red clay embankment around the projected work area. Next they laid down a series of light-brown-and-buff sand floors and began construction on three earth platform mounds in the Enclosed Court area. Whatever else they erected was obliterated by later activities. During Phase II they placed an adobe block wall on top of the red clay embankment and deposited numerous white sand floors, the last placed on a foundation of crushed green serpentine rock. Massive Offerings and Pavements 1 and 3 (see *Offerings and caches* section below, p. 72) were created before construction began on Mounds A-1-d and A-1-e. Phase II activities ended with the construction of Mound A-1-d directly above Pavement 3. Mound A-1-e with its accompanying Massive Offering and Pavement were constructed east of the centerline at the same time.

Phase III was initiated by dumping a thick layer of red, purple, and pink clays over the entire Enclosed Court and covering them with multi-colored sand floors. Massive Offering 3 was excavated into the subsoil and filled with six layers of serpentine blocks. Offering 10, a cruciform-shaped cache of thirty-eight serpentine and jadeite celts was then placed on top of the Massive Offering in a special red clay bed and plastered over with a cap of yellowish sandy clay, and Offering 4, described below, was placed in a deep hole cut into the plaza floor west of Mound A-1-f.

33

pl. III

Complex A attained its fullest, most flamboyant glory in Phase IV. Eleven low mounds covered with red clay were constructed, although any buildings that may have existed on their summits have disappeared without a trace. Multi-colored floors were laid down to the top of the surrounding adobe walls and a fence or palisade of prismatic stone columns was erected on top of the adobe walls, apparently to maintain privacy by preventing outsiders from looking into the Court. Similar enclosures were created on top of Mounds A-1-d and -e at the south end of the Enclosed Court and Mound A-2 was enlarged to receive several burials, thereby completely closing off the north end of the Enclosed Court. Numerous stone sculptures were discovered on the plaza surfaces. Hidden away from view were mound interiors constructed of adobe blocks and carefully selected clays, buried tombs with rich offerings and elaborate caches, creating a three-dimensional ritual setting that replicated the Olmec Underworld, the World of the Living, and the Heavens.

Construction began with the excavation of a steep narrow pit 14.8 x 6 x 4.8 m (49.5 x 20 x 16 ft) deep and depositing a single layer of serpentine blocks laid in a bed of red clay (Massive Offering 2). The pit was refilled immediately with soil that contained three offerings. One contained thirty-

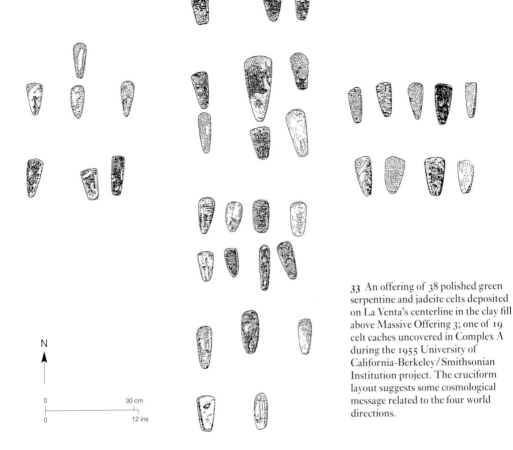

N

0   30 cm

0   12 ins

33 An offering of 38 polished green serpentine and jadeite celts deposited on La Venta's centerline in the clay fill above Massive Offering 3; one of 19 celt caches uncovered in Complex A during the 1955 University of California-Berkeley/Smithsonian Institution project. The cruciform layout suggests some cosmological message related to the four world directions.

seven jadeite and serpentine celts arranged in a cruciform pattern, the others were placed in shallow pits excavated in the sand equidistant from the site centerline. Their contents were identical: nine celts laid in three rows of 4-4-1 and an iron ore mirror north of the single celt and cinnabar stains at the south end. Tomb B, a large sandstone sarcophagus carved with the likeness of the Olmec Dragon on its exterior, was placed directly above the offerings. Tomb A was constructed from basalt columns identical to those in the palisade above the northern edge of Massive Offering 2, and numerous other offerings and caches were placed in Mound A-2.

Did the Olmecs who laid down Phase I have a clear vision of how the precinct would look at the end of Phase IV? This seems unlikely, especially if construction spanned four centuries as the excavators maintained. I personally believe that the entire project was carried out over 100 or 150 years, and that the planners did have a basic vision of its ultimate appearance. However, I also suspect that someone, perhaps La Venta's last ruler, imposed a new, more grandiose vision on the project that resulted in what we see as Phase IV.

Complex A probably functioned for several generations before it fell into disuse when the entire city was abandoned at about 400 BC. Yet the Olmecs did not simply walk away from this sanctuary, leaving it open to the elements. Their last construction act was to ritually bury the entire area under a 30-cm (12-in) cap of red clay, sealing it off from the world until inquisitive archaeologists began to poke holes in it in 1940.

Stone monuments

At least a dozen carved monuments formed part of the Complex A Phase IV architectural program. Most are very fragmentary but four are sufficiently complete to show significant details. Stela 1 portrays a standing woman, one of the few reasonably certain human females in Olmec art. The front of Stela 3, a large irregular basalt shaft, is covered with a complex low relief scene that seems to depict a historical event or legend. Two elaborately costumed men confront each other while smaller, perhaps mythical figures fill the air around them. Monument 5 depicts a small rotund human with a pronounced baby-face and "Mohawk-style" hair bundle or crest, holding what looks like a bowl. The sculptor probably intended to portray a dwarf or archetypal Olmec were-jaguar baby, but local folklore has firmly identified the creature as "La Abuelita," a kindly grandmother offering a bowl full of hot, homemade tortillas to her adoring grandchildren. Monument 13, nicknamed "the Ambassador," shows a profile view of a walking man who holds a banner or flag in his left hand. Four glyph-like symbols shown around him may represent some of the oldest-known writing on stone in Mesoamerica. The only one that can be identified with any certainty is a footprint behind the man, the oldest-known example of this pre-Columbian glyph for travel.

Tombs

Five formal tombs were created during Phase IV. They are so elaborate and so integrated to the architecture that it seems clear that Complex A really was a mortuary complex dedicated to the spirits of deceased rulers. Tombs A, B, and E lay beneath Mound A-2 directly on the site centerline, while Tomb C was under Mound A-3. Tomb D, the only burial lacking a formal structure, also lay under A-3 but was slightly offset to the west. These are among Mesoamerica's oldest formal tombs and the offerings placed with them would be considered lavish at any time period. Unfortunately, all the skeletons have completely disintegrated in La Venta's acidic soils. Despite the lamentable disappearance of the skeletons, the elaborate tomb architecture, privileged location, and rich offerings all indicate that the deceased belonged to the highest echelon of La Venta society.

34   Tomb A's walls and roof were constructed of basalt columns. Limestone slabs covered with dark clay paved the floor. Large deposits of red cinnabar that stained the soil and the floor probably covered the corpse or corpses. The excavators tentatively identified two clusters of badly decomposed bone splinters and teeth as remnants of two human juveniles. Each cluster contained sets of exquisitely carved jadeite objects that included four stand-
pl. xv   ing figurines, a seated female figurine who wears a tiny obsidian

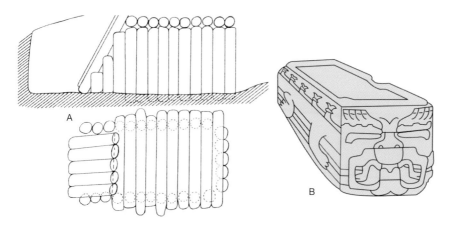

34 La Venta Tombs A and B. Tomb A contained almost completely disintegrated human skeletal remains thought to be those of two juveniles, along with numerous jadeite ornaments. Tomb B is a sandstone sarcophagus covered with a depiction of the Olmec Dragon. Ht 180 cm (89 in).

pendant-mirror on her chest, two ear ornaments, a clamshell pendant, beads, numerous ornaments that probably were sewn onto a cloth backing, and a bloodletter in the form of a stingray spine. Other grave goods included authentic stingray spines and an exquisitely polished magnetite mirror. After the burials were placed on the floor and liberally covered with red cinnabar, the chamber was filled with reddish–orange clay and Mound A-2 constructed above it using the same material.

Tomb B, a large hollowed-out rectangular sandstone sarcophagus with a closely fitted lid, lay a few meters south of Tomb A. The sarcophagus exterior featured an Olmec were-jaguar figure whose face filled the north side and body covered the long sides facing east and west. The well-finished interior was filled with compact clay. No traces of human remains were visible but archaeologists found a standing human figurine carved from serpentine, a jadeite bloodletter, and two large jadeite ear spools, each accompanied by jaguar canine tooth pendants of the same material, on the sarcophagus floor. Did Tomb B ever contain a corpse or was it a "pseudo-burial," an interment that imitated a human burial but lacked a human corpse? Did the bones simply disintegrate over the centuries or were they removed when Complex A was abandoned? We will never know, for even the badly eroded and fragile sarcophagus has disappeared or been destroyed since its discovery.

Tomb E lay between Tombs A and B. A layer of horizontal basalt columns covered a mixed deposit of red cinnabar and clay containing 108 jadeite celts, ornaments, and other objects. One outstanding celt depicts an 35 Olmec were-jaguar whose features were highlighted by placing red hematite in the incised crevasses of the light greenstone. Ear ornaments, a necklace, and other ornaments were arranged as they might have been placed on a corpse, but as with Tomb B, no skeletal remains were identified.

35 Jadeite celt, La Venta. This spectacular celt was found south of Tomb A in an offering containing more than 100 celts, beads, and other objects. Cinnabar in the crevices may be an intentional accent to the carving or simply residue from a rite in which the entire object was coated with a substance symbolic of life or blood. Ht 13 cm (5 in).

Tombs C and D lie under Mound A-3. Tomb C was a rectangular cyst constructed of sandstone slabs that was covered with red clay after the slabs were in place. The builders only partially filled the interior with clay, causing the roof to collapse when the red clay cover was dumped on it. A thick bed of cinnabar that probably covered the now-disappeared corpse was discovered near the floor. The burial offering placed in the cyst included three pottery vessels, an incised obsidian prismatic blade core, several fragments of rock crystal, and a trove of greenstone objects. The latter included 37 serpentine and jadeite celts, 2 decorated jadeite ear spools and pendants, a large jadeite tubular bead, a jadeite perforator, 2 jadeite "turtle carapace" pendants, a serpentine figurine and 110 jadeite spangles that may have been attached to a shroud or cloth. This treasure may be the very last offering deposited in Complex A, and thus perhaps includes the last great collection of greenstone wealth controlled by the last rulers of the site.

Tomb D, the only interment that lacked a formal container, was marked by a layer of cinnabar found near the north edge of Mound A-3, slightly west of the site centerline. Excavator Waldo Wedel considered it a possible child's burial, based on the jadeite ear spools and pendants he found placed as though they originally decorated the head of the deceased. He also found a pottery vessel, two cylindrical jadeite beads, and a jadeite disk associated with this enigmatic burial.

Offerings and caches

The numerous caches of objects deposited in Complex A in contexts other than burials are classified as Massive Offerings, Pavements (also referred to as Mosaic Masks), and Small Dedicatory Offerings. Massive Offerings were placed in large, purposefully excavated pits that were then filled with tons of serpentine blocks encased in special clay matrices. Five Massive Offerings have been identified in Complex A. Massive Offering 1 is typical; a rectangular pit 23.1 m (77 ft) on a side was cut through existing floors and constructions down to clay subsoil. The builders immediately deposited twenty-eight layers of serpentine blocks weighing more than 1,000 tons, surrounded with specially selected olive and blue clay. Next, they laid down Pavement 3, a gigantic, single-layer mosaic constructed of 485 green serpentine blocks placed in yellowish-olive clay. The subject of this large 4.8 x 4.4-m (15.8 x 14.5-ft) and highly abstract design has sparked endless debate, in part because we do not know which end the Olmec considered the top. Most archaeologists consider it an extremely stylized depiction of an Olmec were-jaguar. The mottled pink clay fill above it contained a Small Dedicatory Offering of jadeite and serpentine celts arranged in a cruciform pattern, together with a small iron-ore mirror. Similar cruciform caches have appeared at other places in Complex A, either alone or associated with Massive Offerings, Pavements and burials.

Small Dedicatory Offering 4, an unusual set of greenstone figurines and   pl. XIII
celts, provides a fascinating glimpse of an Olmec courtly scene or ritual in progress. During Phase III someone excavated a deep, narrow hole into the plaza floor west of Mound A-1-f and carefully placed 16 human figurines   36
and 6 celts upright in the bottom of the hole. The long thin celts form a backdrop or wall reminiscent of Complex A's basalt column enclosures. Four of the celts had been cut out of a larger existing celt or plaque that had an engraved scene on one face, yet another example of the Olmec practice of recarving existing objects of precious stone into new forms. Despite this obvious reworking, one self-styled expert in ancient writing systems recently misidentified the engraved lines on the four as examples of Chinese writing, offering them as "evidence" that the Olmecs were pre-Columbian migrants from China!

Eleven of the human figurines stand in a semicircle observing four others that walk single file towards a central character, represented by a spectacular, highly polished jadeite

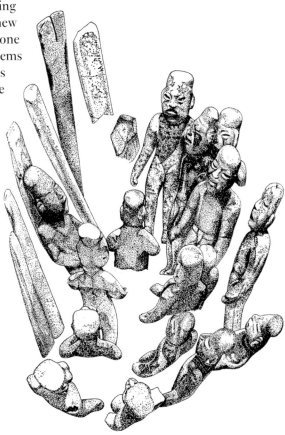

36 Offering 4, Complex A, La Venta. Sixteen stone figurines depicting men stand in front of a wall-like structure constructed of four celts carved out of an older, larger celt that bore an inscribed figure. Four figures were placed as though passing for inspection between a local figure standing with his back to the wall and eleven onlookers.

figurine. The remaining figurines are carved from serpentine, with the exception of one badly eroded basalt piece. Every object in Offering 4 is worn and battered, suggesting that they were already well-used heirlooms when they were placed in the ground. Does this scene replicate an event that actually took place inside Complex A? We suspect so, but of course will never know for certain. Whatever the cache signified, later generations knew its precise location: many years later someone excavated a small hole through the accumulated floors above it, exposed the figurine heads, perhaps to verify that they were still there, and covered them up once again without disturbing them.

The total quantity of the treasures uncovered in Complex A, only a portion of which are described here, brings to mind the royal treasures of European monarchs or pharaonic tombs. La Venta's Olmec rulers valued serpentine and especially jadeite above all other materials. The effort and costs they expended to obtain these materials was so substantial that the word "staggering" is not an exaggeration. For example, the five Massive Offerings contain hundreds of tons of serpentine brought from unknown quarries somewhere outside Olman's alluvial lowlands. Scientists have recently identified the source of La Venta's jadeite in Guatemala's Sierra de las Minas district more than 480 km (300 miles) to the southeast. Olmec artisans turned the raw quarry blocks of serpentine and jadeite into exquisitely polished figurines, ornaments, and celts used by rulers and their kin in the course of daily life as well in the rituals that put them where archaeologists find them today. More than 250 greenstone celts and axes have been scientifically excavated in Complex A, most lying in carefully arranged rectangular or cruciform patterns; looters may have removed many more. Most are undecorated except for a high polish, but a few are carved with depictions of Olmec supernaturals.

La Venta sculpture

La Venta was one of the two great centers of monumental stone sculpture in the Olmec world. Ninety stone monuments are known today and new examples continue to appear. Certain classes of La Venta sculpture are so similar to analogues at San Lorenzo that they may be contemporaneous. Both communities featured Colossal Heads, thrones, drain systems, and other royal or dynastic monuments. Both had permanently installed sculptures as well as smaller, more portable pieces that may have appeared only on special occasions. Nevertheless, notable differences separate the sculptural corpuses of the two centers. La Venta's sculptors created many flat, single-dimension depictions, while those at San Lorenzo favored fully sculpted, in-the-round monuments. These differences are not absolute and may simply reflect the different sources of stone available to the artisans at each center, or different approaches to carrying out their basic mission of depicting rulers and their supernatural patrons.

37–39

37 La Venta Monument 4. Matthew Stirling unearthed this Colossal Head in his first field season at La Venta. Along with two other heads it forms a line which may have marked La Venta's northern limit or entrance. Ht 226 cm (88 in).

38 (*below*) Scene on La Venta Stela 3. This large, irregular stone slab was found in Complex A. Two elaborately garbed men of high rank, including perhaps La Venta's ruler, face each other. Five other figures that may be ancestors or supernaturals surround them in a setting suggestive of a spirit world.

39 La Venta Monument 19. This dynamic portrayal of a rattlesnake with a feathered crest is the oldest-known feathered serpent in Mesoamerican art. The human nestled within the serpent's coiled body wears a cape, breechcloth, and an elaborate helmet while holding a bag in his right hand. Ht 95 cm (37 in).

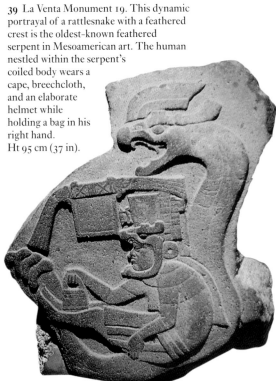

La Venta as a sacred landscape

What did these mysterious mounds, monuments, and offerings mean to the people who created them? Why did the Olmecs put so much effort into transforming their community into a "sacred landscape" full of features that make no sense in ordinary utilitarian terms? Although questions like these have puzzled archaeologists for sixty years, two recent developments open new avenues of investigation into the meanings behind the physical remains. The first – publication of the long-awaited La Venta site map – allows archaeologists finally to grasp the spatial and functional relationships among mounds, monuments, and offerings. At the same time, decipherment of Maya hieroglyphic writing has revolutionized our view of ancient Mesoamerican cultures by demonstrating that Classic Maya architecture and art express basic pan-Mesoamerican beliefs about the cosmos and the creation of the world. The story of this creation is told in the Popol Vuh, a sixteenth-century Quiché Maya text that tells of the origin of the universe, humankind, and maize, Mesoamerica's staff of life.[15] Central elements related in the Popol Vuh are depicted in Olmec sculpture and portable art extending back in time to the early occupations at El Manatí. Finally, the dawning realization that Olmec imagery reflects these same basic beliefs and practices has led to new and innovative interpretations of Olmec art and architecture. F. Kent Reilly III, for example, argues that like later Mesoamerican centers La Venta was created as a sacred landscape that served as a portal, channeling supernatural power into the human community. If this is true, how was this landscape organized and what principles guided its creators?

David Grove attempted to exploit some of these new insights in a pioneering study of the distribution of La Venta monuments related in some fashion to rulership.[16] Grove reasoned that most sculptures remain close to the spot where the Olmecs left them, and thus their modern locations provide clues to their uses by the Olmecs. Thus three Colossal Heads occur together at the north edge of the site while a fourth lies in the middle of the Central Plaza. Eight of nine thrones ("altars") cluster in or near Plaza B; two occupy the apron in front of the Great Pyramid; five sit in Complex B on or near the site centerline; and one lies east of Mound D-8. Finally, two large stelae that appear to portray rulers in action are found in Complex A, while a third is in Plaza B next to the Colossal Head. These distributions suggest to Grove that the Great Pyramid divided La Venta into two sectors. The south sector, including Complexes B, D, and most of the major monuments, was designed for large public performances in which the sculptures functioned in rituals dedicated to the living ruler and his relationship to the supernatural world. The north sector (Complexes A and I) was a mortuary complex where major tombs mark the world of the ancestors and the past. The Great Pyramid dividing them represents a sacred mountain that may have served as the portal connecting the two worlds.

In a closely related study, F. Kent Reilly III attempted to integrate La

Venta's mounds, monuments, and buried caches into a unified reconstruction of its scared geography. Like Grove, Reilly detects two sectors, but places the boundary at Plaza B rather than the Great Pyramid. He views the northern sector as a three-dimensional model of the Olmec cosmos, with the Great Pyramid symbolizing what the Maya called "the First True Mountain, the source of maize, potable water, and the site of the creation of human beings."[17] The line of Maize God stelae on the C-3 apron depict vegetative fertility and the Cosmic Axis, the Axis Mundi of the Mesoamerican world. Together with the two nearby thrones, they created a stage where La Venta rulers publicly reaffirmed their elite status by reenacting world creation events in front of crowds standing below in Plaza B.

Reilly suggests that celebrants moved from this public stage to the private confines of Complex A's South Court along the passageway on the east side of the apron. The Enclosed Court was the centerpiece for a royal mortuary complex that replicated the spot in the cosmos where First Father raised the World Tree during the creation of the present world. Here, living rulers sought access to supernatural power. The buried Massive Offerings represent the primordial ocean on top of which the Olmec Dragon, god of earth, water, agriculture, and fertility, represented by the Mosaic Pavements, floats. Mound A-2 is a royal burial mound surrounding the Tomb B sarcophagus, final resting-place for a true Olmec king. The actual burial deposit included the stone coffer, Massive Offering 2, and numerous other caches and offerings. The dead ruler plays out an eternal role in an endless cycle of creation, world renewal, and regeneration, protecting his subjects and their living royal interceder with the supernatural world.

Reilly and Grove examine the possible meanings of the mounds, monuments, and caches to the people who created them. But why did the Olmecs invest so much effort into transforming their community into such a strange place? I believe this investment reflected their faith in Olmec leaders as mediators between them and the supernatural world. Like later Mesoamerican rulers, Olmec shaman-kings were considered living participants in the eternal universe and continued to serve that function after physical death. Thus the ruler's surroundings, the stage on which he played his divine roles, had to duplicate the Otherworld. This stage included his eternal resting-place, the spot where his successors could summon his spirit and seek his help and guidance. In view of this, it is not surprising that archaeologists have occasionally lost sight of the fact that La Venta was also a place where ordinary people lived, worked, raised families, and died. The next great archaeological challenge at La Venta is to identify these Olmec citizens and learn more about them.

La Venta's hinterland

The hinterland controlled by La Venta surely fluctuated constantly as its fortunes waxed and waned and as leaders in peripheral communities alternately aligned themselves with or broke away from their counterparts in the city. Three archaeological surveys in the swampy terrain east of La Venta have located hundreds of sites, including many buried beneath thick alluvial deposits laid down in more recent times.[18] Anyone standing on the Great Pyramid when it was in use would have seen splotches of light-colored thatch roofs in a patchwork of maize fields, recently abandoned swidden farmlands, and high forests.

William F. Rust was able to define a three-tiered regional settlement hierarchy in the region east of La Venta. La Venta occupied the top rung of the hierarchy, followed by large villages with one or two central mounds and, finally, numerous low house mounds, and numerous smaller villages and hamlets lacking central mounds.[19] San Andrés and Isla Alor are the only hinterland communities that have been scientifically excavated.

Rust's excavations at San Andrés, an intermediate-level village, yielded high-status and ceremonial items that included incised pottery vessels placed in offerings, La Venta-style figurines depicting helmeted males, ballplayers, and slender nude females, and polished greenstone ornaments, tablets, and celts. The occupants enjoyed a varied diet that included maize, fish, turtles, venison, crocodiles, and domesticated dogs. More recent excavations at San Andrés have already shed light on the pre-Olmec occupations in the region as well as the existence of true Olmec writing and promise to provide an abundance of data on the middle range of Olmec society during La Venta's florescence.[20]

Isla Alor occupies a spot of high ground, actually an ancient river levee between La Venta and the coast. Excavations into the subsoil revealed the typical debris that remains of Olmec households in this region: remnants of prepared clay floors, postmolds, hearths, broken pottery, figurines, spindle whorls and ground-stone tools.[21] Obsidian blades and manufacturing debitage show that stone tools were actually manufactured on the spot. Carbonized organic remains created by a fortuitous fire included wood, maize cupules, palm nut fragments, and fish bones. Scanty though they are, the data from Isla Alor and San Andrés provide important glimpses into the daily lives of the vast majority of Olmecs, the "silent majority" who were the critical core of Olmec society.

La Venta's contemporaries

Any reconstruction of La Venta's Realm must take into account potential rival cities in other parts of Olman. If none existed, as may have been the case at times, La Venta's Realm probably extended from the base of the Tuxtla mountains eastward to the Mezcalapa river and south to the Chiapas mountains. Potential rivals included San Lorenzo, Laguna de los Cerros, and La Encrucijada, Tabasco. Surveys have detected substantial Middle Formative-period populations in San Lorenzo's hinterland and the Tuxtla foothills near modern Hueyapan.[22] However, as noted in Chapter 2, San

40 Greenstone pectoral from La Encrucijada, Tabasco. This chest ornament depicts an Olmec were-jaguar baby wearing wavy ear streamers thought to signify rain or fertility. A symbolic maize cob emerges from the V-shaped cleft in the top of the creature's head. Ht 8.5 cm (3⁵⁄₁₆ in).

Lorenzo apparently was a minor center at best during this time and the dates for Laguna de los Cerros are problematical. Both centers may have been subject to La Venta in one way or another for at least part of the period.

La Encrucijada, a large site 40 km (25 miles) east of La Venta, was apparently large enough to be either a secondary center or even an independent polity in Middle Formative times. A beautiful greenstone pectoral with an Olmec were-jaguar face appeared in a road cut through the site, but its precise findspot and context are not known.[23]

In 1969 Río Pesquero (also known as Arroyo Pesquero), near Las Choapas, Veracruz, was the site of one of the most spectacular Olmec discoveries ever made, when fishermen accidentally uncovered jadeite and serpentine objects in the river bottom. It soon became apparent that they had encountered an immense cache that included dozens of life-sized greenstone masks, at least 1,000 celts, as well as figurines, ornaments and ritual paraphernalia.[24] University of Veracruz archaeologists managed to salvage a few pieces, but virtually the entire cache was smuggled out of Mexico and sold to eager collectors in North America and Europe. Río Pesquero objects are very similar to La Venta in style and iconography, and archaeologists suspect the entire cache was a gigantic offering like those in Complex A. No serious archaeology has ever been done at Río Pesquero so we do not know whether it was a major settlement on the scale of La Venta, or perhaps an isolated shrine to a water deity as at Manatí. Any study of the site would be invaluable, even after thirty years.

The cloud-covered summit of the volcano San Martín Pajapan has always been one of Olman's most inaccessible places. The steep slopes receive rain almost daily and the dense forest is virtually impenetrable. Given the Olmecs penchant for tackling exceedingly difficult projects, it is not surprising that they chose this spot to erect a stunning masterpiece of stone sculpture on top of a platform.[25] Like later Mesoamericans, the Olmecs believed that cloud-covered mountain peaks were home to the rain and water gods while earth deities lived inside the mountains. The San Martín shrine is the oldest known evidence for these beliefs. The sculpture depicts a kneeling life-sized man who wears an elaborate helmet decorated with feathers and an Olmec greenstone "mask." His head and headdress are so

40

41–43

pl. XVI, XIX

44

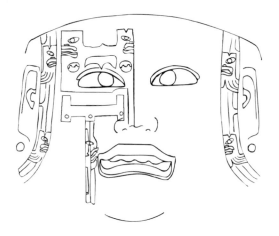

41 Human mask with incised design, attributed to Río Pesquero, Veracruz. The life-sized mask could actually have been worn by an adult human. Facial features seem to project a smiling, friendly attitude coupled with a piercing glance. Fine-line incision depicts repeated Olmec design elements that may have been tattooed or incised on the faces of living high-status individuals.

similar to a fragmentary head found at La Venta that both could be the work of the same sculptor. He grasps a bar in both hands while leaning forward in a dynamic pose that almost vibrates with tension. F. Kent Reilly III believes the man is shown in the act of raising the World Tree, the Axis Mundi of Mesoamerican cosmological thought, into its upright position at the moment of creation. Regardless of what he is doing, his Olmec creators went to unbelievable lengths to move the finished sculpture (or the stone from which it was carved) uphill to the mountaintop over extremely rough terrain. People continued to venerate the monument long after Olmec times; the Veracruz archaeologists who moved it to the Museum of Anthro-

42 Greenstone figurine attributed to Río Pesquero. This exquisite small sculpture is thought to be an "official portrait" of an elaborately dressed Olmec ruler wearing a Maize God headdress. Ht 16.3 cm (6.25 in).

43 Celt attributed to Río Pesquero. This rare incised celt shows a profile Olmec head above a ceremonial bundle or staff held by disembodied hands. Maize symbols surround the face and form a trefoil headdress element.

44 San Martín Pajapan Monument 1. Found on top of San Martín Pajapan volcano in the Tuxtla mountains, this monument continued to be venerated from Olmec times until it was removed to the Museum of Anthropology in 1967. The position of the young man's hands and legs suggests he is in the act of rising up as he lifts a staff thought to represent the World Tree from a horizontal to a vertical position. Ht 142 cm (55⅞ in).

pology in Xalapa in 1967 recovered broken offering vessels of all pre-Columbian time periods mixed in with modern objects in the area around the sculpture. Unfortunately no one has searched the mountaintop for other Olmec remains. I suspect the kneeling lord was part of a much larger shrine and that other monuments may lay hidden in the dense cloud forest.

La Venta's demise and the end of Olmec culture

Olmec civilization had run its course by 400 BC. La Venta, San Lorenzo, and large sections of the riverine lowland zone lay abandoned, artisans no longer created Olmec-style sculptures, jades, and pots, and the extensive trade networks that had once connected Olman with the rest of Mesoamerica ceased to function. Nevertheless people continued to occupy the area and a new civilization sometimes called Epi-Olmec evolved at Tres Zapotes on the northern edge of the Tuxtla mountains (Chapter 8).

What happened to Olmec culture? When and why did it disappear? After decades of speculation, archaeologists finally have partial answers to these questions. The period of the decline can be narrowed down to the fifth and fourth centuries before Christ. Thus construction Phase IV at Complex A not only marks the greatest achievements of La Venta's rulers but also the onset of their decline. La Venta's Great Pyramid, and probably the rest of the city as well, was abandoned by the beginning of the fourth century BC. Palangana-phase San Lorenzo and the numerous villages and hamlets surrounding it were deserted at approximately the same time. These were not temporary population movements; the lower Coatzacoalcos region was uninhabited for at least a millennium and La Venta's hinterland remained virtually uninhabited until the mid-twentieth century.

Having dated the Olmec decline, what might account for it? Cultural decline and decay are normal occurrences in human history, the kind of regular transformations that happen to all civilizations. However, only rarely do farming populations abandon entire regions for centuries, unless something prevents them from returning. Archaeologists concerned with the Olmec collapse have focused on two basic explanations: environmental changes and human actions. At the moment our best evidence relates to the former, but archaeologists have only recently begun seriously to investigate the problem.

Recent studies by Mexican geomorphologists show that the rivers around La Venta and San Lorenzo are dynamic systems that experienced constant changes over the past 4,000 years.[26] San Lorenzo's decline at the end of the Early Formative period coincided with pronounced channel shifts in the Coatzacoalcos river and the same happened at La Venta 500 years later. Natural processes triggered these shifts: tectonic uplift and coastal subsidence created new topographies,while rising sea levels worldwide drowned coastal margins and silt and volcanic ash clogged rivers. The silt was washed off from expanding agricultural fields while the ash came from eruptions in the nearby highlands. These ashfalls had a dramatic impact on pre-Columbian human settlement in the Tuxtla mountains and the same probably was true in the adjacent lowlands.[27] Other less catastrophic environmental changes may also have contributed to the Olmec decline: secular fluctuations in rainfall have been suggested as a possible factor, although no one has collected the information needed to prove or disprove this hypothesis. Human activities almost certainly had a negative impact on the environment as well. Frequent forest clearing for agriculture probably led to erosion and river channel silting, just as occurs throughout the tropics today.

Whatever environmental changes occurred, the demise of Olmec culture was ultimately a cultural process that reflected human actions and responses to the natural challenges. Such actions could have included civil unrest on the part of disgruntled peasants or breakaway subordinate groups, dynastic rivalries, claims to the throne by upstarts, or the loss of control over long-distance trade routes. If Olmec rulers lost access to the exotic goods they needed to maintain the loyalty of their comrades and subjects, further unrest and eventual chaos could have resulted.

In the final analysis, however, these factors fail to explain the complete depopulation of eastern Olman. That must reflect very serious environmental changes that rendered the region unsuited for large groups of farmers over a period of centuries. But what happened to the people? Some probably emigrated to surrounding areas, yet we lack concrete evidence for these movements. Populations in western Olman grew, but those increases are modest enough that they could reflect nothing more than local natural growth.

4 · Olmec Daily Life and Culture

Our preoccupations with monuments, jades, and the other trappings of elite Olmec life frequently obscure the fact that most Olmecs were ordinary commoners. They passed their lives in the small communities where they were born, and followed daily routines that revolved around farming, fishing, and household activities carried out within a small circle of friends and relatives. Truly "People of the River," they lived adjacent to the rivers, streams, oxbow lakes and swamps that provided fertile agricultural land, aquatic foods, and transportation arteries so essential to their lifeways. As rivers changed their courses through time, human settlements followed in response. Until recently, the daily lives of these villagers were totally neglected by archaeologists. Fortunately this is no longer the case. Thanks to recent excavations at San Andrés, Isla Alor, San Lorenzo, and other sites, we can begin to appreciate what life was like in America's first civilization.[1]

Olmec villages and hamlets

There was probably no such thing as a standard Olmec village, but they must all have shared many basic characteristics. Archaeological evidence suggests that Olmec villages were similar in many ways to rural villages found in the area prior to the inroads of modern civilization. Typically a village consisted of a few houselots scattered haphazardly about the landscape on local elevations that placed them above the annual floods. Larger villages may have included a modest mound that supported the residence of the senior family or perhaps a small temple dedicated to the villager's patron deity or revered ancestor. Such mounds would have been lacking in smaller villages and hamlets where everybody enjoyed more or less the same status appropriate for their age and sex.

45

Houselots probably included a main building, lean-to shelters, a courtyard, a small house garden, and a simple fence or boundary marker of living plants. The main building served as a dormitory, dining room, and shelter from inclement weather. Most daily activities took place under the lean-to shelters and the protection they offered from the fierce tropical sun. Courtyards were merely zones of compacted earth beaten hard by constant traffic. Gardens were planted with vegetables, pot herbs, and medicinal plants.

45 A modern house in Tenochtitlán village with wattle and daub walls and a palm thatch roof similar to those constructed by the Olmecs.

They probably received much more constant care than the larger outfields where maize and other major crops were grown, including hand irrigation when necessary and fertilization as a by-product of their use as trash dumps and latrines. Dense stands of trees surrounding the buildings provided shade as well as avocados, palm nuts, cacao (chocolate) seeds, and many other fruits and nuts. Fish nets, traps, farming tools, and other useful things probably lay about in seeming disorder, but at hand when someone needed them. If we were magically transported back to an Olmec village, we would doubtless see many vignettes of daily life that escape the truncated vision of archaeology: women grinding corn, mothers dandling fat babies on their knee, little boys torturing the household pet dog (destined, sooner or later, for the stew pot or roasting rack), the orphaned monkey tied to a tree limb, the anxious look on the faces of observers during a curing ceremony.

This reconstruction owes more to conjecture and ethnographic analogy with modern houselots in the region than to actual hard archaeological data, but excavations have verified some aspects of it. Excavations at the village of San Andrés, Tabasco, revealed earth floors, postholes, fragments of mud daub, hearths, subterranean storage pits, human burials, and middens containing broken pottery, figurines, tools, kitchen utensils, and food remains. Houses at San Andrés had pole walls plastered at times with clay daub, compacted earth floors and peaked thatch roofs. Most were square or apsidal (parallel-sided with rounded corners) in shape. Some rested directly on the ground while others crowned low earth mounds. Cooking hearths were placed on the packed earth floors inside houses. Most houses probably contained rude benches and sleeping platforms covered with woven mats;

baskets, net bags, and wooden utensils, and shrines or altars dedicated to the occupant's ancestors. Cylindrical and bell-shaped pits excavated into the subsoil inside and adjacent to the house probably served for storing food-stuffs in baskets or pottery vessels. When these pits collapsed or turned sour, the residents filled them in with trash-laden midden soil, perhaps as much to prevent cave-ins as to dispose of the trash. One storage pit was filled with lime powder presumably used in cooking maize for *nixtamal*, a special kind of corn dough that played a critical role in the Olmec diet (see below).

Olmec houses reflected the social status and economic means of their residents. High-status families occupied larger-than-average houses erected on earth platforms that were located close to temples, palaces, and other public buildings. These houses contained exotic ceremonial pottery vessels, figurines and greenstone objects. San Lorenzo's "Red Palace" is the most elaborate Olmec residence excavated so far. Its distinctive features included a platform substructure, L-shaped steps carved from basalt, red gravel-coated floors and walls dressed, a 4-m (13-ft) high columnar basalt roof support carved from a single block of stone, and a winding drain constructed of basalt troughs.[2] Certainly a vast gulf separated Olmec leaders from their supporters.

Diet and subsistence

Ordinary Olmecs, like many ancient peoples, enjoyed a diet as good and perhaps much better than that of their modern descendants. Here we can look to the testimony of both archaeology and historical linguistics. Linguists Lyle Campbell and Terrence Kaufman have argued fairly convincingly that the ancient Olmecs spoke proto-Mixe-Zoquean, an extinct ancestor to numerous modern languages of the area. They also reconstructed a basic vocabulary for the language that contains numerous very informative food terms. These include maize, cacao, squash, tomato, bean, sweet potato, manioc, cotton, and tropical fruits such as *chayote*, *guava*, *zapote*, and papaya. This reconstructed Olmec grocery list was partially verified when ethnobotanists identified maize, manioc, beans, cacao, and cotton, as well as sunflower and corozo palm nuts, in trash excavated at San Andrés. The same deposits yielded remnants from the harvest of the adjacent swamps and river, including clams, turtles, catfish, gar, snapper, and crocodiles, as well as bones of deer and domestic dog. San Lorenzo has yielded remains of most of these same plants and animals, with a surprising number of dog bones attesting to the importance of this animal as a source of high-quality protein.

While all these foods contributed to the larder and the well being of the average Olmec villager, the evidence strongly supports the somewhat controversial idea that maize was the Olmec staple, the core element of the diet. 46 Wild maize, a native highland Mexican grass, was apparently domesticated in Guerrero's Balsas river valley sometime during the Archaic period. It did

46 Modern native maize varieties grown along the Coatzacoalcos river. Such "primitive" maize strains are better adapted to local climatic and soil conditions than those scientifically created.

not take humans long to transplant it to the humid tropical lowlands: domesticated maize pollen appears in soil cores dating to 6200 BC at San Andrés, Tabasco. Larger pollen grains of an improved strain are evident a scant 200 years later and the first kernels, cobs, and other macroscopic remains appeared there by 2500 BC.[3] Early domesticated maize was a relatively unproductive plant with small ears and few kernels, but it quickly evolved into a highly productive and dependable staple crop.

Maize is one of mankind's most versatile foods. It can be eaten in various forms and at various stages during its growth cycle, fermented into an alcoholic beverage, and even dried and stored for long periods of time (an important advantage in the humid tropics where many foods rot quickly). These characteristics made it an ideal plant for farmers who needed to store seed for the next planting and food for the lean months, as well as rulers interested in hosting their followers and allies at large feasts. Some archaeologists even suggest that maize owed its initial popularity to its role as a feast food and fermented beer, and only later achieved its potential as a daily food.

Just when that critical shift occurred is not known for certain. I believe it was well under way long before 1200 BC but others prefer to date it to after 800 BC. The really critical question is, when did some nameless Olmec housewife discover the process of "nixtamalization"? *Nixtamal* (Aztec, Sp. *masa*) is finely ground corn dough that has been prepared by cooking the kernels with lime, wood ash, or burnt shells. After letting the corn sit overnight, the cook washes off the hulls and can grind the kernels into a fine dough, suitable for preparing flat corn cakes called tortillas, or tamales, plump patties of maize dough steamed in corn husks. *Nixtamal* not only opens the door to new foods but the process vastly enriches maize by

47 Olmec maize symbols and the Maize God: (*top row*) depictions of maize cobs and their leaves; (*bottom row*) maize symbols in the headdresses serve to identify this basic Olmec deity.

enhancing amino acids and augmenting the protein content of the dough to the point where the average person is protected from the most common deficiency diseases.[4]

We know that Olmec cooks ground maize into flour on stone *metates* with hand stones called *manos*, but did they simply used boiled maize or were they acquainted with the entire nixtamalization process? Carbonized lime deposits on *tecomates* (neckless jars, see below) interiors suggest the latter, but have never been tested to prove or disprove it. The linguistic evidence can be construed to support this hypothesis, the proto-Mixe-Zoquean language apparently including terms for grinding and leaching maize. In any case, by 1500 BC maize was so important to the early Olmecs that they had deified it and endowed that god with some of the most important symbols of the Olmec world. *47*

Olmec leaders may have controlled certain special foods not ordinarily available to the population at large: cacao was perhaps one such delicacy, meat another. According to William F. Rust, Middle Formative Río Barí villages that contain central mounds also contain deer, crocodile and domestic dog bones in their midden, species apparently absent in smaller villages that lacked mounds. Perhaps only elites were permitted to consume these animals or perhaps leaders distributed these special foods to their followers during festivals and celebrations. It is worth noting that deer and crocodile pelts were also important raw materials for elite Olmec costumes and ritual paraphernalia. I suspect that when archaeologists have excavated enough village middens and studied their contents, we will see that everybody ate these prized foods when possible, but may have rendered portions of any kill to the local chief. *48*

Although Olmec farming techniques are not well understood, the ancient farmers almost certainly practiced some form of swidden or slash–and–burn agriculture. This would have involved felling the forest with stone axes, burning off the "slash" after it had dried for a few weeks, and planting seeds and cuttings in the ash with digging sticks amongst the semi-consumed vegetation. Olmec farmers may have created artificial planting platforms by mounding up earth in swampy terrain, but this remains to be demonstrated. They may also have planted crops on different sections of sloping lands as the annual floodwaters receded.

Modern studies suggest it is not much more difficult to clear mature forests with stone axes than with modern steel tools, but clearing the thick brush of secondary forests without a steel machete must have been truly arduous work. Rich silt deposited each year on the river levees by receding floods made it possible to cultivate them annually and inhibited the growth of dense brush. Less fertile inter-fluvial lands away from the rivers were probably more difficult to clear and less fertile, and no doubt farmers cultivated them as little as possible. Indeed, they may have served primarily as

reserves for valuable game and forest products. Archaeologists working near Lake Catemaco in the Tuxtla mountains uncovered the surface of a Middle Formative agricultural field fortuitously preserved by thick volcanic ash.[5] Furrows and hillocks on the field surface indicate that farmers mounded the soil around the bases of growing maize plants, a practice that lowland cultivators surely employed as well.

48 A cacao orchard with seed pods growing out of the tree trunks. Portions of Olman are prime cacao-producing regions today and the Olmecs consumed cacao seeds in a highly prized beverage.

Technology

The Olmecs were heirs to a long tradition of human adaptation to their humid tropical environment. They improved upon this legacy by inventing new tools, techniques, and ways to organize human labor. In the realm of technology, they created tools and utensils from clay, stone, bone, deer antler, wood, basketry, and other perishable materials. In all but rare instances, only those of clay and stone have survived the ravages of time.

Olmec potters, most likely women, transformed the incipient ceramic technology of their ancestors into a craft that produced finely made pottery vessels, solid and hollow figurines, and other objects from locally available clay. Although pots break easily, they are also easy to replace. Thus Olmec archaeological sites contain literally millions of broken sherds which provide archaeologists with the raw material for ceramic chronologies as well as important information about ancient daily life.

Crudely made grit-tempered cooking and eating vessels decorated with brushed surfaces may have been manufactured at San Andrés as early as 2300 BC, but our most complete information on Olmec ceramics comes from San Lorenzo.[6] Pottery vessels served both ritual and utilitarian functions. Basic vessel forms included flat-bottomed bowls with out-flaring walls, deep hemispherical bowls, necked bottles, jars, and *tecomates*. "Camaño Coarse" vessels, the basic cooking pots at San Lorenzo for centuries, were an unslipped ware with tan-to-brown surfaces, coarse sand temper, and grass-brushed exteriors. Other kitchen wares included jars and bottles for storing liquids, and bowls for serving foods. Some were highly decorated with surface modeling and gadrooning, paint, incision and excision on the exterior, and punctated designs. San Lorenzo-period ceramics varied considerably in quality and decoration, with the best-made examples apparently reserved for ritual occasions. They may have served as containers for ritual offerings or as special eating utensils used, like Mother's fine china, only for festive occasions. The two most notable ritual wares – Calzadas Carved and Limón Carved-Incised – include thin, finely made bowls, jars and small *tecomates* decorated with exquisitely carved and incised designs on their exteriors depicting rich and highly stylized Olmec icons and symbols.

49, 50, 51, 52, 53

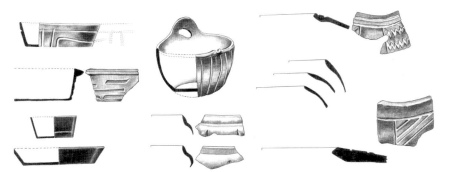

49 San Lorenzo pottery vessels: (*left to right*) bowls, collared jars and *tecomates*.

Olmec ceramicists produced human and animal figurines, maskettes, and other miscellaneous objects as well as pots. The most common of these are small, solid human effigies or figurines; males and females are both portrayed, although in many cases the sex of the individual is unclear. Male effigies include ballplayers who wear loin cloths, protective gear, helmets and masks over their lower face; females are often depicted in advanced

54, 55, 56

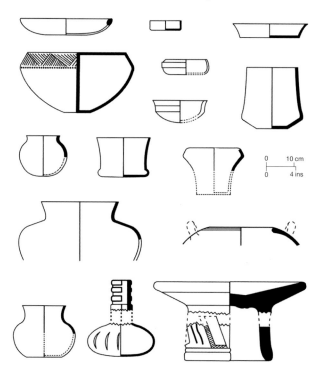

50 (*above*) San Lorenzo ceramic decoration techniques included differential firing to create black and white zones, incision, rocker stamping to produce zig-zag designs, and excision. The three pieces bottom right show humanoid monster faces and a fish effigy.

51 (*right*) La Venta ceramics: La Venta potters manufactured jars, bowls, and bottles like their San Lorenzo predecessors but with different shapes, appendages and forms of decoration.

52 (*left*) La Venta potters employed cross-hatching, mat-like and curvilinear designs, and punctuation on their ceramics.

53 (*below*) A cylindrical vase found in La Venta's Complex A. The highly abstract designs are repeated in three bands around the vessel's entire circumference.

pregnancy and on occasion nurse infants. Chubby, bald "baby-faces" with puffy cheeks, downturned mouths and slit eyes are common in Early Formative deposits; Middle Formative examples often have punched holes to represent the pupils of the eyes. Larger, hollow figurines slipped with white paint are less common than the small solid ones but represent one of the masterful achievements of ancient American potters of any time period. Their functions elude us, beyond the reasonable hypothesis that they served as ritual objects. Their rarity and high quality suggest that they were reserved for very special occasions, whereas a more common and widespread function may be considered for the small, solid examples.

Stone tools played a crucial role in the daily lives of every Olmec family. Olmec craftsmen manufactured the ubiquitous *manos* and *metates* found in every kitchen by pecking and grinding basalt and other fine-grained volcanic stones. Other ground-stone implements included mortars, pestles, celts, wedges, polishers, hammer stones, abraders, sandstone "saws," and flat "paint palettes." Knappers chipped and flaked obsidian, chert, and flint into razor-sharp blades for cutting, projectile points, scrapers, burins, engravers, and drills. The volcanic glass called obsidian is not native to the Tuxtla mountains or any other part of Olman and thus had to be imported from distant sources. Neutron activation analyses show that San Lorenzo imported it from numerous sources but the majority came from Guadalupe Victoria, Puebla, Otumba, Estado de Mexico, and El Chayal outside

57

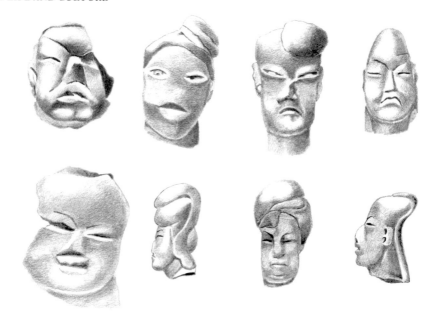

54 San Lorenzo-phase solid figurine heads. All have been separated from their original bodies, some of which may have been constructed from perishable materials. Distinctive coiffures and facial features probably denoted actual living persons.

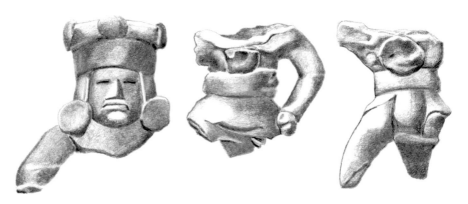

55 San Lorenzo-phase ballplayer solid figurines. Protective helmets, padded waist and groin protectors and round chest ornaments that may be iron ore mirrors appear to be common ballplayer garb at San Lorenzo and Olmec-era centers elsewhere in Mesoamerica. The leg of the figurine on the right is covered with black asphalt.

Guatemala City.[7] The Mexican obsidian was probably transported from the "quarries" (more likely outcrops rather than true mines) to San Lorenzo through central and southern Veracruz, while the El Chayal material traveled a circuitous route through the densely populated Soconusco and then northward across the Isthmus of Tehuantepec. The presence of manufacturing debris at San Lorenzo suggests that obsidian blocks or cylindrical cores were imported rather than finished tools.

56 San Lorenzo-phase hollow figurines. The star-shaped hollow on the back of the third example allowed super-heated air to escape during the firing process and prevented the figurine from exploding, but also may have served as an ethnic or kin-group marker.

57 Solid ceramic figurine heads from La Venta illustrating various hairstyles, headdresses, and facial characteristics. Most figurine heads appear to have been attached to bodies, as with the female on the left, and broken in use.

Although the Olmecs had a Stone Age technology, they did work the iron ores magnetite, hematite, and ilmenite into beads, mirrors, and at least one marvelous little human figurine – nicknamed "Oddjob" for his uncanny resemblance to the James Bond villain.[8] Ilmenite may have been quarried somewhere near San Lorenzo, where Ann Cyphers and her colleagues uncovered two workshops containing tons of small rectangular "beads" perforated with conical holes.[9] The holes suggest they were strung on cords or threads, and one San Lorenzo Colossal Head (Monument 17) wears a net-like head covering held together by what appear to be actual beads. Furthermore, the soil around the head contained seven of these enigmatic cubes. However, the sheer quantity of objects turned up by Cyphers suggests they must have had some other use as well. She proposes that they functioned as drilling platforms used in the manufacture of something else, and were discarded after being perforated. Other writers have suggested they served as a form of currency.

The most spectacular Olmec iron ore creations are large, beautifully polished, parabolic concave "mirrors" made from magnetite and ilmenite. Seven were uncovered in Complex A at La Venta.[10] While their backs are roughly shaped, the concavity on the front is as carefully ground as many modern optical lenses, and the optical qualities of some allow them to be

58

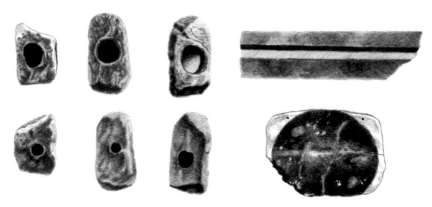

58 The iron ore beads may have been strung on necklaces or head coverings, while rectangular mirrors served as chest ornaments. The bar is thought to be a magnetic compass needle.

used to ignite fires and project "camera lucida" images on flat surfaces. The grinding was apparently done by hand with a substance similar to jewelers' rouge. They all have suspension holes drilled at the edges and many Olmec figurines show people wearing such mirrors on their chests. Similar mirrors have been found at San Lorenzo and a few are attributed to Río Pesquero and even distant Guerrero. Olmec lapidaries also constructed mosaic mirrors out of small polished iron ore plaques, perhaps placed on wooden backs. Tests have shown that a workshop at San José Mogote in the Valley of Oaxaca produced some and perhaps all of the plaques recovered at San Lorenzo.[11] Did the workshops also produce the large single-piece mirrors as well? That question remains to be answered.

Social and political organization

The social and political aspects of Olmec culture have fueled endless archaeological debates and even the vast body of new information has not resolved the disputes.[12] While everyone agrees that kinship was the basis of Olmec social life, the specifics of who lived with whom, how they were related, and what kinds of ties bound together neighbors and people living in different villages remain unresolved. The questions of how much power and authority existed and who wielded it lie at the center of the disputes. Some authorities argue that the Olmecs were organized into lineages, groups of individuals who traced their descent to a single real or fictitious ancestor, and that each lineage member was ranked hierarchically in accordance with his or her genealogical closeness to the lineage founder. According to this scenario, the living lineage head or chief was the person of the appropriate sex most closely related to the founder. Lineages themselves were ranked in the same manner as individuals, with the highest-ranking or paramount lineage forming a nobility of sorts and its own leader serving as chief or ruler of the entire society.

Societies of this sort are called chiefdoms, and they occurred commonly in the foundation stages of many of the world's ancient civilizations. They are also well documented historically in Polynesia, sub-Saharan Africa, lowland South America, and the Pacific Northwest coast of Canada and Alaska. Chiefdoms are intermediate-level societies – larger and more complex than more egalitarian societies of simple food foragers and farmers but lacking the sharply defined socio-economic classes, complex integrated economies, political territories, standing armies, government bureaucrats, and hereditary ruling classes characteristic of more highly evolved archaic states. Chiefdoms have frequently foreshadowed the development of ancient states throughout human history. Was the same true in Mesoamerica?

Some authorities reject the chiefdom model and argue that Olmec societies were so large and complex that they had to be true states.[13] They cite the large regional populations, the substantial labor required to transport monuments and construct other public works, and the well-developed long-distance commercial contacts. In the past I have championed the chiefdom model, but the new data on Olmec urbanism has me forced me to reconsider my position. I remain undecided. Whichever position turns out to be correct, there can be no doubt that Olmec society had a well-developed hierarchical structure. This is apparent in the settlement patterns, craft specialization, architecture, sculpture, art, religion, ritual activities, and high status burials.

Writing, calendrics, and astronomy

Writing, calendrics, and astronomy were fundamental aspects of Classic and Postclassic Mesoamerican elite life. Today we know that writing and calendrics can be traced back to 650 BC at La Venta (see below), but the case for Olmec accomplishments in astronomy is not so evident. Mesoamerican scribes recorded symbols, called "hieroglyphs," in books (*codices*) made from bark paper or animal skins and on stone, pottery, and other imperishable media. Classic Maya writing is the best known and most sophisticated Mesoamerican writing system, but at least a dozen other scripts existed at various times and places. The most common subject matter of the texts was history, particularly the deeds of rulers and social groups. Inscriptions normally included dates recorded in one or more of four major calendars in use throughout much of the region. They included a 260-day ritual almanac composed of 13 numbers and 20 day names, and the 365 solar or "Vague Year" with 18 "months" and 20 days. When run simultaneously, these two cycles produced the 52-year eras known as the "Calendar Round," a period that dominated much of Mesoamerican life and thought. Some authorities believe that the Olmecs observed the 260- and 365-day cycles, and perhaps even the Calendar Round, although we lack hard evidence of this. The final important Mesoamerican calendar was the "Long Count," a much longer time cycle that the Classic Maya believed began on 13 August 3114 BC.

Scholars once considered the Long Count a Maya achievement, but today we know it was in use in the Trans-Isthmian zone of Veracruz, Chiapas, and Guatemala centuries before the Maya adopted it, and some authorities believe it too may have been an Olmec invention.

Writing and calendrics were so important in later Mesoamerican culture that their apparent absence in Olmec culture seemed an anomaly. Only one monument, La Venta Monument 13, "The Ambassador," contains a possible contemporaneous text. This sculpture depicts a striding person holding a banner accompanied by a human footprint and three possible glyphs that cannot be deciphered. A few Olmec celts and other portable objects contain short hieroglyphic inscriptions, but in every case the text appears to be a later addition to an Olmec heirloom.

Prior to 2002, it was generally agreed that *pars pro toto* "pseudo-writing," in which specific elements stand for a large invisible item – for example, the "paw-wing" as shorthand for the deity called the Olmec Dragon – was the closest the Olmecs came to true writing.[14] Symbols of this sort are common on pottery, facial "tattoos," rulers' costumes, and other media but do not qualify as real writing because they do not represent spoken words. Then in December 2002 a fortuitous discovery established the existence of Olmec writing and calendrics by at least 650 BC. Archaeologists excavating at San Andrés, Tabasco, a mere 5 km (3 miles) east of La Venta reported finding a roller stamp and two fragments of a greenstone plaque in a trash deposit laid down during a feast or festival.[15] The stamp shows a flying bird with two speech scrolls and two glyphs emanating from its mouth. The glyphs incorporate U-shaped elements, scroll and bracket motifs, and a double merlon placed inside a cartouche, forming logographs, words or concepts existing in the spoken language. Similar logographs occur on the sculpture known as the "Young Lord" from the Pacific coast of Guatemala (Chapter 6), the probable representation of an Olmec ruler. The greenstone fragments probably functioned as costume elements or jewelry and depict two complete and

59 La Venta Monument 13. The footprint was a universal Mesoamerican symbol for travel. His elaborate feathered headdress, necklace, nose ornament, bracelets, fancy loincloth and elaborate sandals all proclaim this man's high status. Diameter 80 cm (31 in).

60 Clay roller stamp with glyph from San Andrés, Tabasco. The rollout drawing of the excised design shows a bird emitting sounds depicted as glyphs and curved speech scrolls. Ht 7 cm (2.75 in).

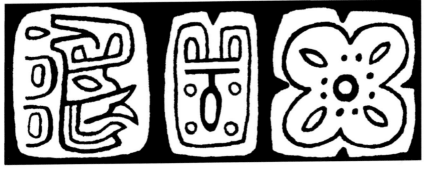

61 A roller stamp from Tlatilco found in the Basin of Mexico: the glyphs are typically Olmec.

at least two partial glyphs. Comparisons with glyphs in later Isthmian and Maya writing systems help identify one of the glyphs as 3 "ajaw," a day name in the later Maya 260-day Calendar Round. "Ajaw" also translates as "king," suggesting a reference to a ruler named "king 3 Ajaw" at La Venta during the fifth century BC. Similar roller stamps with possible glyphs have been identified at La Venta and Tlatilco, but most scholars rejected claims 61 that they were an early form of writing.[16] As we shall see in Chapter 8, this newly identified Olmec writing system led directly into the later Isthmian and Maya scripts and perhaps others as well.

Olmec accomplishments in the realm of astronomy are unclear. La Venta's orientation 8 degrees west of north is thought by some to reflect a celestial alignment, perhaps to the constellation Eta Draconius, but others argue that it is linked to volcanoes in the Tuxtla mountains or other terrestrial features.

Religion

Religion was the force that bound Olmec culture together, providing coherence to its members and a unified sense of expression to modern observers. Olmec religion had five primary components: deities or supernatural forces that controlled the universe while sanctioning the human social and political order; a cosmology that explained and structured the universe; rituals that expressed the cosmology; priests and shamans who conducted the rituals; and natural and manmade sacred settings.[17] This "public" religion served the entire society and coexisted with localized beliefs and practices that small kin groups carried out in the privacy of the family houselot.

Much has been written about Olmec religion in recent years; most of it is speculative and almost none can be proven beyond a reasonable shadow of doubt. Archaeology provides the raw data on Olmec religion but these facts do not "speak for themselves," they need to be interpreted. Scholars draw on three lines of evidence to provide insights into Olmec religion: icono-graphic analyses of sculptures and other artifacts; Spanish accounts on Contact-period Aztec and Maya religions; and modern ethnographic studies of Mesoamerican Indians and other Native Americans. They are the base for what Peter D. Joralemon, a leading authority on Olmec art, iconog-raphy, and religion, has called the "Continuity Hypothesis." According to Joralemon, "there is a basic religious system common to all Mesoamerican peoples. This system took shape long before it was given monumental expression in Olmec art and survived long after the Spanish conquered the New World's major political and religious centers."[18] This hypothesis allows scholars to project later religious concepts and practices back onto the Olmecs and other early cultures for which there is no contemporary documentation.

62   Miguel Covarrubias first connected the Olmecs to the Continuity Hypothesis sixty years ago with his famous chart that graphically illustrated the derivation of all later Mesoamerican rain deities from an Olmec progen-itor. Recent studies confirm the Continuity Hypothesis by showing that many scenes depicted in pre-Columbian art depict events discussed in the great Quiché Maya Creation Story known as the Popol Vuh or "Book of Counsel."[19] This pre-Columbian epic tale recounts the origins of the world and humanity together with the deeds of the Twin Maize Gods and their sons the Hero Twins. The Twin Maize Gods battle the evil Gods of Xibalbá, the Underworld, on the ballcourt of that nether region, only to lose and be sacrificed. Their sons, fruit of a miraculous conception, follow in their father's footsteps but defeat the Lords of the Underworld in a series of trials, ultimately tricking them into committing suicide. Finally they resur-rect their fathers, create the fourth great cycle of existence, the one we live in today, and organize the universe. There is mounting evidence that Aztec, Mixtec, Zapotec, and especially Maya cosmological beliefs were grounded in some version of the Popol Vuh. F. Kent Reilly III, Karl Taube, Linda Schele and others have identified numerous Popol Vuh-related images in Olmec art.[20] Thus it appears that the *ur*-myth behind the epic was an Olmec creation, or perhaps even an older account that they were the first to express visually in media that have survived the ravages of time. In either case, Joralemon's Continuity Hypothesis receives strong support from this evidence.

62 The genealogy of Mesoamerican water and rain deities. Miguel Covarrubias' classic chart relates all of them back to an Olmec ancestor shown on the bottom (a).

Although most scholars accept Joralemon's premise, two reservations must be kept in mind. First, as any student of religion realizes, symbols and motifs do not always retain their same basic meanings over time and across space. Second, Aztec religion, the best-documented Mesoamerican system and the one that serves as the primary model for comparisons, may not be an altogether appropriate analog for the Olmecs. Aztec populations numbered in the millions and the tremendous disparity in social complexity between them and the Olmecs may have led to fundamental differences in the religious institutions and beliefs of the two groups. Despite these caveats, judicious use of historical and ethnographic analogy grounded in the Continuity Hypothesis remains our best (and probably only) way to understand Olmec religion.

Olmec cosmology, their beliefs about the origins and structure of the world, is very difficult to reconstruct in the absence of written accounts, but the Continuity Hypothesis does provide important clues. Scholars have realized that all Mesoamerican cultures shared a basic set of cosmological beliefs at the time of the Spanish Conquest thanks to Eduard Seler's pioneering investigations into the subject over a century ago. This shared cosmology included a creation story in which the universe was created and destroyed by the gods on four or five occasions, with the current world being the latest in the series. But where did these ideas come from and how did the Olmecs shape them into their own unique religion?

Joralemon identifies three basic traditions in Olmec religion: an ancient shamanistic ideology brought to the Americas by the first Paleo-Indians, a more recent agricultural/fertility cult that emerged as farming became the primary subsistence activity, and finally an Olmec creation he calls the "Cult of the Ruler."[21] Together, these defined an Olmec cosmological vision of the natural and supernatural worlds while situating the human actors in these worlds.

The shamanistic ideology conceived the world as a three-tiered entity composed of sky, earth, and underworld, bounded by the four cardinal directions and balanced on the central *axis mundi*. Each cardinal point probably had specific trees, colors, birds, and gods assigned to it. Shamans, the actual religious practitioners, were men and women whose special powers allowed them to establish contact with the supernaturals and intercede on their client's behalf. While in trances, often induced by fasting and psychotropic substances, shamans traveled the cosmos accompanied by their animal familiars as they attempted to heal the sick, establish contact with the ancestors, and propitiate the forces beyond human control.

The agricultural/fertility complex focused on the sun, earth, rain, weather, spirits of the agricultural plants themselves, and other supernatural forces that control the growth of life-giving plants. These supernaturals were thought to live in caves, springs, mountain tops, and agricultural fields, as well as in temples, shrines, and other supernatural homes that worshipers constructed conveniently close to their own houses.

The Cult of the Ruler involved a special set of rituals focused on the unique place of rulers in the cosmos. By 1200 BC, Olmec rulers had emerged as the most important point of contact between their subjects and the supernatural world, sanctifying the differences in status and rank that evolved as Olmec culture grew. We do not know whether rulers claimed supernatural protection, supernatural descent, or even actual divinity, but at its most fundamental, Olmec art serves visually to portray this special relationship in one form or another. In this new world order, rulers gradually assumed the more formal role of first priest, usurping some of the powers and activities once reserved for shamans. Shamans continued to function, however, just as they did in every later Mesoamerican culture. Indeed, the distinction between shamans and priests is difficult to identify in the archaeological record and was probably quite blurred in the reality of the day.

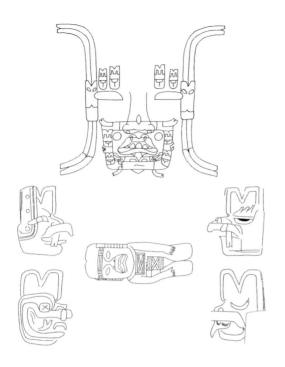

63 Las Limas Monument 1, the "Lord of Las Limas." Incised designs on the man's shoulders and legs, together with the inert baby in his lap, provide the key to understanding the Olmec supernatural world. Ht 55 cm (21 in), estimated weight 0.06 tons.

Olmec supernaturals have generated more controversy than any other aspect of their religion. Some scholars even argue that Olmecs did not worship gods with recognizably distinct personalities. Others accept their existence but disagree on their specific identifications. For example, the deity known as the Olmec Dragon has been variously identified as a were-jaguar combining human and feline traits, a caiman, a toad, and a manatee! The relative importance of various deities is another hotly debated topic. Was the jaguar the supreme Olmec god or did the serpent hold this exalted position? Historian of religion Karl Luckert devoted an entire book to this question, concluding that what we have identified as a feline really is a snake.[22] Joralemon identified the reason for such confusion when he observed that Olmec art is filled with "creatures that are biologically impossible," things that "exist in the mind of man, not in the world of nature."[23] Olmec supernaturals not only blended symbols and attributes but also apparently shared functions in a highly fluid, non-compartmentalized world with diffuse boundaries between their specific roles.

Michael D. Coe, together with his students Peter D. Joralemon and Karl Taube, have proposed the "Las Limas Hypothesis," the most generally accepted reconstruction of the Olmec pantheon. They believe that Las Limas Monument 1 provides a key, an Olmec Rosetta Stone of sorts, to 63 understanding Olmec deities. This magnificent greenstone sculpture depicts a seated youth holding an inert were-jaguar baby on his lap. According to Coe, the infant and four incised tattoo-like designs on the youth's shoulders and legs form an Olmec Pentateuch, with each figure displaying the oldest known representations of later Mesoamerican supernaturals.[24]

Building upon Coe's insights, Joralemon identified eight primary deities in the vast corpus of Olmec iconography, creatures that combine human, reptilian, avian, and feline attributes in endless and bewildering arrays.[25] In deference to those archaeologists who question their actual relationship to later gods, Joralemon assigned them descriptive names rather than the proper names of later Nahuatl or Maya deities. The Olmec Dragon and the Olmec Bird Monster are the most commonly depicted supernaturals; other denizens of the pantheon include the Fish Monster, Banded-Eye God, Water God, Maize God, Were-Jaguar, and Feathered Serpent.

64

Three deities – the Olmec Dragon, Bird Monster, and Fish Monster – combined to form the Olmec cosmos, conceptualized as a crocodilian Earth Monster lying between the celestial realm and the surface of a watery under-world. The Olmec Dragon, depicted as a crocodilian with eagle, jaguar, human, and serpent attributes, is the Earth Monster. The Dragon appears to signify earth, water, fire, and agricultural fertility, and may also have served as the patron deity of the elite. His basic icons include flame-eye-brows, L-shaped eyes, a bulbous nose, elongated upper jaw, bifurcated tongue, and limbs drawn using what is called the "paw-wing" motif. As the name implies, the Dragon's body generally takes a crocodilian form, although at times it looks more like a toad. Joralemon suggests that the Olmec Dragon was a predecessor of the Aztec gods Cipactli, Xiuhtecuhtli, Huehueteotl, Tonacatecuhtli, and Quetzalcoatl and the Maya god Itzamná.

The Bird Monster is a raptorial bird tentatively identified as a harpy eagle. It has both mammalian and reptilian features. Joralemon associates it with the sun, the heavens, and the celestial realm located above the Dragon's abode, as well as maize, agricultural fertility, rulership, and mind-altering psychotropic substances. The Bird Monster occurs frequently at La Venta,

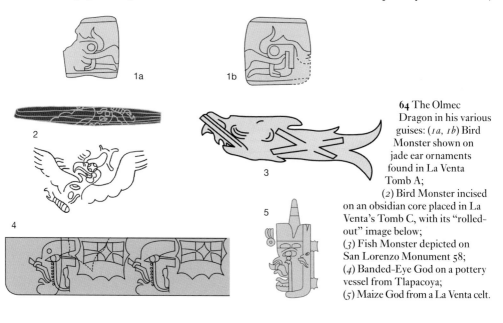

64 The Olmec Dragon in his various guises: (*1a, 1b*) Bird Monster shown on jade ear ornaments found in La Venta Tomb A; (*2*) Bird Monster incised on an obsidian core placed in La Venta's Tomb C, with its "rolled-out" image below; (*3*) Fish Monster depicted on San Lorenzo Monument 58; (*4*) Banded-Eye God on a pottery vessel from Tlapacoya; (*5*) Maize God from a La Venta celt.

where it appears on the upper register of Altar 4, an incised obsidian core, jade celts and bloodletters. Mural 1 at Oxtotitlán cave, Guerrero, contains an outstanding example, and it is common on pottery found outside the Olmec homeland. Bird Monster insignia can often be detected on costumes and ornaments worn by rulers.

The Fish Monster, symbolic of the watery Underworld on which the Dragon floats, is the least frequently depicted member of the cosmological triad and thus we know less about it than the others. A flat stone slab at San Lorenzo shows it with shark's teeth, crossed bands covering the body, a dorsal fin, and a split tail.

The Banded-Eye God is the most puzzling of the Las Limas quintet. Known only from facial profile depictions, it features almond-shaped eyes connected to the curving band which identifies it, an open mouth with an elongated upper lip, toothless gums, and downturned corners. Some scholars consider it the ancestral version of Xipe Totec, the Aztec god of spring and renewal, but recent studies by Sue Scott make this seem very unlikely.[26]

The Olmec Maize and Water gods form an agricultural-fertility dyad that must have been extremely important to rulers and farmers alike.[27] The Maize God has germinating seeds, corncobs, and at times entire plants sprouting from a cleft in the top of his head. His symbols commonly occur on rulers' costumes and ornaments, testimony to the symbolic and practical roles maize played in Olmec life as well as rulers' responsibility for promoting fertility, abundant harvests, and general well-being. The Water deity is depicted as a lifeless, asexual, full-bodied infant or pudgy dwarf with a were-jaguar face. He frequently wears a headband decorated with pleated

47, 65

65 San Lorenzo Monument 52 depicts the Olmec Water God as a dwarf with his legs drawn up.

streamers. He appears on large stone sculptures, either alone or held by an adult, as well as on celts, figurines, and other portable objects. Although often called the rain god, his realm probably included springs, rivers, and all forms of water utilized by humans. Joralemon suggests, no doubt correctly, that the Olmec Water God is an early form of Tlaloc, Chac, and other later Mesoamerican water deities.

The were-jaguar is one of the most easily recognized, frequently discussed, and least understood Olmec supernaturals. Basically a human infant with felinized facial characteristics, the were-jaguar is identified by a cleft in the top of his head, slanted almond eyes in enlarged sockets, and a large flared upper lip with downturned corners. At times, the gums lack teeth but a few representations depict large fangs with split tips. How did the Olmecs believe such a creature came to exist? No one really knows, but years ago Matthew W. Stirling proposed the "Stirling Hypothesis," a courageous and often criticized attempt at an explanation.[28] Stirling suggested that two

66 monuments from San Lorenzo depict the sexual union of a female human and a male jaguar, an event celebrated by the Olmecs as the conception of a race of were-jaguars. Alas, the Stirling Hypothesis remains unproved. For one thing, the sculptures in question are too badly destroyed to identify clearly who or what is doing what to whom. Even Kent V. Flannery and the author, two very open-minded observers, could not verify Stirling's identification after a detailed examination of one of the sculptures in the Tenochtitlán village school yard in 1967. On the other hand, the Olmec mural in Oxtotitlán cave, Guerrero (Chapter 5), seems to depict a jaguar with an erect penis apparently about to engage in what the television wildlife programs refer to as "copulatory behavior" with a human. Perhaps Stirling's conjecture is not as farfetched as it may seem, but it hardly provides conclusive evidence that jaguar–human mating formed a central tenet in Olmec explanations about the origins of the universe.

The Feathered Serpent is the final Olmec supernatural identified with any confidence. It is generally shown as a rattlesnake with a coiled or undulating body with the feathers occurring as individual elements that form a crest on the top of the head (compare La Venta Monument 19). This may be the ancestor of the Feathered Serpent that occupied such a prominent place in later Mesoamerican religions but, if so, its rarity suggests it was a minor member of the Olmec pantheon.

66 Tenochtitlán Monument 1 is believed to depict a jaguar that is either dominating a woman or having sexual intercourse with a woman. Ht 80 cm (31 in).

The prominent role agricultural and fertility deities played in the Olmec pantheon is striking. This is no surprise given the importance farming played in Olmec subsistence, but it marks the oldest extant evidence for these deity concepts in Mesoamerica and thus stands as a major Olmec contribution to Mesoamerican culture.

The Olmecs carried out their rituals in both manmade and natural sacred settings. The former included temples, plazas, enclosed precincts, ball-courts and water systems, while springs, caves, and mountaintops served as natural sacred places. Archaeologists have not yet excavated an identifiable Olmec temple, but they assume most were pole-and-thatch sanctuaries that housed the holiest cult images, and where priests and leaders gathered in seclusion to conduct esoteric rites only they could witness. After La Venta, Olmecs adopted the mound-and-plaza concept: temples were probably placed on mound summits, allowing the public gathered in the courtyards below to observe at least portions of the celebrations. Other ceremonies were conducted in secluded precincts like La Venta's Complex A. The objects looted from Río Pesquero may have come from a similar precinct at that site. Examples of natural settings include the Manatí springs, the shrine on top of San Martín Pajapan, and Juxtlahuaca and Oxtotitlán caves.

Olmec ritual included a rubber ball game similar to those played in later times. It appears likely that the game was primarily a religious observance in which players representing supernaturals and culture heroes played out predetermined scenarios that often ended in the sacrificial death of at least one protagonist. Olmec clay figurines depict men wearing protective clothing reminiscent of that used by later ballplayers and some even hold what appears to be a ball. The only Olmec ballcourt identified so far is the Middle Formative Palangana mound group at San Lorenzo; it appears to lack the rings and benches of later courts, but residue from a rubber ball was uncov- 67 ered during the very limited testing of the court floor and one mound. More recently, well-preserved rubber balls have been recovered at nearby Manatí. Archaeologists once believed that Colossal Heads depict ballplayers wearing helmets, an idea that re-emerges from time to time despite the absence of any supporting evidence.

67 A solid rubber ball preserved in the protective environment of the El Manatí bog. Its inclusion in a ritual offering reinforces the idea that the ball game was a ritual event rather than simply a sport or pastime.

The elaborate stone aqueducts at San Lorenzo and La Venta surely had ritual functions in addition to whatever utilitarian purposes they may have served. Their construction involved inordinate amounts of labor and they are always associated with palaces and stone sculptures displaying water symbolism. The San Lorenzo system may have carried fresh potable water but the source of water for the La Venta system is unclear, given its location at the summit of the Stirling Acropolis. In all likelihood, these lavish water works symbolized both the link between rulers and water deities and the real and metaphorical control the elite exerted over this substance that was so essential for daily life and spiritual well-being.

Caves are virtually absent from the alluvial lowlands of Olman, but possible cave depictions appear in Olmec art. Sculptured scenes showing people seated in caves or emerging from cave-like niches suggest an early occurrence of the later pan-Mesoamerican belief that deities and even entire ethnic groups entered the world's surface through caves that served as doorways to the supernatural realm inside the earth. In some cases, these depictions clearly represent the mouth of the Olmec Dragon. The paintings in the Guerrero caves, surely the work of ethnic Olmec artisans, imply that Olmecs sought out sacred spots in distant lands. Whether this was their primary reason for venturing into these unknown regions, as opposed to economic or political motivations, is a fascinating question that we cannot answer.

Religious practitioners

Who was in charge of religious activities in Olmec societies? Rulers and their close kin probably fulfilled the most important religious posts, serving as mediators between the supernaturals and the populace at large. Indeed, religious power of this sort must have underlain their claims to legitimate elite status. This does not mean that Olmec societies were theocracies, but simply that sharp divisions between the religious and secular realms of life were absent.

Like later Mesoamerican civilizations, the Olmecs undoubtedly had both full-time priests and part-time shamans who performed healing ceremonies that mixed practical medicines with supernatural cures. Peter D. Joralemon believes that full-time priests led cults devoted to specific deities, although they are difficult to identify in Olmec art because they frequently wear the costume of their supernatural patrons.

The evidence for shamans is strong and convincing. In addition to the shamanistic ideology underlying Olmec beliefs discussed earlier, Peter T. Furst has identified stone figurines depicting Olmec shamans undergoing the transformation from humans to jaguars and F. Kent Reilly III has even proposed the actual sequence of steps in that transformation.[29] The sequence opens with a kneeling human who proceeds through the motions of rising on one knee while assuming were-jaguar characteristics and ends with a completely jaguarized creature who stands in a highly charged,

68, 69

combative human stance. This sequence appears to recapitulate the actual transformation living shamans experienced after ingesting hallucinogens such as native tobacco (*Nicotiana rustica*) or the psychoactive venom found in the parathyroid gland on the marine toad *Bufus marinus*. Bones of this totally inedible toad appeared in trash deposits at San Lorenzo, while the magnificent kneeling figure known as the "Princeton Shaman" has one of these amphibians incised on the top of his head.

While we have difficulty separating rulers, priests and shamans in Olmec art, their ritual regalia is much in evidence in museums and private collections all over the world. They include anthropomorphic and zoomorphic figurines, masks, mirrors, celts, "spoons," "stilettos," and a vast miscellany of objects decorated with esoteric designs that charged them with religious meaning.[31] Attempts to identify their functions have fueled a virtual cottage industry of speculation. "Stilettos" and similarly pointed objects with handles are proposed as bloodletters used in ritual penis perforation and other forms of autosacrifice, while "spoons" – discussed more fully in Chapter 5 – are said to be snuff tablets used to administer hallucinogenic substances. There is no indisputable evidence for Olmec use of mind-altering substances, but most scholars assume that they were taken.

Conclusion

This brief and incomplete reconstruction of Olmec life cannot begin to do justice to the richness of the daily existence of even the lowliest farming family. Only an ethnography conducted by a sympathetic observer magically transported back in time could capture the fullness of their lives and the dynamic aspects of Olmec culture as it changed through time. The songs, dances, quarrels, acts of treachery and bravery, fears and exhilaration have disappeared into ancient mists that archaeologists can never enter. Nevertheless, they can learn much more than we know at the moment, a challenge that younger archaeologists must take up with gusto.

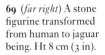

68 (*right*) San Lorenzo Monument 47. A powerful human, perhaps a ruler or shaman, subjugates a deadly snake. Ht 70 cm (27 in).

69 (*far right*) A stone figurine transformed from human to jaguar being. Ht 8 cm (3 in).

5 · Olmec Art

Olmec artisans created some of ancient America's most striking and beautiful objects in a unique style that stands as the visual hallmark of their culture. Olmec art expresses the relationships between humans and the supernatural world, especially those that connected rulers with their deified patrons. This bold and complex art system developed in Olman simultaneously with the emergence of hierarchical societies as early as 1500 BC. Its origins are unknown but surely lie buried at the bottom of some early village site, and may even be lost forever if the earliest objects were made in perishable materials. Olmec craftsmen and women worked clay, wood, rubber, shell, bone, plant fibers, feathers, animal skins and other locally available raw materials, as well as imported volcanic and metamorphic stones. Virtually their entire output, save for objects made of clay and stone, has perished in the humid tropical environment, but the remaining objects are stunning testimony to the skill and vision of their creators.

Olmec art presents an enigma to most modern observers. For one thing, the subject matter runs a seamless gamut from naturalistic humans to surreal creatures in a way completely foreign to western sensibilities. Furthermore, our ingrained expectations demand that the large stone monuments and three-dimensional naturalistic carvings characteristic of the Olmecs should signal an advanced stage of Mesoamerican artistic development, not its beginnings. Art historian Esther Pasztory notes that the earliest manifestations of ancient Egyptian and other art styles in the Old World are stiff and rigid, and that naturalistic creations full of movement, like those of ancient Greece, only appear after a long history of development. However, Olmec art is different. It appears very suddenly, with no known predecessors, and the most naturalistic Olmec pieces are the earliest, with the tendency through time towards greater conventionalization rather than less.[1]

Miguel Covarrubias, the great Mexican artist and pioneering historian of pre-Columbian art, defined Olmec style forty years ago based upon his decades of collecting and studying Olmec art. According to Covarrubias, the Olmec aesthetic ideology emphasized "simplicity and sensual realism of form, vigorous and original conceptions." He went on to say that Olmec artists were preoccupied with representing human beings made up of solid, ample masses, powerful and squat individuals like certain modern Indians of southern Mexico, and that they handled these forms with architectural discipline and sensitivity. "They delighted in the smooth, highly polished surfaces of their jades, broken occasionally by fine incised lines to indicate such supplementary elements as tattooing, details of dress, ornaments, and glyphs. These lines are sharp and precise, soft curves and angular shapes with rounded corners."[2] Despite the many discoveries in the past fifty years, Covarrubias's words remain as valid today as when he first penned them.

Monumental sculpture

Archaeologists traditionally divide Olmec art into two basic categories: monumental sculptures and small, portable pieces. Most monumental sculptures were carved from stone, although the wooden busts uncovered at El Manatí remind us that Olmec sculptors probably carved scores of perishable wooden monuments for every one executed in stone. Indeed I suspect that stone sculptures were truly exceptional works of art reserved for only the most important ritual occasions and leaders, and that wooden sculptures littered the Olmec landscape. Basalt and other volcanic stones were the preferred raw material, although limited quantities of limestone, sandstone, and schist were also used. Petrographic analyses show that the basalt found at San Lorenzo and La Venta came from Cerro Cintepec volcano in the Tuxtla mountains, but archaeologists have not determined sources for the other stones.

Approximately 250 Olmec stone monuments are known and additional examples appear every year. While archaeologists occasionally uncover Olmec sculptures in controlled excavations, local farmers make most of the discoveries and frequently destroy the contextual evidence in the process of exposing the find. Olmec sculpture displays a tremendous diversity of size, ranging from small, almost portable pieces to gigantic basalt blocks weighing more than 30 metric tons. The subject matter is so diverse that every modern classification leaves residual categories larger than any of the classes. Apparently the Olmecs did not share our "logical and scientific" taxonomies, although they surely had a classification of sculptures that we have failed to recognize.

Beatriz de la Fuente, today's leading authority on Olmec sculpture, identifies three pervasive themes in Olmec monumental sculpture: mythic images, effigies of supernaturals, and human figures.[3] Mythic images portray events that occurred at the beginning of time, and explain creation as a sacred process of transformation directed by the gods. They include larger-than-life-size humans emerging from interior spaces, seated humans holding babies, and the jaguar–human "copulation figures" discussed in Chapter 4.

Larger-than-life-size humans emerging from interior spaces occur on large rectangular thrones (often mislabeled "altars") at La Venta, San Lorenzo, Laguna de los Cerros, and elsewhere. According to de la Fuente

70

70 La Venta Monument 4. This, the largest Olmec throne known, rested in the plaza south of the Stirling Complex. The Olmec Dragon mask in the upper register is very similar to the throne in the Oxtotitlán cave painting (see plate X). Ht 160 cm (62 in).

they depict the widespread Mesoamerican origin myth that marks humankind's emergence from the cave of the earth at the beginning of life. Seated persons holding a baby occur on small, portable greenstone objects, monumental thrones, and freestanding sculptures. The baby frequently lies in an inert, death-like pose, suggesting the offering of a sacrificed infant, reminiscent of the remains of sacrificed infants uncovered at El Manatí.

Supernatural beings, de la Fuente's second major theme, include were-jaguars and other animals depicted more or less realistically. Were-jaguars, as we saw in the previous chapter, are composite, abstract beings that combine human and animal features, generally human bodies with felinized facial features. Other commonly depicted animals include felines, birds, serpents, and crocodilians; while some are rendered very naturalistically, all contain imaginary features that signal their otherworldly origin.

De la Fuente's class of human figures includes Colossal Heads, men under supernatural protection, and "mediators." All are naturalistic portrayals of either living individuals or fully human, idealized men. Colossal Heads apparently are ruler portraits, while men under supernatural protection have a supernatural being placed above them. Thus, for example, the central figure on La Venta Altar 4 sits under a stylized feline mask and the man depicted on San Martín Pajapan Monument 1 wears a massive were-jaguar headdress. "Mediators" are full-bodied, freestanding sculptures that, like Colossal Heads, seem to portray rulers. However, they generally project a special dynamism lacking in the heads, a sense of control, strength, constraint, and serenity expressed in body posture and facial expressions.

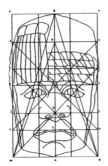

71 San Lorenzo Monument 4. Portions of both rear sides of this sculpture were removed after it had outlived its original purpose. The lines crossing the drawing illustrate the geometric relationships behind de la Fuente's "Golden Section." Ht 178 cm (69 in), weight *c.* 6 tons.

In her writings, de la Fuente has advanced the controversial proposal that Olmec artisans were guided by the "Golden Section," a mathematically based set of proportions created by dividing a length so the smaller part is to the greater part as the greater part is to the whole. Certain other ancient cultures applied this basic set of proportions to sculpture and architecture, and it also occurs in nature. De la Fuente argues that Olmec sculptors employed the Golden Section in Colossal Heads, other sculptures and small portable objects. She also points out that Colossal Heads at Tres Zapotes and La Cobata, generally accepted as the latest heads in the Olmec sequence, fail to achieve this ideal and suggests that it no longer existed in the closing centuries of Olmec culture. 71

Colossal Heads

Colossal Heads are the most widely recognized symbol of Olmec culture in modern times. One La Venta head graced a Mexican postage stamp in the 1970s and there is even a novel with the theft of a head as its central theme.[4] Most were apparently sculpted from spherical boulders, but two San Lorenzo examples were carved out of larger existing thrones. Seventeen are known: 10 at San Lorenzo, 4 at La Venta, 2 at Tres Zapotes, and a rather grotesque and perhaps unfinished example from La Cobata.[5] All portray mature males with jowly cheeks, flat noses, and slightly crossed eyes, a physical type still common in the region today. Their expression combines power with a sense that these men have seen and done it all. The backs of the heads are frequently flattened, as though they were designed to stand against a wall. Many have irregular, unfinished bottoms that slant upward from the chin to the back, leading Sara Ladrón de Guevara to suggest they were intended to be displayed gazing into the heavens, rather than directly at the viewer as they appear in modern museum displays. All wear distinctive 72

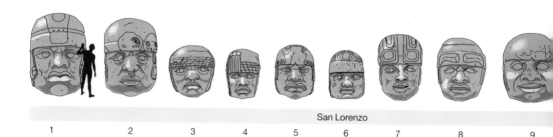

San Lorenzo

1 2 3 4 5 6 7 8 9

72 Known Olmec Colossal Heads. This line-up shows the differences in size that characterize these ruler portraits as well as the considerable variation in facial features and headgear.

headdresses reminiscent of the traditional leather American football helmet of my youth. These headdresses were probably made from cloth or animal skin and some depict the knot of the cloth at the back of the head. Feathers decorate some of them and one La Venta example even includes a bird's head. Similarities amongst the headdresses found on several Colossal Heads have prompted suggestions that they identify specific dynasties or individual rulers. Most wear large plugs inserted into openings in their ear lobes. Remnants of white plaster and reddish paint on one San Lorenzo head suggests that Olmec monuments, like their Greek analogues, were brightly decorated affairs.

pl. VII   Endless speculation surrounds the identities of the men portrayed on Colossal Heads. They were once thought to represent ballplayers, but today scholars agree they are portraits of individual rulers. Of course, rulers may have been featured participants in ballgame rituals, so perhaps the distinction is irrelevant. Whoever they depict, they are surely portraits of living or recently deceased individuals whose physical features were well known to the sculptor, and each face is unique and strikingly realistic.

When José Melgar y Serrano published his pioneering description of Tres Zapotes Colossal Head 1 in 1869 he proposed that it depicted an "Ethiopian." This fiction recently resurfaced in the writings of Ivan van Sertima and others as part of an Afrocentric rewriting of world history. Melgar may be excused for his mistake, but today there can be no doubt that the heads depict the American Indian physical type still commonly seen on the streets of Soteapan, Acayucan, and other towns in the region.[6]

It is impossible to assign a precise date to most Colossal Heads. San Lorenzo's heads were carved, used, and buried before 900 BC, but those at La Venta were found partially exposed on the modern ground surface, and the Tres Zapotes examples were moved out of their contexts before archaeologists could record them. Thus we do not know where the tradition of carving Colossal Heads began or if it lasted 100 years or 1,000 years. We must also not forget that heads carved from wood may predate the imperishable stone examples. I personally suspect that the practice of carving stone Colossal Heads was a short-lived fad that lasted only 50 or 100 years, but obviously have no proof to support this theory.

	Tres Zapotes		La Cobata		La Venta		
10	1	2	1	1	2	3	4

The two San Lorenzo heads carved out of larger pre-existing thrones have forced archaeologists to reconsider many of their ideas about Olmec sculpture.[7] There can be no doubt about the sequence of carving in these two cases: both heads reveal remnants of the niche and seated figure that graced the front the older throne. But, why was it done? Did newly installed rulers commission their own images to be carved from a predecessor's throne to symbolize continuity in the ruling family? Did usurpers recarve old thrones to trumpet the overthrow of their enemies? Or did the practice simply represent ongoing programs of recycling scarce and valuable basalt? These questions cannot be answered until we have more evidence.

Thrones

Thrones are large, flat-topped rectangular basalt blocks with primary images carved on the front, and, at times, subsidiary scenes on the sides. Most intact examples are quite large: San Lorenzo Monument 14 measures 1.38 m by 3.48 m and 1.52 m high (4.5 x 11.4 x 5 ft), while La Venta's "Altar 4" is even larger and weighs an estimated 33 metric tons. Fourteen thrones are known: 7 occur at La Venta and another 4 are found in or near San Lorenzo. Tabletop thrones, the most common type, have flat tops and ledges that project out from the top. They all depict scenes and motifs related to rulership and royal descent, especially Beatriz de la Fuentes' mythic image of larger-than-life-size humans emerging from a niche holding a baby in their hands. Although the infant's features are eroded or destroyed in every case, they clearly depict were-jaguars similar to that portrayed on the well-preserved Las Limas sculpture. The sides of some thrones show adults holding lively, at times highly animated, babies. The true functions of thrones as seats for rulers only became apparent after archaeologists discovered the Olmec-style mural in Oxtotitlán cave, Guerrero, with its elaborately dressed man seated on top of a supernatural face identical to the one on La Venta's Altar 4. Three somewhat aberrant thrones lack niche figures: La Venta's Altar 1 substitutes a were-jaguar face while Potrero Nuevo Monument 2 features two chubby Atlantean figures supporting a ledge carved into an Olmec Sky band (see ill. 14, p. 35), and Monument 18 at nearby San Lorenzo has two similar dwarfs.

Full-figured human and animal sculptures

Olmec achievements in the realm of three-dimensional sculpture surpassed those of every later Mesoamerican civilization, except possibly the Aztecs. While Colossal Heads and thrones are best viewed from the front and sides, full-figured, realistic sculptures of human and animals, especially felines, are obviously meant to be viewed from all sides. Human figures are shown kneeling or seated in a cross-legged "tailor pose." Most appear to be individualized portraits of living men, probably rulers, although a few have either were-jaguar faces or cover their faces with fierce masks. The Lord of Las Limas, the "Prince" from Cruz del Milagro, and La Venta Monument 77 ("The Scribe") are three outstanding examples of this genre. Some seated figures hold ceremonial bars or were-jaguar babies in both hands, while others clasp "torches" or "knuckle-dusters" (ritual bloodletters?) to their chests. La Venta and San Lorenzo have yielded several seated figures, but unfortunately most have suffered decapitation or other mutilation. A recently discovered sculpture at Loma del Zapote, near San Lorenzo, originally had one leg hanging down from the torso, perhaps over the ledge of a throne. The "Wrestler," a seated figure in an incredibly dynamic pose from Antonio Plaza, Veracruz, is the most spectacular sculpture of this sort. His beard, mustache and head shape give him a very Oriental appearance that fuels sporadic speculation about Chinese contacts with the Olmecs, speculations of the sort that crop up whenever someone sees what they take to be non-Indian physical traits in Olmec art.

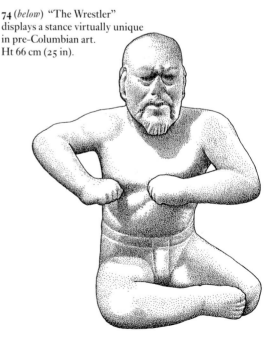

73 (*left*) La Venta Monument 77, mutilated only by the removal of this ruler's headdress. Ht 104 cm (40 in).

74 (*below*) "The Wrestler" displays a stance virtually unique in pre-Columbian art. Ht 66 cm (25 in).

Kneeling figures include San Lorenzo's spectacular Monument 34, a life-sized male whose perforated shoulders once held arms of wood or some other perishable material, as well as the renowned sculpture found at the summit of the San Martín Pajapan volcano. While the San Lorenzo sculpture appears to portray its subject in a resting pose, the San Martín Pajapan piece projects a tension suggestive of a man rising up out of his kneeling stance.

Felines, specifically jaguars (Felis onca), are the most common animals depicted in the round. One San Lorenzo example is actually a jaguarundi (Felis yagouaroundi), a smaller relative of the more common jaguar. They often grasp serpents in their mouths; one La Venta example clearly depicts a serpent with heads at both ends of its body. In most cases, the forelegs are separated from the bodies, but the El Azuzul monument that may be recarved from an older monument depicts them as slightly raised elements attached to the torso.

Stelae

Stelae are large stone slabs with beings or scenes carved on the front face that were set upright in the ground. The carving of stelae appears to be a relatively late development in Olmec art and they only occur at La Venta, Tres Zapotes, and a few post-Olmec sites west of the Tuxtla mountains. Even the Tres Zapotes examples, including Stela C with its famous Epi-Olmec design and Long Count date of 31 BC, are so distinct from earlier Olmec art that they probably belong to a post-Olmec culture.

Four stelae with virtually identical were-jaguar faces formed a tableau at the base of La Venta's Pyramid C (Monuments 25/26, 27, 58, and 66). Their form and thematic content duplicate those found on small portable greenstone celts or axes described below. The same monumental tableau included Stela 5, an irregular slab depicting three standing individuals overseen by a fourth flying above them. Similar themes occur on other La Venta stelae, where central figures, perhaps rulers, surrounded by flying figures are thought to portray supernatural patrons.   75

The standing person on La Venta's Stela 1 is one of the few possible females in Olmec monumental art. The artist endowed her with a hint of discernible breasts, a skirt-like garment, and a feminine cast to her head, but even these do not prove her gender, given the Olmec penchant for portraying androgynous beings.

Olmec uses of sculpture

Most Olmec sculptures lack archaeological contexts that could provide critical clues about their original uses. However, many are found near mounds, terraces, drains, and other architectural forms, suggesting they were functionally related to these constructions. Recent discoveries at San

75 La Venta Stela 2. This large irregular stone slab depicts a standing Olmec ruler surrounded by smaller beings, perhaps supernatural protectors or ancestors. Ht 426 cm (166 in).

Lorenzo and La Venta show that the Olmecs arranged their sculptures into multi-monument scenes or tableaus that may have included architectural backdrops. The line of stelae in front of La Venta's Great Pyramid is an especially impressive monumental tableau, while Offering 4 to its north is a good example in miniature. The four sculptures at El Azuzul and the wooden busts at El Manatí are other settings frozen in time. I suspect that Olmec "ritual choreographers" regularly created and re-created sets of monuments, particularly those smaller and lighter than Colossal Heads, stelae, and thrones. Such rearrangements may have occurred on a seasonal or cyclical basis or according to the needs of the ritual, perhaps even during rituals as mythic storylines unfolded.

At times the general locations of sculptures indicate possible ancient patterns of placement even if they have been moved out of their original context. Rebecca González Lauck believes that a set of three Colossal Heads may mark La Venta's northern boundary, while three badly eroded sandstone monuments perhaps served a similar function to the south. David G. Grove goes further with his suggestion that at La Venta mounds, sculptures, and buried offerings formed a deliberate cosmogram, an integrated and symbolically charged arrangement created for the benefit of the supernatural patrons of La Venta's elite.

Monument carvings and transport

How did the Olmecs manage to carve and move their magnificent sculptures without metal tools, draft animals, and wheeled vehicles? A recent segment of the popular BBC/NOVA television program "Secrets of the Ancients" attempted to answer these questions through field experiments in Olman, but only managed to demonstrate that the Olmecs knew some things we don't. However, recent investigations of monument workshops at Llano del Jícaro and San Lorenzo have shed some light on the problem. Although we cannot say how long it took to carve a throne or move a basalt block 80 km (50 miles), we do have some insights into how these tasks were accomplished. Workshops are marvelous sources of information not available anywhere else. As Egyptologist R. Engelbach observed about the famous unfinished Aswan obelisk, "It must have been galling beyond words to the Egyptians to abandon it [the obelisk] after all the time and trouble they had expended, but today we are grateful for their failure, as it teaches us more about their methods than any other monument in Egypt."[8] Mesoamericanists feel the same way about Llano del Jícaro and the Group D setting at San Lorenzo.

Archaeologist Alfonso Medellín Zenil discovered Llano del Jícaro's workshop in 1960 when he identified an unfinished seated figure at the site.[9] Although he labeled the sculpture Laguna de los Cerros Monument 8, the actual find spot was Llano del Jícaro, located several kilometers from the larger settlement. The sculptor had roughed out the head, body, and pedestal of the sculpture but failed to finish it for reasons we do not know. No obvious cracks or flaws can be detected and it may have been ready for shipment to a "finishing" workshop at its final destination. In any case, Susan Gillespie's 1991 investigations at the site revealed natural rock outcrops, loose boulders, worn stone hammers, quantities of chips, flakes, and other debris, and nine partially carved stones.[10] By the time the sculptors abandoned the largest unfinished monument, a tabletop throne that split horizontally during the manufacturing process, they had begun to delineate the ledge at the top and the head of a person seated in a niche.

The rulers of Laguna de los Cerros probably controlled the Llano del Jícaro workshop but monuments produced there may have reached a much wider market, including perhaps San Lorenzo and La Venta. An extensive program of petrographic testing of native boulders, debris, and

76

76 Llano del Jícaro Monument 8. This unfinished image of a seated person was abandoned in the sculpture workshop. Ht 195 cm (76 in).

117

finished monuments is needed to shed light on the entire problem of the sources of Olmec monuments. Thomas W. Killion and Javier Urcid have uncovered numerous locales with boulders suitable for carving into monuments in the Tuxtla foothills around Laguna de los Cerros, and they suspect that some may contain additional undetected Olmec carving stations.[11]

Olmec sculptors employed stone tools to flake and grind the native basalt. Flaking was accomplished with hammer stones, many showing considerable wear and damage. Another technique involved grinding or drilling circular pits into the stone. Paired shallow pits intrude into existing designs on some Colossal Heads, suggesting they served as some form of mutilation carried out after the initial carving. Deep pits define the corners of the mouths on some heads. Some writers propose that hard jadeite axes were used with sand or some other abrasive for the final finish carving, but there is no evidence to support this speculation.

The techniques Olmecs used to transport large stones over long distances of inhospitable terrain without wheels or draft animals remain a mystery. Although Olmec sculptors left no written records, they created two monuments that may depict the actual transport of basalt blocks. San Lorenzo Monument 15 and Laguna de los Cerros Monument 9 portray rectangular basalt blocks bound with ropes and surmounted by now-badly destroyed human figures whose legs dangled over the edge of the stone. I believe they are depictions of Olmec rulers exhorting their workers to pull the stones destined to become their thrones or portraits.

Historical information from the Egyptians, Assyrians, and other ancient civilizations suggests that whenever possible, the Olmecs used the rivers as transportation routes. Not only is water transport easier and more efficient than hauling huge stones overland, but Olman's vast river network provided easy lines of movement from the quarries and workshops to virtually every known final destination. Joseph Velson and Thomas Clark proposed that the Olmecs moved the stones on large rafts, perhaps towed by lines of canoes,

77 San Lorenzo Monument 15, and Laguna de los Cerros Monument 9. The ropes around these rectangular stone boxes are a graphic representation of the way in which the Olmecs moved stones over solid ground. Ht 30 cm (11 in) and 38 cm (14 in).

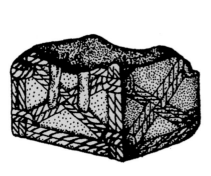 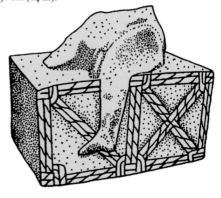

78 San Lorenzo Monument 20, a throne subjected to extensive breakage and defacement prior to its abandonment, perhaps as an initial step to turning it into a Colossal Head. Striations on the bottom that overlap mutilation scars suggest it was dragged to its final resting spot after the sides were removed, accounting for the lack of debris in the surrounding soil. Ht 167 cm (65 in).

during the dry season when currents are less turbulent and fewer fallen trees and other obstacles block the channels.[12] Upon arriving at the disembarkation point, it was still necessary to drag the stones overland and uphill. This task was probably accomplished by hundreds of sweating men pulling the stones on wooden sledges, rollers or log rails. Ropes, levers, wedges, earth ramps, and cleared paths probably rounded out the technology of transport, but motivation, patience, and determination were surely the critical ingredients in these efforts.

Many Olmec monuments show extensive mutilation, a fact that has puzzled archaeologists since Matthew W. Stirling's day. The destruction is clearly ancient since it occurs frequently on deeply buried sculptures. Human sculptures often lack heads and limbs or have had facial features obliterated, giant sections have been broken off tabletop altars, and curious pits often mar the faces of Colossal Heads. Some scholars believe foreign invaders or local peasants who rebelled against their oppressive rulers were the agents of this destruction. Others argue that monuments were ritually destroyed upon the death of their owners. The latest evidence that Olmecs re-carved existing sculptures into new, smaller works of art suggests that much of the "mutilation" resulted from recycling "old" stone. Basalt must have been a very valuable commodity, difficult for Olmec rulers to obtain even in the best of times. Existing monuments must have constituted a tempting source of raw material, especially those that once belonged to a vanquished rival or competing lineage. Furthermore, the competitive political landscape that pitted Olmec centers and their rulers against each other may have made new basalt periodically unavailable when quarries fell into unfriendly hands. All in all, it is likely that old monuments were constantly being recycled into new ones. This brings into question traditional visions of Olmec capitals as huge outdoor museums where the treasures of the ages were displayed for decades for the entire world to see.

78

Greenstone objects

Olmec artists created hundreds if not thousands of exquisite small ornaments and ritual paraphernalia from a wide range of rare metamorphic
stones.[13] Often mistakenly labeled "jade," the raw materials include albitite,
chloromelanite, jadeite or jadetite, marble, and serpentine in colors ranging
from deep green to near white. Nephrite or "true" jade is only found in Asia.
The more generic term "greenstone," although not completely accurate,
has gained general acceptance in modern archaeological circles. The Olmecs
prized green and blue-green jadeite above all others. The source of this
scarce material was a mystery for decades. Miguel Covarrubias proposed
that it came from an undiscovered deposit in the mountains of Guerrero
while others favored Costa Rica's Nicoya Peninsula. Recent investigations in
the Sierra de las Minas mountains overlooking northern Guatemala's
Motagua river have revealed the actual source in a zone strewn with raw
material, including giant boulders weighing hundreds of tons.[14] At one time
archaeologists believed that Olmec craftsmen did not work greenstone until
after 800 BC, but recent discoveries at El Manatí and La Merced push its use
well back into the Early Formative period.

Olmec lapidaries worked greenstone into celts, figurines, beads, ear
spools, pendants, and numerous enigmatic objects with uncertain functions.
Well-made, highly polished celts or "votive axes" are quite common; hundreds appeared in buried offerings at La Venta, El Manatí, La Merced, and
several sites in Chiapas, and more than 1,000 are said to have appeared at Río
Pesquero. Celt caches at La Venta often assumed cruciform and other geometric patterns. Most celts have highly polished though otherwise
undecorated surfaces, but some – among them
four examples from La Venta and
several unprovenienced pieces – have
incised designs. Three La Venta
pieces, all bearing lightly incised,
somewhat whimsical "faces,"
occurred in a cruciform cache. The
fourth, a true masterpiece that
depicts an Olmec were-jaguar
covered with red cinnabar, was part of
Tomb E's rich offering. Celts and

79 Two greenstone celts. Most
celts are plain, but these exhibit
incised depictions of rulers or
other important personages. They
wear elaborate costumes and carry
possible symbols of office in their
hands.

80

80 The Kunz Axe, a "votive axe" or celt, was first published in 1890, long before the Olmec culture and style were recognized. One of the largest Mesoamerican jades known, it portrays an archetypal Olmec were-jaguar face. Ht 30 cm (11 in).

axes generally lack evidence of actual use in the utilitarian functions their names imply. Karl Taube believes that they symbolically represent maize seeds and may have been employed in rituals dedicated to the maize deity. They may also have functioned as units of value or currency, with caches serving as stored wealth that was hidden but easily accessed if needed. Interestingly enough, the carved designs that grace some of them appear to be miniature versions of the supernatural being shown on the four stelae in front of La Venta's Great Pyramid.

Figurines

Hundreds of greenstone figurines depict humans and animals, but only a few have appeared in well-defined archaeological contexts. The best documented come from La Venta, plus a few heirloom items from Yucatan, Puebla, and the Aztec capital of Tenochtitlán. Many are so similar in theme and workmanship that they may be the products of a small group of artisans in a single workshop that only functioned for a few decades.

Humans, jaguars, and were-jaguars are the most common themes depicted on Olmec greenstone figurines. Human renderings tend to be more stylized than naturalistic, and virtually all show complete figures with heads and bodies, although bodies and limbs are normally less detailed than the heads. Humans stand, kneel, sit, recline on their sides, or assume postures reminiscent of contortionists. The quality of the raw material and craftsmanship ranges from mediocre to truly outstanding. Cinnabar and other red pigments often appear on their surfaces and in the crevices. Some are very highly polished while others were either left unpolished or have suffered surface erosion. Delicate fine line incision was used to represent facial and body painted designs or tattoos on a few figurines.

81

81 The Dallas Figurine (pl. XII). Lightly incised tattoo-like designs are common on Olmec jade faces. The were-jaguar face that covers the upper portion of the right side of his face appears attached to the headband that has deformed his skull. Ht 18.4 cm (7 in).

82 Portrayals of adults holding or interacting with were-jaguar babies occur on several thrones but are very rare on jade figurines like this one, called the Guennol figurine. Ht 21.5 cm (8 in).

82, pl. XVII   Standing males are the most common subjects of greenstone figurines. Most are mainly bald, although a few show hair or wear a skullcap. Pear-shaped heads indicate the practice of skull deformation, an apparent marker of elite birth. Ears are commonly shown as long perforated tabs that may have held perishable ornaments. Almond-shaped eyes, fleshy faces, and mouths with downturned lips are standard. Some show short necks, while many lack necks entirely. The most common posture is a straight-legged stance with arms integrated to the body, but a few have independent arms held in various positions. Toes and fingers, when shown at all, are depicted with simple lines. The most common, and frequently the only clothing indicated on males is a loincloth or codpiece. Some authorities believe that figurines were dressed in costumes made from perishable materials, with different sets of clothing for each ritual occasion, a pre-Columbian version of Barbie's friend Ken. In addition to the traditional straight-legged standing posture, we find deformed dwarfs, hunchbacks, and even fetal figures, at times shown holding their hands to their ears as if straining to hear a distant sound.

pl. XII   Seated figurines assume more dynamic poses than their standing counterparts; some occupy benches or thrones while others have one leg bent in front of them, tuck both legs under their body, or assume a cross-legged, tailor posture. Several reclining figures depict a man with one hand to his ear and the other on his stomach, flexed legs that are joined at the feet, and holes in the earlobes that permit them to be suspended horizontally or vertically.

How did the Olmecs use their figurines? Unfortunately there is not much archaeological information on this topic. In all likelihood, the Olmecs, like later Mesoamericans, employed figurines in religious rituals and curing ceremonies. Peter Furst proposed that Olmec transformation figurines were placed on altars and similar settings where they may have functioned as household gods and familiars or spirit helpers.[15] This may have been true for other stone and ceramic figurines as well. The varied poses of transformation figurines suggest that actual sets were used together, perhaps arranged in scenes replicating the ritual being performed. The sixteen standing figures in La Venta's Offering 4 may be one such symbolic ritual frozen in time.

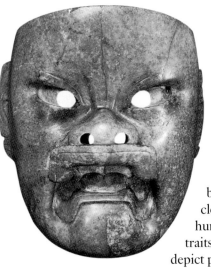

83 A ruler or shaman could have worn this life-sized greenstone mask. Ht 20.8 cm (8 in).

Masks

Stone masks are among the finest creations of Olmec artisans.[16] They occur in two classes: full-sized masks that, while heavy, could be worn on the face, and smaller maskettes designed to be suspended on necklaces or sewn on to clothing. Some portray naturalistic human faces, including a few possible portraits of living individuals, while others depict powerful and awe-inspiring were-jaguar or bird-monster faces. At times, portrait masks project a haunting familiarity, as though they reproduce the face of a long-forgotten acquaintance. Many have openings for the eyes, nostrils, and mouth; parted lips often show the upper teeth, and long tabs stand in for ears. Lightly incised designs suggestive of tattooing cover a few faces. Many masks are discolored owing to ritual burning prior to burial, or prolonged contact with the soil or inlaid substances around the eyes. Most have holes drilled through the sides to facilitate tying the mask on the wearer's face or some other object.

Looters have uncovered virtually every known Olmec mask. Dozens are attributed to Río Pesquero, Veracruz, including some of the finest examples. The absence of reliable information on the actual contexts of masks makes it impossible to know precisely how they were used. Peter D. Joralemon suggests they served as funerary objects, perhaps placed with the dead, or kept as mementos after the deceased was buried. At least some were attached to headdresses, as shown on San Martín Pajapan Monument 1, La Venta Monument 44, and an exquisite diopside figure in the Dumbarton Oaks collections.

Ornaments and ritual paraphernalia

Many Olmec greenstone ornaments and ritual objects do not fit into any of the classes discussed above. The functions of some are obvious, while depictions in art provide clues about how others were employed, but frankly many leave us puzzled. Olmec "spoons," elongated objects carved from fine jadeite with a deep concavity near one end and holes for suspension as pendants, are a good example. The human figure on one Olmec sculpture wears such a "spoon" hung on his chest. Most are plain but a few have incised or carved designs. What do they represent and how were they used? Are they bird monsters or tadpoles? Did they function as snuffing tablets for hallucinogens, paint pots for holding pigments, or accessories used in bloodletting rituals? All these ideas have been put forth at one time or another.

84 (*left*) Fine feathers and bird eyes depicted on the handle of this jade perforator lead to a beak-like appendage, forming a hummingbird effigy for what may have been a ritual bloodletter. Length 17.2 cm (6 in).

85 (*right*) This highly polished jade hand is anatomically correct down to the fingernails. Red pigment residue remains between the fingers. The bottom is hollowed out to resemble a canoe or rectangular punt. Length 20.5 cm (8 in).

Personal ornaments made from greenstone include ear ornaments; chest pendants; perforated celts apparently worn on belts; and oblong and spherical beads used in necklaces, bracelets, and aprons. Tiny replicas of human ears, arms, and legs may have been placed on idols or sewn on to clothing or headdresses. Other objects probably served as symbols of high rank or ruler-
84 ship. These include sharply pointed perforators or ritual bloodletters carved in the shape of awls and sting-ray spines, scepters, punt-shaped jadeite
85 "canoes," including one worked into the form of a human hand, and "yuguitos," U-shaped carved stones decorated with were-jaguar faces and other Olmec symbols that make some sort of ball game paraphernalia.

Manufacture, recarving, and reuse
Archaeologists have not yet identified Olmec greenstone workshops, so our knowledge of their lapidary techniques is based solely upon studies of the finished products. Like monument carving, the process was a subtractive one that removed material from a larger matrix. Once removed, it could not be replaced and the only recourse of the unfortunate artisan who made a mistake was to salvage the raw material for some smaller object.

Philip Drucker's classic study of greenstone objects found at La Venta revealed that Olmec lapidary techniques included sawing, drilling, polish-ing, and incision.[17] He suggested that stone saws were used to reduce the original blocks of raw material. John Carlson's examination of a jade plaque in the Dumbarton Oaks collections revealed that its slightly concave surface had been achieved by grinding it with an equally flat nether stone and abra-sive.[18] Holes were probably drilled with a bow drill or some similar device,
86 and were perforated part way into the stone as the first step in creating eyes, mouths, nostrils, etc. Interestingly, Olmec artisans used solid conical drill

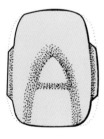
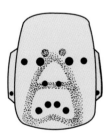
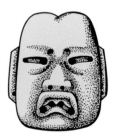

86 Sequence of steps in manufacturing a stone figurine head.

bits rather than the hollow bird-bone and reed drills favored by later Mesoamericans. Suspension holes drilled completely through pectorals, beads, and other objects often have bi-conical profiles indicating that they were drilled from each side to the center. Sandstone saws or strings charged with abrasive were employed to create the engraved facial features of figurines. Polishing must have involved many tedious hours of rubbing the pieces, perhaps with soft deer hide impregnated with quartz sand, powdered jadeite, or some other abrasive. Eyes were often inlaid with obsidian, iron ores and perhaps shell; most have disintegrated but telltale residues remain in a few sockets. Complex designs executed on the faces of figurines with shallow, scratch-like incisions appear at first glance to be later additions or afterthoughts but, if so, they are skillfully integrated into the overall design.

The intrinsic value of rare greenstones led the Olmecs and later peoples to recarve broken objects. In some cases, broken limbs were provided with new fingers. Other objects show multiple modifications over the centuries. For example, a pectoral in the Dumbarton Oaks Collection started out as a   87 winged bar with a were-jaguar face surrounded by incised St Andrew's crosses. Later two large holes were drilled through the crossed bands. At the beginning of the Christian era, centuries after its original manufacture, a seated Maya ruler was inscribed on the back along with a proto-Maya hieroglyphic inscription.

Numerous other instances of later reuse and veneration of Olmec objects can be cited. In the sixth or seventh century of our era Classic Maya mourners placed an heirloom Olmec pendant in a grave on Cozumel Island, Quintana Roo. At approximately the same time, a magnificent figurine depicting a crying baby in polished blue jadeite was deposited in a Classic-period offering at Cerro de las Mesas, Veracruz. Even the Aztecs placed an Olmec maskette in a dedicatory offering at their Great Temple in AD 1470.

Reuse of Olmec objects was so common in ancient times that I suspect pre-Columbian peoples occasionally looted Olmec sites in search of these precious objects. Nor did reuse and veneration cease with the Spanish Conquest. Twentieth-century objects were found in front of San Martín Pajapan Monument 1 and, as described in Chapter 3, the Las Limas sculpture occupied the place of honor as a native Madonna on a village altar. One greenstone mask even retains traces of modern paint, owing perhaps to its use in modern village rituals.

87 An Olmec winged pectoral modified through time. Later users drilled holes through the existing St Andrew's Crosses on the wings and added writing to the back. Length 9 cm (3 in).

6 · The Olmecs Abroad: Eastern Mesoamerica

The Olmec world extended into other parts of Mexico and Central America far beyond Olman's borders. Mesoamerica had undergone a great cultural awakening after 1500 BC as complex societies appeared first in Chiapas and Olman and slightly later in central Mexico and Oaxaca. These societies shared an agrarian-based economy sustained by the cultivation of maize, beans, squash, chilies and (where possible) cotton. Farming families lived in villages, constructed simple houses of perishable materials and employed pottery and stone tools in their daily tasks. Large villages functioned as capitals of loosely integrated chiefdoms ruled by leaders whose high status was evident in their elaborate residences, exotic personal ornaments, lavish burial offerings, and the command of communal labor for the construction of temples and public works projects.

By 1200 BC San Lorenzo Olmecs emerged as Mesoamerica's most complex and highly organized society. Groups in the lands bordering Olman shared many basic cultural characteristics with them but lacked the emerging urbanism, elaborate public architecture, stone sculpture, elite craft traditions, definable art style, and well-developed iconography that characterized Olmec civilization. After 1200 BC Olmec merchants established relationships with local leaders in Chiapas, Central America, and highland Mexico, exposing them to these hallmarks of civilized life. These leaders adopted Olmec ideas about rulership and its social, economic, political, and religious manifestations and quickly began to modify them into new configurations. As time passed by, some of these transformations prospered and became less Olmec while still retaining a clear imprint of Olmec parentage. In this way the Olmecs became Mesoamerica's Mother Culture (see below), creators of a world view and vision of elite culture that was well established throughout Mesoamerica by 600 BC and flourished in modified but still recognizable form until the Spanish Conquest.

Long-distance trade in obsidian and other raw materials and goods was common in Mesoamerica long before 1200 BC. The exact mechanisms of exchange are unknown, but most likely involved down-the-line commerce with diverse groups trading items with their immediate neighbors who passed them on to their neighbors. These exchanges moved goods thousands of kilometers without any trade partners needing to range far from home.

After 1200 BC San Lorenzo-based Olmecs initiated a new approach to commerce by leaving their home territory to search for exotic goods. Their journeys brought these earliest merchants into contact with foreigners who spoke many different languages and had what must have seemed strange customs. Despite these obstacles they managed to establish close personal relationships with local leaders. It is highly doubtful that they ever established an Olmec "empire" or conquered large areas. Instead, they probably cultivated amicable partnerships with local leaders that served to guarantee safe passage through potentially hostile territory. Their tactics may have included gift exchange, marriage to local women, and even bride exchanges between Olmec rulers and their distant associates. From the Olmec perspective, the Mesoamerican political landscape probably comprised archipelagos of friendly groups extending southeastward into Central America and west to Oaxaca, the Balsas basin of Guerrero, and Central Mexico.

While most scholars believe that the Olmecs initiated these contacts, the extent of their impact sparks lively disagreements among archaeologists. These disagreements began in 1942 when Alfonso Caso proposed that all later Mesoamerican civilizations grew out of an Olmec Mother Culture.[1] Miguel Covarrubias[2] and Matthew W. Stirling[3] supported his bold assertion against considerable opposition, particularly from Mayanist J. E. S. Thompson and his colleagues.[4] Today most archaeologists accept it as a fact but dissenters continue to keep the debate alive.[5] My reasons for supporting the Olmec Mother Culture school will become apparent, but this dispute involves basic philosophical beliefs about the nature of human cultures as well as the actual data, and will continue long after the current warriors have retired from the field. The core of the debate revolves around the concept of Olmec horizons during the Early and Middle Formative periods.

Olmec horizons

Archaeological horizons are short episodes of intense interaction between societies that left some evidence in the archaeological record. When these societies differ significantly in size, complexity, and power, the smaller or less-organized group frequently adopts ideas, beliefs, practices, and symbols from their more powerful and prestigious partner. In the Olmec case, the ideas and beliefs adopted by non-Olmec groups are reflected in pottery shapes and designs, sculpture, architecture, religious paraphernalia, personal regalia, and other elite objects.

Archaeologists generally accept the existence of two Olmec horizons: an Early Olmec horizon (1200/1150–900 BC) that emanated from San Lorenzo, and a Late Olmec horizon based at La Venta (850–500 BC).[6] During the Early Olmec horizon, societies throughout Mesoamerica adopted highly unique Olmec ceramic forms and decorative motifs. These included bowls, dishes, and bottles carved with the jaguar paw-wing motif and other characteristic Olmec motifs, as well as large, hollow, baby-faced ceramic figurines.　pl. XI

Polychrome paintings on cave walls may be another marker, but the known examples are undated, making their assignment to a specific Olmec horizon problematic. These signatory traits occur earlier at San Lorenzo than elsewhere in Mesoamerica and are presumed to have originated there.

The Late Olmec horizon is provisionally dated to 850 to 500 BC but may have only lasted for a century within that time span. Its most prominent markers include stone sculpture, especially relief carvings and boulder faces carved with narrative scenes; hard, white pottery incised with the "double-line break" motif; and extensive use of jadeite and other greenstones, including those embellished with carved and incised designs. John E. Clark and Mary E. Pye have recently proposed a third Olmec horizon, provisionally named after the Manantial phase (1000–800 BC) that emanated from the Basin of Mexico during the interregnum between San Lorenzo and La Venta.[7] Their proposal is too recent to have received critical examination but serves as a warning that our current ideas may be too simplistic.

What kinds of contacts created these horizons? Explanations put forth in the past include colonization, conquest, religious proselytization, and trade; of these, the last fits all the evidence much better than the others. By 1200 BC Olmec merchants penetrated highland and Pacific coastal Guatemala, Oaxaca, and central Mexico in their quest for obsidian, jade, serpentine, iron ores, basalt, cacao, salt, marine shells, animal pelts, and exotic bird feathers. Obsidian and basalt already circulated outside their immediate source areas; in these instances, the Olmecs apparently managed to insert themselves into the established networks and export the goods back to their home bases. In the case of iron ores, and perhaps other materials as well, they created demand for things that no one had used before and even colonized unoccupied source zones.

Local leaders must have quickly grasped the potential advantages of amicable ties with Olmec traders who could provide them with exotic goods embellished with motifs and symbols of rulership. Regular visits by Olmec merchants strengthened these ties to the point that some rulers adopted the outward trappings of Olmec elite culture and may even have accepted Olmec women as marriage partners. The intensity and duration of these highly personal relationships depended upon the fortunes of individual Olmec rulers and merchants and their foreign trading partners, and probably waxed and waned from one generation to the next. Unfortunately these short-term fluctuations are not easily detected in the archaeological record, leaving us simplified glosses or palimpsests for what must have been very complex social histories.

The Early Olmec horizon

The Mokaya

While eastern Mesoamerica is well known as the homeland of the Classic Maya, the hot, humid piedmonts and coastal plains of southern Chiapas and

Guatemala played a critical role in the earlier Olmec world. This was especially true of the Soconusco region of southeastern Chiapas. The Soconusco, famous for its high-quality cacao in Aztec times, maintained particularly close ties to the metropolitan Olmec region, ties so strong that at times it practically became an outer hinterland of Olman.

Early Formative Mokaya (Mixe-Zoquean for "the Maize People") living in the Soconusco created Mesoamerica's earliest known chiefdoms at Paso de la Amada and other Mokaya centers where recent investigations show a progressive growth in population, complexity, and sophistication during the second millennium BC.[8] Small independent villages appeared, then coalesced into simple chiefdoms that quickly evolved into larger, more complex chiefdoms. San Lorenzo Olmecs established regular contacts with Mokaya rulers who soon adopted many basic Olmec ideas and practices. San Lorenzo and their Mokaya allies declined simultaneously in the tenth century, but a century or so later La Venta's rulers established new ties with groups in other parts of Chiapas. Archaeologists working in Chiapas have been aware of these long-lived and at times intense relationships for decades, but only recently have they become apparent to other scholars.

The Mokaya are credited with many "firsts" in Mesoamerican history: the oldest-known permanent villages, the first effective agriculture, Mesoamerica's oldest securely dated pottery, and the region's first hierarchical societies. It is not surprising that early Olmecs established strong ties with Mokaya groups, since both probably spoke related proto-Mixe-Zoquean languages. Furthermore, they lived in societies on a similar level of development and enjoyed easy communications across the low hills of the Isthmus of Tehuantepec and along the Gulf lowland rivers that extend deep into Chiapas. Olmec elites could obtain many desirable goods from the Pacific coast including cacao, cotton, salt, bird feathers, and jaguar and crocodile skins. The region also provided easy access to the adjacent Guatemala highland sources of obsidian, jadeite, serpentine, and quetzal feathers.

Paso de la Amada

The best evidence for Olmec–Mokaya contacts is found at Paso de la Amada, a large Mokaya village in the Mazatán section of the Soconusco near the Guatemalan border where archaeologists from the New World Archaeological Foundation have traced six phases of Mokaya culture between 1600–1550 BC and 900 BC.[9] Barra-phase (1550–1400 BC) farmers, the oldest identified in the Soconusco, constructed simple houses with pole walls, thatch roofs, and earth floors. But there is no evidence that they erected temples or other specialized public buildings. Although they cultivated maize and other domesticated plants, they also consumed shellfish, fish, and land mammals just as their Archaic-period predecessors had. In fact, some archaeologists believe they used maize primarily to ferment into beer similar to Andean chicha that they consumed on ritual occasions rather than as a daily staple.

88   Barra-phase pottery is the oldest currently known in Mesoamerica, but is
amazingly sophisticated and much too elaborate and well made to represent
the first fumbling attempts at ceramic technology. Archaeologists suspect
Mokaya potters were heirs to an ancient ceramic-making tradition that first
appeared in northern South America before 3000 BC and gradually spread
northward along the Pacific coast to Mesoamerica. The surfaces of their
well-made deep bowls and incredibly thin-walled *tecomates* were decorated
with monochrome, bichrome and even trichrome slips. Other decorative
treatments included incision, zoned stamping, grooving, and gadrooning.
Vessel shapes appear to imitate gourd containers, suggesting that the earliest
pots replaced everyday gourd containers, perhaps as high-status objects
used on ceremonial or festival occasions that featured consumption of maize
beer, chocolate, or other prized beverages.

Agriculture became more important as Mokaya populations grew in the
Locona and Ocós phases (1400–1100 BC). Social and political hierarchies
emerged when many small independent Mokaya chiefdoms, each with its
own leaders, head village and home territory, appeared throughout the
Soconusco. At Paso de la Amada archaeologists identified fifty-one earth
platform mounds scattered haphazardly around the 50-ha (123-acre) village
core. As many as 1,500 of the estimated 4,000 members of the chiefdom
inhabited the village, while the remainder of the population occupied small
settlements in the hinterland. Five or six generations of chiefly families
occupied a succession of residences on top of Mound 6, the largest raised
platform in the village. By the end of the Locona phase, this mound had

88 Barra-phase pottery from the Mazatán region, coastal Chiapas. The richness and
sophistication of this pottery assemblage is surprising in view of its age.

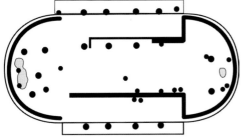

89 Reconstruction drawing and floor plan of a chief's residence, Mound 6, Paso de la Amada, Chiapas. The round holes in the floor held posts that supported the thatch roof; the curved walls were made of tamped clay.

been rebuilt at least eight times and stood 4 m (13 ft) above the surrounding ground level. Mound 6 supported a sequence of chiefly residences and careful placement of a highly polished jade axe beneath the first floor prior to construction indicates that the builders envisioned its special nature from the very start. One apsidal house with rounded corners measured an astounding 22 by 10 m (72 x 30 ft). Artifacts on the house floors included elaborate pottery, well-made stone bowls, large, hollow ceramic effigy figurines, ceramic ear ornaments, greenstone, mica, iron ore mirrors and other items not available to the average Mokaya farmer. 89

Paso de la Amada's greatest surprise, Mesoamerica's oldest formal ball-court, appeared in 1995.[10] The structure included two long parallel mounds, interior benches that face each other, and a long central alley (80 m [240 ft]). Clearly local chiefs could mobilize large labor parties, perhaps fueled with maize beer at the end of the workday, for public works projects in addition to their own residences.

The court also demonstrates that ritual ballgames, a central element of Mesoamerican religion and cosmology, already existed at the very beginnings of settled village life in southern Mesoamerica. Although rubber balls were known from El Manatí and later Olmec ceramic figurines depict ballplayers in full regalia, formal courts were not known to exist prior to about 600 BC.

Mokaya chiefs and the Olmecization of Mokaya society
How did early Mokaya leaders establish and perpetuate their power? John E. Clark and Michael Blake argue that charismatic men enhanced their power and prestige by hosting large periodic feasts with elaborate ritual displays while distributing obsidian and other rare imported goods to their

supporters.[11] In this sense they were similar to the traditional "Big Men" chiefs of highland New Guinea and other small-scale village societies around the world. Resourceful leaders who threw successively larger bashes attracted more supporters until the entire population came to them for economic support, political and military protection, justice in disputes, intercession with the supernatural world, and an occasional good time. At first, ambitious men achieved chiefly status through their own efforts and those of their closest allies. However, status of this sort was quite ephemeral and chiefs who failed to reward their followers soon found themselves leading a one-man parade. As high status came to be inherited within family lines and power and wealth were more tightly concentrated in the hands of a few people, chiefs began to serve important economic, political, and religious functions. At Paso de la Amada, they controlled access to obsidian from highland Guatemalan sources at Tajamulco, San Martín Jilotepeque, and El Chayal, as well as iron ore, greenstone, and other precious materials. Such control was a powerful tool in the hands of an astute leader, but no one could rule by simply manipulating material goods and wealth. Successful leaders also had to win over the minds of their followers, a feat they probably accomplished by claiming special access to the spirit world through putative kinship with deities who determined the course of human events. The Mokaya chiefs who resided on Mound 6 achieved this level of power by 1300 BC when they assumed control of the entire Paso de la Amada chiefdom. Early Olmec leaders at San Lorenzo may have used similar methods at about the same time.

Paso de la Amada continued to dominate the Soconusco in the Ocós phase (1250–1100 BC), but dramatic changes began to occur as the population grew and agriculture became more effective. The most significant of these was the appearance of Olmec merchants at 1150 BC or earlier, their increasingly frequent visits ultimately precipitating the "Olmecization of the Mokaya": a process of cultural interchange in which the leaders of Mokaya groups, "tried to become Olmecs, or become like the Olmecs."[12]

John E. Clark and Mary E. Pye have identified three stages in this process, culminating in a thoroughly reorganized Mokaya culture and society along metropolitan Olmec lines by 1000 BC with a new regional center at Cantón Corralito.[13] Clark attributes the relocation of the regional capital to an aggressive takeover of the entire Mazatán region by San Lorenzo Olmecs. At the same time, people abandoned their traditional religious symbols for imported Olmec models and locally made pottery with abstract Olmec designs, and esoteric deity representations completely replaced the older animal-effigy vessel adornments and figurine styles. The leaders of this new Olmec satellite society were probably local chiefs who proudly announced their identification with the cosmopolitan Olmec world by wearing imported ornaments and finery, using imported Olmec pottery and figurines, and commissioning the two San Lorenzo-style stone sculptures found at nearby Alvaro Obregon and Buena Vista. These sculptures show

90

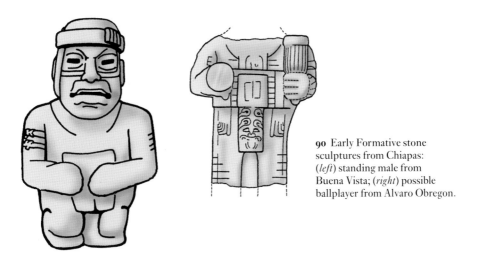

90 Early Formative stone sculptures from Chiapas: (*left*) standing male from Buena Vista; (*right*) possible ballplayer from Alvaro Obregon.

men who are probably local rulers decked out in typical Olmec regalia. Both monuments were no doubt carved by itinerant San Lorenzo sculptors sent to Chiapas by their San Lorenzo lord.

The Early Olmec horizon outside the Soconusco

The Soconusco Mokaya were as Olmec as any foreigners could be by 950 BC, but were not the only "Olmecized" groups in southern Mesoamerica. By then Olmec merchants had ventured into highland Chiapas, Honduras, and El Salvador. San Lorenzo-style pottery and figurines appear at many places in the Chiapas mountains, among them Chiapa de Corzo, Mirador/Plumajillo, Padre Piedra, San Felipe, Mirador/Miramar, Santa Rosa, Amatal, Vistahermosa, San Isidro, Maritano, and Río Totopac.

Mirador/Plumajillo, a settlement located in the Cintalapa valley west of Chiapa de Corzo, is the most intriguing of these.[14] Here Pierre Agrinier found native iron ore deposits, a workshop littered with thousands of broken and partially worked ilmenite and magnetite blocks, chert drills and other tools, and even a fragment from an iron ore mirror, all associated with San Lorenzo-style ceramics and figurines. According to Agrinier, the area was lightly inhabited when colonists from San Lorenzo established a mining outpost at Mirador/Plumajillo, the only known Olmec colony outside Olman. Ann Cyphers recovered several tons of identical blocks at San Lorenzo, where they also appeared in the Yale excavations along with mirror fragments.

No Early Olmec-horizon remains have been identified in the Guatemalan highlands east of Chiapas, but we know that San Lorenzo imported obsidian from the El Chayal source near Guatemala City and greenstone from the Sierra de las Minas further down the Motagua river valley.

A similar lack of information prevailed in Honduras until Rosemary A. Joyce and John S. Henderson uncovered a long Early Formative ceramic sequence at Puerto Escondido near the Caribbean coast of Honduras a few years ago.[15] The Archaic foragers who occupied the site until 1600 BC were followed by Barahona- (1600–1400 BC) and Ocotillo-phase (1400–1100 BC) farmers who lived in perishable houses and used ceramics similar to those found in the Soconusco. Olmec-style vessel forms and surface treatments appeared during the Chotepe phase (1100–900 BC), a clear signal of contact with the wider world of southern Mesoamerica, perhaps motivated by the desire to acquire obsidian. Although there is no evidence for direct Olmec involvement in these contacts, neither can it be ruled out.

The Late Olmec horizon in eastern Mesoamerica

John E. Clark and Mary E. Pye have called the Early Olmec horizon "a brief historical interlude in a much longer history of interaction" between the Olmecs and their neighbors to the south and east.[16] It was also the prelude to the even more widespread and pervasive Olmec intrusion we call the Late Olmec horizon. This horizon was the work of La Venta's rulers and it triggered a major cultural florescence that transformed societies all over Chiapas and northern Central America. Social stratification, public art, architecture, and long-distance trade in exotic goods appeared for the first time in regions where they had never existed, as one group after another adopted Olmec symbols, beliefs, and practices. The horizon's visible manifestations included architectural designs, monumental stone sculpture, ceramics, specific styles of stone and ceramic figurines, and the use of plain and decorated jades. Some archaeologists believe that Olmecs even transformed local food preferences, agricultural practices, and basic religious beliefs by promoting widespread use of maize as a basic food staple and veneration of the Olmec Maize Deity.

La Blanca and the Soconusco

The large village of La Blanca in westernmost Guatemala near the Mexican border emerged as the Soconusco's most important center by the Conchas phase (850–650 BC).[17] Mound 1, a monumental construction measuring at least 25 m (82 ft) high and 100 m (330 ft) wide at its base, dominated the village. Excavations at the site have yielded a full inventory of local ceramics and Olmec-style vessels, hundreds of ceramic ear ornaments, fifteen ear ornaments carved from jadeite and other imported greenstones, polished mica jewelry, and two fragmentary Olmec-style carved stones. Two additional spectacular Olmec-style sculptures that lack provenance are attributed to the La Blanca environs while a third appeared at nearby Ojo de Agua, Chiapas. One, known as the "Tuxtla Chico Dancing Jaguar," depicts a standing anthropomorphized jaguar. The other, said to come from Ojo de Agua, shows a fantastically costumed male sporting a cape and headdress that make him look like a background figure in the movie Star Wars.

The final sculpture said to be from the region is the enigmatic "Young

91 A standing male in elaborate costume, Ojo de Agua, Chiapas. The chest plate shows an Olmec seated on a throne inside a cave.

92 Dancing Jaguar, Tuxtla Chico, Chiapas. Its human body and feline face suggest a "transformation figure" like the smaller figurines (ill. 69). Ht 102 cm (40 in).

93 (*right*) Serpentine statuette from coastal Chiapas. Known as the "Young Lord" or "Slim," this masked male holds a scepter in one arm and a bloodletter in the other. His arms, thighs, and legs are richly decorated with tattoo-like designs. Ht 65 cm (25 in).

Lord," a 65-cm (26-inch) high serpentine figurine also known as "Slim" owing to his almost anorexic appearance. Today Slim resides in a private collection in the United States, but is believed to have originated near La Blanca. He wears a tall headdress, a facemask, and loincloth, while clutching two celts or scepters close to his chest. His lower torso and limbs are covered with elaborate incised designs. Some students of Olmec art believe that Slim represents a shaman, but Peter D. Joralemon considers him a ruler, perhaps shown at the moment of his accession to power. Indeed the youth may have filled both roles simultaneously. In any case, his costume incorporates an unusually rich and complex display of Olmec rulership iconography.[18]   93

Chiapas beyond the Soconusco
Archaeological surveys and limited excavations in the Chiapas highland and coastal zones have revealed major Late Olmec-horizon occupations.[19] The best evidence for Olmec contacts and influence is seen in architecture, community plans, stone sculpture, Olmec and Olmecoid ceramics, greenstone objects and dedicatory offerings.

La Venta-inspired architectural forms, including high pyramids, long mounds, large rectangular or square acropolis-like platforms, and buried offerings appeared quite suddenly at San Isidro, Mirador, Tzutzuculi, La Libertad, Chiapa de Corzo, Finca Acapulco, San Mateo, and other Chiapas sites. In addition, at least a dozen Late horizon Olmec-style monumental stone sculptures have been identified between the Isthmus of Tehuantepec and El Salvador. All lack good contextual information, making it difficult to place them in time, but thematic and conceptual ties to La Venta sculpture suggest they were created after 800 BC. Their size makes it virtually certain that they were created at or near their modern locations and although most fall short of the highest levels of artistic execution found in Olman, they appear to be the work of itinerant Olmec carvers rather than local imitators. If they were the work of local carvers, we would expect to find a much larger corpus of monuments, including perhaps some in non-Olmec styles. However, most locales have only one sculpture, invariably in the Olmec style.

Low-relief carvings on natural boulders are the most common format, but a few monuments were carved in the round. Interestingly enough, no Colossal Heads or thrones have been reported, perhaps because their close identity with metropolitan Olmec rulers and rulership made them inappropriate for foreign regions. Two basic themes dominate the sculptural corpus: single individuals, and group scenes depicting three or more people. The single figures may represent deities, deity impersonators, local rulers, or even Olmec kings. Maize cobs and other representations of the plant are common adornments, leading Karl Taube to identify the individuals who bear them with the Olmec Maize God.

94 Finca Acapulco, Chiapas. This Late Olmec Horizon community was the largest in the Central Depression region of the Chiapas highlands.

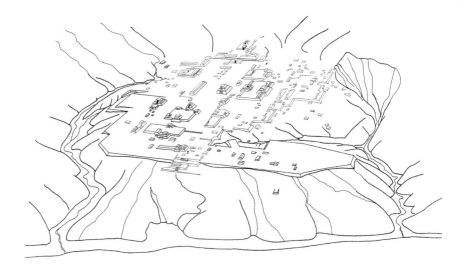

X Rendering of Mural 1 at Oxtotitlán cave, Guerrero. An Olmec ruler in a bird costume sits on his flat-topped throne in the form of the Earth Monster.

XI This seated hollow white ware ceramic figure is said to be from Zumpango del Río, Guerrero. Similar effigies assume various poses that must have held some unknown meaning to their makers. Ht 36 cm (14 in).

XII Seated figure carved from serpentine, known as the Dallas Figurine (see ill. 81, p. 121). His dynamic yet relaxed pose suggests a young but self-assured and powerful ruler. Cinnabar residues imply the entire work was once covered with red pigment. Said to be from San Martín Texmelucan, Puebla. Ht 18 cm (7 in).

XIII La Venta Offering 4 was found deeply buried in Complex A, the ritual court behind Pyramid C. Jade figurines were used to create a scene in which several men parade before a gathered assembly and a principal figure who stands with his back to a wall of upright celts.

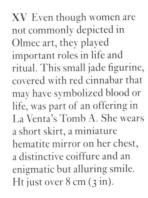

XIV Four wooden busts from El Manatí feature rudimentary bodies topped with individualized faces. These 3,000-year-old sculptures provide the oldest evidence for the Olmec use of wood in ritual contexts.

XV Even though women are not commonly depicted in Olmec art, they played important roles in life and ritual. This small jade figurine, covered with red cinnabar that may have symbolized blood or life, was part of an offering in La Venta's Tomb A. She wears a short skirt, a miniature hematite mirror on her chest, a distinctive coiffure and an enigmatic but alluring smile. Ht just over 8 cm (3 in).

XVI, XIX (*right* and *opposite*)
Two views of a life-sized mask
carved from dark serpentine.
It is one of several stone masks
attributed to Río Pesquero,
Veracruz. Ht 17.8 cm (7 in).

XVII The Bliss Figure. This standing male
with outstretched arms wears a beard and penis
sheath. Named for Robert Woods Bliss, who
purchased it in Paris in 1912, it shows more
musculature and movement than most Olmec
jade carvings. Ht 29.3 cm (9 in).

XVIII This unique black-ware ceramic duck effigy,
attributed to Las Bocas, Puebla, apparently served as a
censer. Incense placed in the duck's stomach received air
through the openings in the belly while smoke emerged
from the enlarged mouth aperture. Ht 23 cm (9 in).

XX The Lord of Las Limas, a seated youth holding an inert were-jaguar baby, has four major Olmec supernaturals carved on his limbs while the baby represents a fifth. Ht 55 cm (21 in), weight 60 kg (132 lbs).

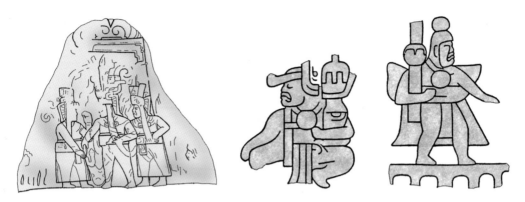

95 Low-relief Olmec rock carvings in southern Mesoamerica: (*left*) Pijijiapan Monument 1, (*center* and *right*) Chalchuapa Monument 12.

Pijijiapan Monument 1 is an outstanding example of a group scene composition. This boulder sculpture from coastal Chiapas shows a central male figure and two female companions dressed in typical Olmec finery accompanied by two diminutive attendants.[20] The three primary figures stand under a sky-band panel that may signify a cave opening. The scene seems to portray a frozen moment in the courtly life of a local ruler surrounded by his entourage, perhaps a marriage scene celebrating his union with an Olmec woman. A similar three-figure composition occurs at nearby Tiltepec northwest of Pijijiapan. 95

Olmec-style monuments in Chiapas are found in out-of-the-way locales in or near passes leading up into the mountains rather than within communities. This distribution pattern is quite different from that of most monumental sculpture in ancient Mesoamerica, suggesting that they marked territorial boundaries, way stations along pilgrimage or ritual circuits, or merchants' guide-signs through uninhabited countryside.

Many Chiapas sites have yielded the distinctive ceramic hallmarks of the Late Olmec horizon; jade and greenstone Olmec-style celts, figurines, maskettes, scepters, and beads are equally widespread but less common. Plain celts commonly occur in large La Venta-style caches or offerings. The large highland site of San Isidro yielded many such offerings before being flooded by the waters behind the Netzalhualcoyotl Dam.[21] Salvage excavations in one mound (Mound 20) revealed eighty-five offerings containing pottery vessels and large numbers of celts placed directly on its east–west axis. Most of the celts were carved from a soft, tuff-like stone but a few were jadeite and serpentine. Cache 11, the most elaborate offering, occupied the center of the alignment and included twelve celts surrounding two sets of large jadeite ear ornaments placed at right angles around a central pottery bowl. San Isidro is the only highland site to yield so many caches, but the new lake behind the dam covered many unexcavated sites. 96

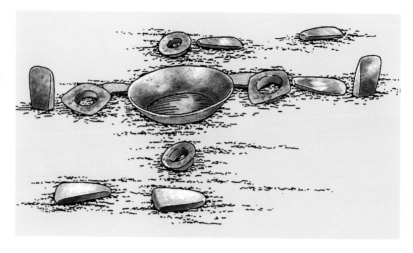

96 La Venta-style offering at San Isidro, Chiapas. Cache contents include a ceramic bowl, celts, and flares from earplug assemblies.

While most celts found in Chiapas are undecorated, a few incised pieces are known. The most famous of these, the Simojovel Celt, is a large black slate object that depicts a profile Olmec face with an elaborate headdress set amid complicated glyph-like vertical designs. A similarly decorated celt is reported from Escuintla, Guatemala.

Pacific Guatemala
The Guatemalan piedmont and coast are dotted with large Late Formative centers that frequently cover earlier remains. Abaj Takalik is one of the most important of these. To date, archaeologists have identified fifty-seven sculptures carved from local andesite boulders, including four Olmec-style pieces.[22] Monument 23 is a large stone that the excavator believes was initially carved as an Olmec Colossal Head and later recarved to depict a seated person in a niche or mouth holding a baby. This sequence of creating a throne from a Colossal Head is the reverse of the San Lorenzo practice of reworking existing thrones into Colossal Heads. Other Abaj Takalik Olmec monuments include a squatting figure wearing an Olmec-style helmet and breechcloth and holding a small animal in each arm, an Olmec

97 A decorated celt from Simojovel, Chiapas. The owner of this black slate celt donated it to Mexico's National Museum of Anthropology at the urging of Matthew W. Stirling. Ht 31 cm (12 in).

98 An Olmec-style low-relief panel from Suchitepéquez, Pacific coastal Guatemala. A contortionist surrounds a central figure. Diameter 81 cm (32 in).

head separated from its body, and a kneeling Olmec in a very dynamic pose. Abaj Takalik was obviously an important place for the Olmecs, and archaeologists eagerly await full publication of the research carried out there since the 1970s. The most striking Olmec carving known from the Guatemalan piedmont is the   98 Shook Panel, a flat circular stone depicting two contortionists in one of the most striking compositions ever attempted by any Mesoamerican sculptor. Said to come from San Antonio Suchitepéquez, it is named for Edwin Shook, the archaeologist who saved it from almost certain illegal export.[23]

A large Formative village named El Mezak lies down-slope from Abaj Takalik. El Mezak may have served as a node in an Olmec trade route that traversed the coastal lowlands.[24] When its leaders came under considerable Olmec influence after 950 BC they began to use Olmec and Olmec-inspired pottery, baby-face figurines, imported obsidian, and jadeite axes. Cleft heads, flame eyebrows, clover leafs, stars, lozenge shapes, and other typical Late Olmec horizon ceramic design elements are common, and one vessel even depicts a complete Olmec were-jaguar. A 6.5-m (21-ft) mound constructed with carefully selected pink, yellow, and green sands is reminiscent of La Venta's Complex A.

El Salvador

Olmec merchants passing through El Mezak apparently continued southeastward to Chalchuapa, El Salvador, where Colos-phase (900–600 BC) inhabitants erected a huge conical mound similar to La Venta's Great Pyramid; used Olmec-style pottery vessels, figurines, greenstone celts, and clay stamps; and commissioned Monument 12, the southeastern-most known Olmec-style monumental sculpture.[25] The sculptor engraved four men on the sides of a natural boulder. Three hold bundles or staffs while approaching a seated individual who cradles a staff in the crook of his arm. Their clothing and ornaments recall depictions at La Venta while they assume postures found on Olmec-inspired sculptures at Pijijiapan, Chiapas, and San Miguel Amuco, Guerrero. The scene may represent an actual historical encounter between Olmec visitors and an Olmecized ruler who had adopted Olmec regalia and symbols of rulership. Was Chalchuapa an Olmec outpost at the uttermost end of their world? Perhaps so; no other site in northern Central America has yielded convincing evidence for direct contact with the Olmec metropolitan homeland.

Honduras

Pre-Columbian Honduras was a cultural borderland where Mesoamerican cultures melded into those of lower Central America and northern South America. The Ulua river formed Mesoamerica's eastern boundary at the time of the Spanish Conquest, but Formative-period cultures east of the river were indistinguishable from those to the north and west. Olmecs maintained contacts of variable intensity with the region between 1000 and 600 BC. These contacts may have been indirect, perhaps through Olmecized leaders at Chalchuapa and points further west, but were not nearly as intrusive as those in Chiapas.

The great Classic Maya center of Copán northeast of Chalchuapa was initially settled by Rayo-phase (1300–900 BC) farmers whose pottery shows Early Olmec horizon affinities.[26] Later Uir-phase (900–300 BC) inhabitants deposited 47 human interments, including the richly appointed Burial VIII-27. The offering accompanying it contained 4 pots, 9 polished jadeite and serpentine celts, and almost 300 jadeite beads and pendants, including 2 shaped like jaguar claws. A decapitated human skeleton flanked the offering on one side, a human long bone the other, and the jades rested on top of two children's skulls. Is this the burial of a fallen chief whose enemies beheaded him before his body could be recovered, or merely the remains of a wealthy leader whose grave was disturbed by later building activities? In either case the pots were Olmec-style bottles and bowls decorated with flame-eye-brows, paw-wings, sharks, serpents, and other typical Olmec images. Similar vessels are found in burials placed in caves high above the Copán valley floor. The absence of Olmec-style sculptures suggests that while Copán's leaders used Olmec-style objects, they did not engage in face-to-face contact with Gulf coast Olmecs. In all likelihood they occupied the end of a down-the-line trade system managed by non-Olmec neighbors at Chalchuapa or some other Olmec outpost.

The village of Puerto Escondido on the banks of Honduras's Chamelecón river near the Caribbean coast was already centuries old at 900 BC when the inhabitants razed existing structures and erected a large stepped platform on the ruins simultaneously with the first appearance of Olmec-style ceramics in the region.[27] The pottery included polished black, gray, and brown wares, and differentially fired white-and-black ware. The predominant forms were flat-based cylindrical and flaring-walled bowls with carved designs, often decorated with red pigment. Design motifs include

99

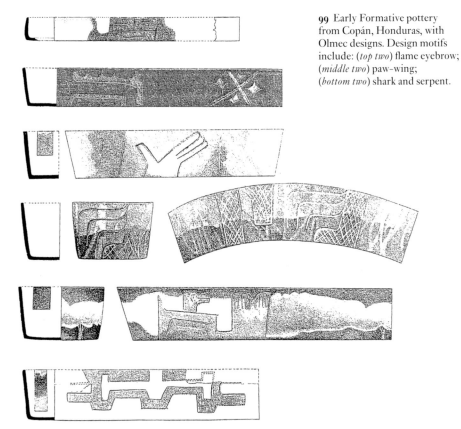

99 Early Formative pottery from Copán, Honduras, with Olmec designs. Design motifs include: (*top two*) flame eyebrow; (*middle two*) paw-wing; (*bottom two*) shark and serpent.

typical San Lorenzo-derived stars, diamonds, St Andrew's crosses, and the paw-wing motifs. The inclusion of two human burials with pottery vessels and jadeite costume ornaments in the platform terraces may have marked a significant change in the local socio-political structure and the symbols that expressed leadership. At the very least, whoever directed the construction of the platform had the power to demolish existing homes and enjoyed the right to wear greenstone jewelry.

Playa de los Muertos, a large ruin inland from Puerto Escondido on the banks of the Ulua river, has yielded numerous Formative-period burials over the course of four archaeological projects over the past century.[28] Most of the artifacts closely resemble material found at Los Naranjos, Chalchuapa, and other nearby sites, but some vessels and figurines are strikingly similar to Early Olmec-horizon Tlatilco-culture objects from the Basin of Mexico. The similarities include vessel forms (bottles, flat-bottomed bowls with flaring walls, stirrup spout and effigy vessels), incised decoration, flat and cylindrical stamps, white-slipped figurines, double-headed figurines, and the use of figurines as grave offerings. Similar materials also occur at Yarumela, another large Honduran site located on the Comayagua river.

The large village of Los Naranjos on the shores of Lake Yojoa in the Honduran highlands apparently attracted occasional Olmec visitors during the Jaral phase (800–400 BC).[29] In addition to numerous large mounds and a fortification ditch, the site boasts several stone monuments, including a muscular Olmecoid, standing human torso that recalls Rodin as much as it resembles metropolitan Olmec sculpture. Other Olmec-style objects recovered at Los Naranjos include a jadeite axe covered with red cinnabar, a well-stocked elite burial accompanied by pottery vessels and jade artifacts, and an Olmec-style ceramic figurine. The fortification ditch suggests unsettled times, but whether Olmecs played any role in this drama is unknown.

Middle Formative villagers in several parts of Honduras practiced an unusual burial cult focused on caves in isolated mountain settings.[30] Evidence for this cult has appeared in the Copán valley, the Cuyamel caves at the headwaters of the Aguán river, and Talgua cave in northeastern Honduras. Despite their notable isolation, these caverns yielded hundreds of human burials accompanied by pottery vessels made in both local and Late Olmec-horizon styles. Many are secondary interments in which fleshless bones, pottery vessels, and greenstone objects were placed in niches and hidden passages. At Talgua cave some skeletons became encased in calcite deposits precipitated by dripping water, leading one writer to name it "The Cave of the Glowing Skulls." Surveys near the caves failed to identify significant contemporaneous habitation sites, suggesting the deceased were brought from considerable distances for burial in these sacred underground sanctuaries. Was this burial cult an Olmec-related phenomenon or a local indigenous cultural practice that incorporated symbols and objects from distant lands? The latter appears more likely but, as we shall soon see, Olmecs conducted rituals in caves in Guerrero and perhaps other places as well.

Costa Rica

Costa Rica is famous for the hundreds of greenstone "axe gods," pendants and other objects found in pre-Columbian tombs. Most postdate Olmec culture but at least fifteen are Olmec or show Olmec stylistic affinities to one degree or another.[31] They include a winged-figure pendant, a hand-paw-wing pendant from Guanacaste province, and a beautifully polished spoon. Given the absence of any other Olmec remains, all may be heirlooms imported centuries after the Middle Formative period.

The Maya lowlands

One of ancient Mesoamerica's great mysteries is the absence of significant human populations in Yucatan, Belize, and the Guatemalan Peten before 800 BC. Earlier remains have been identified at various places in the northern Peten and Belize, but the entire area was very lightly settled until 600/500 BC.[32] Given the region's extremely light and scattered populations, Olmecs would have had no knowledge of its resources and thus lacked any reason to

100 Olmec jades from a cache discovered at Chacsinkin, Yucatan. This cache, the largest set of Olmec jades known from the Maya lowlands, may indicate as-yet undiscovered connections between the Olmecs and early Maya.

enter it. The only evidence for actual contacts between Formative Maya and Olmecs occurs near the eastern frontier of Olman at Seibal where Real-phase (900–600 BC) villagers deposited Cache 7 in a cruciform pit.[33] Cache 7 was a La Venta-style offering that included five Middle Formative pottery vessels, six jadeite celts, and a jadeite "bloodletter." Other Olmec objects that have appeared in the Maya lowlands include a spectacular cache of jadeite spoons and other objects uncovered by local farmers at Chacsinkin in southern Yucatan, and a beautiful greenstone pendant placed in a Postclassic-period burial on Cozumel Island. Most archaeologists consider these as heirlooms that entered the Maya region long after the demise of Olmec culture. Future investigations may reveal local populations that maintained direct contacts with Olmec traders. David Freidel has suggested that La Venta Olmecs actively engaged in salt extraction and/or commerce along the Gulf coast of Campeche and Yucatan.[34] It also seems likely that Olmecs maintained an as-yet undiscovered mining colony at the Sierra de las Minas jadeite source in Guatemala's Motagua river basin.

100

7 · The Olmecs Abroad: Western Mesoamerica

The earliest inhabitants of western Mesoamerica were foragers who exploited the region's rich natural flora and fauna. Their descendants began to domesticate primitive maize and other plants in the middle of the fourth millennium BC, if not earlier. By the Initial Formative period (1800–1200 BC), people lived in settled villages, grew much of their food and manufactured pottery.[1] Archaeologists call this incipient farming culture the "Red on Buff" horizon based on its distinctive brown-to-buff pottery with red-painted designs. Red on Buff-horizon village sites are known over a broad region encompassing the Basin of Mexico, Morelos, Puebla, Oaxaca, Guerrero and west Mexico. Red on Buff-horizon farmers constructed small villages on high ground adjacent to river bottoms or lakeshores that provided access to naturally humid farmland, abundant aquatic products, and terrestrial plants and game. Villages were clusters of pole-and-thatch houses surrounded by outdoor work areas, refuse zones, and conical-shaped subterranean storage pits. The deceased were buried in simple pits beneath or adjacent to the houses. Farmers cultivated house gardens as well as more distant *milpas* or outfields devoted to maize and other staples and supplemented their diet with wild plants and the flesh of birds, fish, land

101

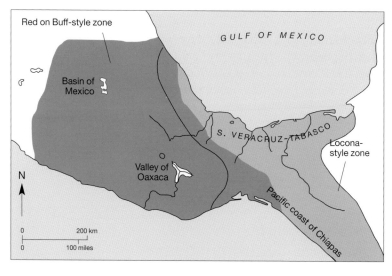

101 Early Formative Ceramic Spheres in Mesoamerica. These two fundamental ceramic traditions persisted as geographically discrete entities for many centuries.

mammals, and domestic dogs. Clearly defined temples, ballcourts, and other public buildings have not been identified, although the Valley of Oaxaca has yielded a few structures that may be either high-status residences or public buildings of some sort.

The Basin of Mexico and the Tlatilco culture during the Early Olmec horizon

By 1200 BC the Tlatilco culture began to emerge in certain favored locales in the Basin of Mexico and adjacent areas.[2] At that time the Basin of Mexico was a rich, well-watered highland valley with forested hillsides, deep fertile soils, and many streams that fed shallow marshes and lakes on its floor. Today Mexico City's 20 million inhabitants blanket the entire Basin in one of the world's largest human aggregations. Uncontrolled urban sprawl, erosion, deforestation, and some of the worst air pollution on the planet signal a virtually unprecedented ecological disaster. Whatever direction the post-industrial world of the twenty-first century is headed, the Basin of Mexico occupies the vanguard. Humans have transformed it so drastically in recent decades that one can barely visualize the environment described by the Spaniards less than 500 years ago. The land was even more bountiful in Tlatilco culture times before human populations became numerous enough to exert a lasting impact.

Tlatilco, Tlapacoya, and Coapexco, the three best-known Tlatilco-culture sites, flourished during Early Formative-period Ayotla (1250–1000 BC) and Manantial (1000–800 BC) phases. Tlatilco and Tlapacoya were chiefdom capitals while Coapexco was a small, short-lived settlement that specialized in the manufacture of stone tools. Tlatilco culture was distinguished from its Red on Buff-horizon predecessors by the presence of large villages that served as capitals of small chiefdoms, multi-tiered settlement systems, hierarchical social structures, religious specialists, community- and regional-level economic specializations, and long-distance exchange. The archaeological markers of Tlatilco culture include a rich ceramic repertoire of utilitarian and ritual pottery vessels, human and animal effigy figurines, masks and

102

102 Map of the Basin of Mexico in Early Formative times. The three population centers drew support from many smaller communities.

153

other exotic ritual objects, and elaborate burials. Tlatilco and Tlapacoya shared very similar material culture inventories but each possessed certain unique ritual objects and ceramic motifs that may simply reflect minor temporal or regional variations or perhaps indicate more basic differences in religion, ideology, and expressions of group identity.

Tlatilco has been the focus of archaeological disputes since Miguel Covarrubias first reported Olmec forms, motifs, and figurines from the site sixty years ago. Was Tlatilco an Olmec center or an Olmec colony? Was it older than the Gulf coast Olmecs? Did Olmecs pass through Tlatilco after leaving their Gulf coast homeland on their way to Guerrero? Was the Basin of Mexico homeland too high and cold to support early civilization? Questions such as these served as a warp thread (or a red herring, depending upon one's view) through Olmec studies for decades. Today the answers are finally becoming apparent.

Tlatilco village covered a 65-ha (160-acre) area on Los Remedios hill overlooking the Hondo river west of Lake Texcoco. This location afforded easy access to fertile, well-watered soils, wild plants, terrestrial game, migratory birds, and lacustrine resources. Today Tlatilco is covered by Mexico City's urban sprawl but before that happened brickmakers, looters, and archaeologists removed thousands of beautiful pottery vessels and clay figurines. Back in the 1930s when brickmakers began digging for clay, they frequently encountered potsherds, stone tools, and human burials. The simple pit graves often contained complete pots, beautifully hand-modeled figurines, and other objects that soon attracted the attention of artists Miguel Covarrubias and Diego Rivera and pre-Columbian art collectors. Looting proved more profitable than brickmaking and by 1941 the site was so endangered that Covarrubias organized the first scientific excavations. Mexican archaeologists from INAH took charge in 1942 and conducted four projects of varying scope and complexity over the next three decades.

Tlapacoya covered the flanks of a volcanic island originally surrounded by freshwater Lake Chalco-Xochimilco in the southern Basin of Mexico. According to Christine Niederberger, the combination of its pink andesite rock, dome shape, grottoes, and springs may have marked it as a sacred mountain in the eyes of its inhabitants. The rich lacustrine environment supported a densely populated Early Formative village that rivaled Tlatilco

History of Investigations at Tlatilco

Institution	Chief Investigators	Years
INAH	M. Covarrubias and H. Moedano	1942
INAH	M. Covarrubias and D. Rubin de la Borbolla	1947–49
INAH	R. Piña Chan	1955
INAH	A. Romano	1962–69
CUNY	P. Tolstoy	1963

in size and importance. Tlapacoya's modern destruction is one of the great tragedies of Mexican archaeology. Since 1950 the national government and the archaeological community alike have watched uncaringly as highway construction, looting, and urban sprawl obliterated one of ancient America's most important sites. Niederberger relates that antiquities collectors and vendors purchased an untold number of intact objects and even sacks of earth for later recovery of restorable pieces in 1958 when one large platform mound was bulldozed for highway fill. These objects included many exquisite Olmec-style "Dragon Pots" (discussed below) and masterfully crafted clay figurines now found in private and museum collections around the world. Salvage excavations by Paul Tolstoy, Christine Niederberger and Beatriz Barba de Piña Chan, along with a systematic survey of the area by Richard Blanton documented a long sequence of Archaic and Formative-period cultures preceding the Ayotla- and Manantial-phase occupations.[3] In addition to the densely settled residential and civic zones, Niederberger reports Olmec-style rock paintings near the top that may be part of an isolated ceremonial or ritual zone that loomed above the ancient settlement similar to the layout of Chalcatzingo, Morelos a few centuries later.[4]

Coapexco covered a 50-ha (124-acre) zone at 2600 m (8515 ft) on the Amecameca pass that connects the Basin of Mexico and Puebla.[5] The frequent frosts at this altitude make the modern environment poorly suited for maize cultivation, but things may have been different during the Ayotla phase. If the climate had been slightly warmer, higher temperatures would have reduced the danger of destructive frosts considerably. In any case, the villagers did not depend solely on farming for their livelihoods, they also manufactured *manos*, *metates*, and other ground-stone tools from raw materials gathered at a nearby quarry, and processed raw obsidian from several different sources outside the Basin into blades and other finished tools. Their home territory may have been marginal for maize agriculture but its location astride the best route between the Basin and lands to the east worked to the villagers' advantage in the growing Early Formative economy. Despite this advantage, Coapexco only existed for a few generations before the inhabitants abandoned their high outpost.

Life in Tlatilco-culture times

Studies of the skeletons unearthed at Tlatilco show that the villagers were relatively short and robust: males averaged 1.65 m (5 ft 5 in) and females about 6 cm (2.5 in) shorter. Parents of high status deliberately modified the skulls of their infants with a cradleboard and adults filed their teeth, practices that presumably reflected prevailing ideals of beauty and social status. General health conditions, although poor, were probably normal for the time and place; tooth decay and arthritis were common adult afflictions, and death rates for women in their child-bearing years and children aged four to six were quite high.[6]

Houses were simple but effective shelters that ranged from 12 to 30 sq. m (130 to 320 sq. ft) with sand or trampled-earth floors, hearths marked by stones, smoothed daub-covered walls occasionally painted red, and numerous subterranean bell-shaped storage pits. Coapexco's houses rested directly on the ground while clay-surfaced earth platforms at Tlatilco and Tlapacoya may have supported elite residences, temples, or other special-purpose buildings. Trash dumped into the storage pits after they had ceased to serve their original function included broken pottery, stone tools, animal bones and carbonized plant remains, testimony to an ample and varied diet.

103 So many burials appeared at Tlatilco that some archaeologists once considered it a necropolis rather than a living site. The deceased were normally buried extended on their backs in crude pits beneath or adjacent to their homes. Most corpses were oriented east to west, although a few faced north to south. Paul Tolstoy believes the distinct orientations reflect two different

---

Food Refuse Identified at Tlatilco*

Common Name		Scientific Name
PLANTS	maize	*Zea mays*
	sieva beans	*Phaseolus Iunatus*
	amaranth	*Amaranthus spp.*
	squash	*Cucurbita spp.*
	prickly pear	*Opuntia spp.*
ANIMALS	mud turtle	*Kinostern spp.*
	hawk	*Buteo spp.*
	horned owl	*Bubo virginianus*
	ducks and geese	family *Anatidae*
	turkey	*Meleagris gallopavo*
	pelican	*Pelicanus spp.*
	American coot	*Fulica americanus*
	crane	*Grus spp.*
	hare	*Lepus cagotis*
	rabbit	*Silvilagus floridanus*
	volcano rabbit	*Romerolagus diazii*
	ground squirrel	*Spermophilus mexicanus*
	gopher	*Pappogeo mys spp.* and *Thommomys umbrinus*
	dog	*Canis familiaris*
	grey fox	*Urocyon cinereoargentus*
	racoon	*Procyon lotor*
	striped skunk	*Mephitis macroura*
	badger	*Taxidea taxus*
	puma	*Felix con color*
	white-tailed deer	*Odocoileus virginianus*
	pronghorn antelope	*Antilocapra americana*
	javelin	*Dicotyles tajacu*

* Based upon García Moll *et al.* 1991 p. 10

103 Tlatilco burials. Later burials often intruded into older ones in the restricted space beneath house floors.

social groups, perhaps moieties that exchanged marriage partners.[7] Most burials included modest offerings of pottery vessels, figurines, and other objects but a few offerings were much more lavish than others. People at society's bottom rung lacked any offerings at all while higher-status individuals entered the afterlife accompanied by pots that may have held food, figurines, obsidian projectile points, and personal ornaments. Signs of *in-situ* fires suggest that the burial rites included burning. One high-status woman was laid to rest with 15 pots, 20 clay figurines, 2 pieces of red-painted bright green jadeite that may have formed part of a bracelet, a crystalline hematite plaque, a bone fragment with traces of alfresco paint, and miscellaneous stones. Another burial held the remains of a male whose skull had been deliberately modified in infancy and whose teeth were trimmed into geometric patterns as an adult. He may have been a shaman since all the objects placed with him were likely part of a shaman's power bundle. They included small *metates* for grinding hallucinogenic mushrooms, clay effigies of mushrooms, quartz, graphite, pitch, and other exotic materials that could have been used in curing rituals. A magnificent ceramic bottle placed in his grave depicted a contortionist or acrobat who rests on his stomach with his hands supporting his chin while his legs bend completely

104

104 This hollow effigy vessel, known as the "Acrobat," accompanied a lavish burial at Tlatilco. An opening on his left knee served for pouring liquid. Acrobats and contortionists occur sporadically in Olmec art, suggesting an important role in society. Ht 25 cm (9 in).

around so that his feet touch the top of his head. Could this masterpiece be an effigy of the actual occupant of the grave?

    Tlatilco-culture potters created some of pre-Columbian America's most beautiful ceramics.[8] The vivid imaginations and deft fingers of the artisans (almost certainly women) more than compensated for their lack of sophisti-
105, 106   cated kilns, molds, and other technological aids. Common forms included

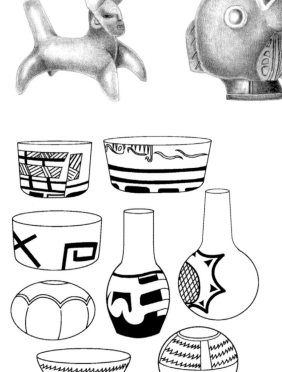

105 Tlatilco–culture pottery shapes and decorations. Shapes: (*above*) dog, fish, and peccary effigies; (*left*) flat-bottomed everted walled bowls, jars, and restricted orifice *tecomates*. Decoration: rocker stamping (peccary and bowl), incision, excision, cross-hatching, and painting.

106 A polished black pottery bottle from Tlatilco with Olmec designs on the body.

round bottles with high necks, stirrup-spout jars, neckless *tecomates*, flat-bottomed bowls with out-flaring walls, and composite-silhouette bowls; rarer exotic vessels included spouted trays, ring-shaped vessels and hollow effigies of humans, plants, and animals. Potters lavished great attention on the surfaces of their vessels, employing black, brown, and reddish-brown slips, red-and-white paint, polishing, burnishing, painted and incised designs, excision, zoned rocker stamping, and alternating matte and polished surfaces. They often rubbed red hematite into incisions and excised areas. Painted and incised designs include triangular patterns, swirls, parallel lines, and cross-hatched scoring on the floors of bowls.

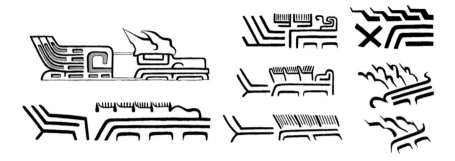

107 Olmec Dragon designs on Tlatilco pottery vessels. This sample suggests the variation on a single theme in such designs at one community.

107 Common Olmec-style motifs include the St. Andrews cross, flame-eyebrows, paw-wing motif, circles, double spirals, bars, four-petaled flowers, dots, torches, and V-shaped clefts in heads with plants emerging from the cleft.

Tlapacoya was the manufacturing center for Pilli Blanc and Paloma Negatif, two related types of ritual cylindrical bowls with flat bottoms and white-to-buff surface slips adorned with incised Olmec were-jaguar faces.[9] 108, 109 These Dragon Pots, as they are called, occur sporadically across central Mexico, but Tlapacoya is the only site that has yielded enough broken sherds to suggest frequent use. Clay analyses suggest they were manufactured locally. They feature two or more profile or frontal-view were-jaguar

108 (left) Tlapacoya-style Dragon Pot from the Basin of Mexico. Frontal view of the Olmec Dragon. Ht 16 cm (6 in).
109 (right) Pilli Blanc-type Tlapacoya Dragon Pot. This profile view incised on the exterior of a pot from Tlapacoya, called "a veritable hymn to the [Olmec Dragon]," exemplifies the complex imagery that characterizes much of Olmec art.

faces around the exterior. These quintessentially Olmec creatures feature a V-shaped cleft in the head, almond eyes with round irises, bulbous noses and mouths with flaring upper lips, downturned corners, toothless gums, and a narrow vertical band passing through the eye. Peter D. Joralemon identifies this being as the Banded-Eye God, an enigmatic creature also inscribed on the Young Lord sculpture described in Chapter 5, and suggests that Tlapacoya was a center for its devotees.

Tlatilco-culture artisans produced clay roller stamps and masks. Roller stamps (often misidentified as "cylinder seals") are round cylinders with excised paw-wing and other Olmec designs that probably served to create the tattoo-like designs occasionally shown on figurine bodies. Years ago several writers proposed that the designs on these stamps were a form of "proto-writing." No one accepted their bold assertion at the time but the roller stamp with Mesoamerica's oldest known glyphs (600 BC) found recently at San Andrés, Tabasco, may have vindicated them (see Chapter 4).

Clay masks have appeared sporadically in burials at Tlatilco and private collections. Most are circular and concave with cutout eyes and mouths, and an occasional protruding tongue. Some portray elderly men; others depict grotesque, twisted faces suggestive of paralysis. One face is split down the middle portraying a living person on one side and a skull on the other. Most are too small to completely cover an adult human face and if worn in real life, they probably covered only the lower part of the wearer's face.

Tlatilco-culture potters produced a rich repertoire of human and animal figurines numbering in the thousands. The vast majority are small, solid, 110 hand-modeled effigies of mostly women, followed in frequency by males. Larger, hollow effigies also occur, albeit in much smaller numbers. Most of the solid examples are found in trash that was strewn around the houses or swept into abandoned storage pits, although a few were placed in burials. The images they portray provide unique glimpses into the clothing, ornaments, and daily life activities of Tlatilco's inhabitants, especially the women who most likely created them.

Some of the women appear to be dancing while others show signs of advanced pregnancy or nurse infants. So-called Type C figurines emphasize scantily clad females who wear turbans, necklaces, bracelets, anklets, and elaborate body painting while Type D "Pretty Ladies" figurines depict well-proportioned young women with large bosoms, elaborately painted bodies, and occasional short grass or fiber skirts. Mothers often hold infants on their hips while dancers frequently wear rattles on their wrists and ankles. However, not all was sweetness and light in the Tlatilco-culture figurine repertoire: grotesque humans with two heads, three eyes, two noses, two mouths, twisted faces, hunchbacks, and other deformities occur side by side with the happy females. Gordon Bendersky, a medical practitioner interested in ancient cultures, believes these odd figurines depict an extremely rare and always fatal birth defect known as diprosopus and considers them to be the oldest scientific medical images known anywhere in the world.[10]

110 Tlatilco solid figurines and Tlatilco–culture figurines. This selection includes females, shamans and a ballplayer.

Depictions of males are relatively rare and tend to portray ballplayers, acrobats, and musicians. At Tlapacoya we find distinctive, solid male figurines that wear tall hats, ear ornaments, large waistbands with round objects (mirrors?) mounted on the front, and leg, ankle, and wristbands. Some may represent ballplayers while others may invoke some other public ritual. Pillistyle figurines at Tlapacoya show men with deliberately deformed skulls, partially or completely shaved heads, and star symbols incised into the back of their heads. Niederberger believes that figurines with this symbol may be portraits of real individuals.

How did people use these figurines and what meanings did they have? Although none seem to portray deities, their placement in graves suggests some ritual function. However, most ended up as broken fragments in ordinary household trash. Repeated patterns of breakage suggest deliberate destruction, but why would someone do that? Joyce Marcus believes that women in Oaxaca at the same time created figurines as ancestor images for use in household divination rituals that ended with their destruction.[11] Other archeologists argue that figurines served as children's toys, a persistent explanation I have never found convincing.

Tlatilco-culture artisans created spectacular large hollow human and animal effigies. Two basic types can be discerned: a localized type known only from the Basin of Mexico and Puebla, and the much more widely distributed large white-ware Olmec-style effigies dubbed "Hollow Babies." The localized type often portrays what appear to be dwarfs, perhaps sufferers of achondroplastic dwarfism. Seated females are frequently shown with large heads, small stubby arms, small breasts, and prominent navels. Some are bareheaded while others wear headdresses, hats, or "pill-box" coiffures. Some males have horn-like projections springing from the top of their heads that may be emblematic of shamans or simply a hairstyle of the day. Hollow animal effigies depict the broad range of creatures native to the region: ducks, parrots, troupials and other birds, fish, opossums, armadillos, bears, dogs, and peccary. Oddly enough deer, an important element in the diet, do not appear in the ceramic menagerie.

111 Tlapacoya ballplayer figurines. Elaborate belts with mirrors and limb guards are thought to represent ball-game protective devices. The figure on the left wears over his lower face a buccal mask of the sort found archaeologically. Ht (*left*) 16 cm (6 in); (*right*) 19 cm (7 in).

112   White-ware Hollow Baby figurines are excellent Early Olmec-horizon markers found in many parts of Mesoamerica. Michael D. Coe dubbed them "the 'Jaguar's Children'…." Olmec were-jaguar babies, offspring of feline father and human mother, deities of thunder, lightning, and rain. Nude and generally sexless, their obesity is that of eunuchs, while their expressions and slanting eyes often give a strong impression of mongolism. Their jaguar ancestry shows only in the down-drawn corners of the mouth."[12] Only 3 of the 40 complete examples known have appeared in controlled scientific excavations, while San Lorenzo has yielded broken fragments but no complete examples.

Hollow Babies have highly polished white-to-orange surfaces and sit with their legs either splayed open or crossed. A unique example attributed to Las Bocas, Puebla, crawls on his knees while another reputed to be from the same site wears a tightfitting helmet or cap while sucking its forefinger. A few seem to depict adults in the guise of a baby: one particularly famous example from Atlihuayan shows an adult male wearing a cape and headdress in the form of the Olmec Dragon while another shows a man's head complete with a goatee atop an infant's body.

Their wide geographical distribution and limited numbers suggest Hollow Babies were rare iconic ritual objects that signified specific religious concepts. Recent studies by Jeffrey Blomster and others showed that while all Hollow Babies share many conceptual and thematic features, each was manufactured locally using clays from nearby sources.[13] Blomster suggests that itinerant craftsmen produced these esoteric images on demand for local leaders. Where did these craftsmen come from? I suggest San Lorenzo, although there is no solid evidence to support my proposal.

Tlatilco-culture communities in the Basin were engaged in some form of exchange with societies scattered across western Mesoamerica. Their exports included locally made pottery and figurines and obsidian from Otumba, Paredón, and Pachuca. In return, they imported pottery from Morelos, Oaxaca, and the Panuco region of northern Veracruz, flint and onyx from Puebla or Guerrero, greenstone from Guerrero, marine turtle shell and pearl oyster shells from the Pacific coast, and probably cotton from Morelos.

112 Hollow white-slipped ceramic baby wearing a tightly fitting helmet from Las Bocas, Puebla. Rolls of fat and pose suggest an infant less than one year old. Ht 34 cm (13 in).

(*left* to *right*) **113** Hollow two-piece clay human effigy. The seated figure either holds an anatomically correct human heart, or is an anthropomorphized heart. Ht 11.4 cm (4 in).
114 Standing jadeite figure from Tehuacan, Puebla. This exceptionally large figure may once have had inlaid eyes. The loincloth and apron are covered with low-relief incised Olmec icons. Ht 52 cm (20 in). **115** The Necaxa Tiger. This small figure of grayish and mottled green jade has the appearance of a human child with a were-jaguar face. Ht 8 cm (3 in).

Puebla

While the river valleys of Puebla contained numerous Early Formative settlements, only those in the Tehuacan valley have been investigated and reported in a systematic fashion. Unfortunately, the Tehuacan valley was off the beaten track for Olmecs and the places they did go, like Las Bocas and Atlihuayan, are known exclusively through the activities of looters. Las Bocas is (in)famous for the looted Olmec-style pottery vessels, figurines, and other objects that began to appear on the pre-Columbian antiquities market in 1958. The actual find spot for many of these is unknown and some archaeologists suspect that objects from numerous unidentified archaeological sites are erroneously attributed to Las Bocas. These include black-ware *tecomates*, bottles, and straight-sided bowls, many with excised paw-wing motifs highlighted with red pigment, fine-paste white Kaolin-ware spouted bowls and trays possibly used for pouring libations. Roller stamps with Olmec designs, large hollow effigies of fish, ducks, and other birds; and the two hollow human babies mentioned above are also believed to have come from Las Bocas. A particularly spectacular Hollow Baby appeared at nearby Atlihuayan during highway construction. The valleys of Puebla clearly played an important role in the Early Olmec horizon, making it especially unfortunate that virtually every known site has been so badly destroyed by looters.

pl. XVIII

113

114, 115

Morelos

The river valleys of western Morelos were ideal settings for early Red on Buff- and Tlatilco-culture farmers, but only three Early Olmec-horizon sites – Gualupita, San Pablo Nexpa, and Chalcatzingo – have been identified so far. Since Chalcatzingo was a primarily Late Olmec-horizon community, we will hold discussion of it until later in this chapter.

While visiting Cuernavaca in 1932 archaeologist George C. Vaillant and his wife Susannah saw what they immediately identified as Formative-period pottery vessels and figurines. These objects came from disturbed burials at a brickyard at Gualupita and were so similar to the artifacts they were uncovering in the Basin of Mexico at that time that they immediately turned their holiday into a salvage excavation.[14] This excavation revealed the first Formative remains in Morelos as well as two unique hollow ceramic figurines. Vaillant immediately recognized their stylistic connection to the Necaxa Tiger, a greenstone figurine in the American Museum of Natural History, and to other objects now recognized as Olmec. Although the evidence was tenuous, Vaillant argued that the Gualupita figures and the Olmec style they exemplified preceded later Classic-period civilizations by centuries. His bold assertion, virtual heresy at the time, was vindicated a few years later by Stirling's research on the Gulf coast.

Like many modern villages in Morelos, San Pablo Nexpa covers the ruins of an Early Formative settlement.[15] On a hillside above lies the only known Tlatilco-culture burial mound. Looters had already churned up the mound when David C. Grove discovered it in 1967. Despite the almost total destruction, Grove could identify an exterior basal facade constructed of river cobbles, and suggests that the structure once held 150–250 burials. Most of the Tlatilco-style bottles, jars, and figurines that accompanied the burials had already been sold to dealers and collectors, but Grove did recover a few Early Formative potsherds with Olmec motifs and figurines in the looters' spoil piles.

Guerrero

Guerrero is surely the neglected stepchild of Mesoamerican archaeology, a virtual archaeological terra incognita. The lack of information on Formative cultures is particularly frustrating because we know that looters have recovered scores of Olmec-style jades from sites in various parts of the state. Miguel Covarrubias purchased numerous outstanding pieces for his personal collection sixty years ago and although he correctly identified them as Olmec, he mistakenly concluded that the Olmecs originated in the region and migrated across central Mexico to Olman. Of the many outstanding Olmec-style objects known from Guerrero, four are especially notable: a greenstone mask from San Jerónimo; the justly famous Olinalá plaque; an oddly shaped hollowed-out stone known as a "yuguito" with an archetypal

116
117

116 Greenstone mask from San Jerónimo, Guerrero. This mask is marked by the three-dimensionality of its strongly everted upper lip size.

117 (*below left*) Stone "yuguito" from Tlacotepec, Guerrero. The face on this domed, horseshoe-shaped object is clearly Olmec but features a rather flat nose and unusually sensuous lips. Its function is unknown. Ht 19 cm (7 in).

Olmec face; and the unique wooden mask encrusted with jade mosaic found in a dry cave at Cañon de la Mano. If the Olmecs did not originate in Guerrero, who made these objects and how did they get there?

In 1964 Charles and Ellen Brush began to search for answers to these questions at sites near Acapulco. In the course of their excavations they recovered very crude fragments of "Pox" pottery, an Early Formative pottery named for its pockmarked surfaces.[16] Although Pox pottery is not quite as ancient as the Brushes thought, it does show that Guerrero was inhabited by about 1800 BC. In the 1970s Yale anthropology students Louise

118 (*above*) Wood mask from Cañon de la Mano, Guerrero. This extraordinary mask, the first-known example of Olmec woodcarving, was discovered in a dry cave. Jade mosaic inlays once covered the lower face. Ht 18 cm (7 in).

167

119 One of four virtually identical T-shaped sculptures carved from travertine depicting the Olmec Maize God placed in the upper walls of the Sunken Court at Teopantecuanitlán, Guerrero.

I. Paradis and John S. Henderson excavated Early and Middle Formative sites along the Balsas river and in eastern Guerrero, respectively.[17] Thus by 1980 archaeologists had identified small Early Formative settlements but had not located major centers with prominent Olmec remains.

Mexican archaeologist Guadalupe Martínez Donjuán made that critical discovery in 1983 when she learned that looters were ransacking a large archaeological site near the confluence of the Mezcala-Balsas and Amacuzac rivers.[18] Her subsequent excavations at the site, which she named Teopante-cuanitlán, revealed a large Early and Middle Formative-period regional center adorned with Olmec-style stone sculpture. The Main Precinct consists of platforms surrounding the Sunken Patio, a large courtyard bounded by two natural hill slopes. She identified four construction phases between 1200 and 600 BC.

During Phase 3 (1000–800 BC), artificial platforms constructed of stone masonry were placed on the natural slopes above and below the Sunken Patio and Olmec-style sculptures were in use. The rectangular Sunken Court was excavated into the original subsoil and two double stairways descended into the courtyard. Stone sculptures depicting stylized Olmec feline heads with flame-eyebrows decorated each balustrade and four large sculptures resembling an inverted T crowned the east and west walls of the courtyard. All four depict virtually identical were-jaguars with headbands, almond-shaped eyes, bulbous noses, and turned-down mouths. Each holds a torch or bundle in its hands. Martínez Donjuán believes they marked the solstices or equinoxes, Karl Taube identifies them as the Olmec Maize God while F. Kent Reilly III argues they represent sacred mountains at the four corners of the Mesoamerican universe. All three interpretations may be correct. Two rectangular platforms mark the playing field of what may be a very small ballcourt in the interior of the Sunken Court while a much larger ballcourt lies 900 m (2,950 ft) to the northeast.

The functions of the Sunken Patio have provoked as much speculation as its sculptures. While it surely served as a ritual gathering place, it has a few hydraulic features that complicate matters. Rainwater runoff from the slopes above the court presented a drainage problem that the builders resolved by constructing two outlets and drains from U-shaped stone troughs and flat covers identical to those at San Lorenzo and La Venta. Some archaeologists believe the drains were just part of a larger hydraulic system that emptied water *into* the Sunken Court from the east to create an artificial pond before it exited though the west drain. Karl Taube believes local leaders deliberately flooded the court during rituals devoted to agricultural fertility.[19] If so, the Maize God sculptures seeming to emerge from the water at the edge of an artificial pond set in the arid Guerrero countryside must have been a spectacular sight! Teopantecuanitlán's leaders also engaged in more mundane water management and large-scale irrigation, constructing a dam and storage reservoir high on the hillside and a stone-lined canal to bring water to lower-lying agricultural fields.

Three post-Olmec-style stone monuments rested on the esplanade known as the North Platform, one of western Mesoamerica's largest Early or Middle Formative constructions 53 m long and 3 m wide (174 ft x 10 ft). They include a large altar shaped like a frog, a plain stela, and a 1-m (3.3-ft) high human head. All three resemble Late Formative-period carvings from coastal Guatemala and El Salvador and probably date to Phase 4 (800-600 BC), the final occupation at Teopantecuanitlán.

Christine Niederberger's excavations of several Early Formative houses in a Teopantecuanitlán residential zone called Lomeríos revealed houses erected on low stone and rubble platforms clustered around a courtyard.[20] Bell-shaped subterranean storage pits associated with the houses contained refuse that yielded maize pollen and remains of dog, deer, rabbit, catfish, crab, and freshwater mollusks. The inhabitants of the houses were artisans who transformed iridescent pearl oyster (Pinctada mazatlanica) shells and other Pacific Ocean mollusks into beads, bracelets, pendants, and other ornaments for export to places like San Pablo Nexpa, Tlatilco, and Tlapacoya.

Teopantecuanitlán declined after 700 BC, perhaps in response to Xochipala's emergence as a large settlement further down the Balsas river. Xochipala flourished in Late Formative times, but looted pottery and figurines portraying Olmec themes in a local style attributed to Xochipala may belong to an Early Olmec horizon or even more ancient occupation.

Martínez Donjuán believes Teopantecuanitlán's inhabitants were true Olmecs and in a revival of Miguel Covarrubias' thesis, she proposes that a splinter group from the original Guerrero Olmecs migrated to the Gulf coast. Niederberger believed that Teopantecuanitlán only attracted the attention of Gulf coast Olmecs *after* emerging as a regional power, pointing out that while its public art imitated Olmec models, the rest of the culture had indigenous roots. As we shall see, this apparently was also the case at Chalcatzingo.

Cave paintings

Archaeologists were amazed when unique Olmec-style wall paintings first appeared in Juxtlahuaca and Oxtotitlán caves approximately 65 km (40 miles) southeast of Chilpancingo, Guerrero, in the late 1960s. Today many still consider them the most sophisticated and complex cave paintings known in the Americas. They have not been accurately dated but I suspect they belong to the Early Olmec horizon, slightly earlier than the Middle Formative date normally given.

Princeton University art historian Gillett Griffin and Italian businessman Carlo Gay explored Juxtlahuaca in 1966.[21] In his account of the discovery, Gay describes passing through the Hall of the Dead, a huge cavern littered with human skeletons, on to the Hall of the Ritual located over 1,000 m 120 (3,400 ft) in from the entrance. Here they encountered Painting 1, a life-sized standing male thought to be an Olmec ruler, towering over a much smaller seated figure. Both men are painted in vibrant polychrome colors. The tall figure is outlined in black and wears an elaborate headdress of green (quetzal?) feathers, a beard, a large round ear ornament, a multi-colored shift or jerkin, and jaguar pelt leggings and gauntlets. He points both arms towards his companion, a trident-shaped device in his right hand and a serpent-like staff in the left. The seated person wears a beard and a possible mask over his face and grasps his knees in a posture that suggests supplication or homage.

Additional paintings further on in the Hall of the Serpent include a bright red serpent painted with a cross-band motif in its eye and short green feathers above its brow. The serpent confronts a red feline (jaguar?) that appears to leap towards it. Elsewhere in this sacred subterranean space, black line drawings depict a standing human, jaguar and serpent heads, and hatched circles.

Oxtotitlán's paintings occupy two shallow grottoes eroded into the cliff face at the cave mouth.[22] David Grove identified two murals in the South Grotto. Mural 2 is badly weathered but seems to depict a human who is either dressed in jaguar-skin clothing or in some way associated with an pl. x actual jaguar. Mural 1, fortunately much better preserved than its companion, is one of the most important pieces of Olmec art outside Olman. It measures 3.8 x 2.5 m (12.5 by 8.2 ft) and was painted 10 m (33 ft) above the cliff base. A seated man assumes a dynamic posture on the head of a jaguar monster. His elaborate headdress incorporates an owl face, green feathers,

and a bird mask. He wears a feather cape or cloak over his arms and back, a green belt and loincloth, and a red-fringed skirt decorated with two hand-and-scroll motifs. His rich array of ornaments includes a green nose plug, an ear ornament with a hanging pendant, and a pectoral decorated with the crossed bands of the St Andrew's cross. He raises his left arm while extending the right towards his right knee. His right leg dangles over the edge of the jaguar's face, a face virtually identical to those in the top registers of La Venta's Altar 4 (see ill. 70, p. 110) and Chalcatzingo's Monument 22. This vibrantly painted scene provided the first clear evidence that Olmec "altars" were actually thrones.

Paintings on the other side of the North Grotto include a human face encased in a four-petal flower; a quizzical-looking owl and a magnificent rep-tilian creature with a fierce countenance; and what Grove calls a "*cipactli*-type" creature with a long, pointed bill, fangs, and a sly expression. *Cipactli* is the Nahuatl name for the crocodilian-like monster ancient Mesoamericans believed supported the universe on its back. Painting 1-d, the most striking creation in the North Grotto, shows a man and a jaguar standing in profile. The man is painted black except for his facemask, head-dress, and exaggerated genitals. His mask depicts a typically Olmec face, surmounted by a relatively simple headdress. His outstretched arms extend

121

121 Cave painting 1-d at Oxtotitlán, Guerrero. One of the very few depictions of a human and feline in the same scene. 1.5 sq. cm (58 sq. in).

in opposite directions while his large penis points toward the rear of the quasi-erect jaguar. That creature turns its head back towards the person. Is this a depiction of a human copulating with a jaguar, the mythical event Matthew W. Stirling proposed as the origin of the Olmec were-jaguar beings? It is certainly a serious possibility.

Additional Olmec-style cave paintings have appeared recently at other Guerrero caves.[23] Although none compare with Juxtlahuaca and Oxtotitlán in complexity or sophistication, they highlight the Olmecs' abiding interest in the caves of the region as ritual settings. One can imagine small parties of celebrants making their tortuous way through the low, narrow, hot passages of Juxtlahuaca guided only by smoking pine torches. Why did the Olmecs create places of worship in such highly inaccessible locales so far from their homeland? Human burials placed in the cave may be grisly remains of ritual sacrifice but may be post-Olmec. Grove believes Oxtotitlán was a shrine to rain, water, and fertility and was sanctified because it embodied cosmological ideas about mythical origins in caves. Juxtlahuaca's murals and drawings appear to emphasize a secular theme of rulership rather than strictly religious imagery. Even the implicit competition between serpents and felines, a procrustean theme in Mesoamerican mythology, surely had real-life political and social dimensions as well as more strictly religious ones. Regardless of the artist's intent, the style and iconography of the paintings show clear Olmec inspiration and direct, sustained contacts between Olmecs and local populations in Guerrero.

Oaxaca

Speakers of Zapotec, Mixtec, and other languages have occupied the fertile valleys, rugged mountains, and Pacific coast of Oaxaca for millennia. The civilizations they created have been traced back to their origins in numerous regions, including the valleys of Oaxaca, Nochixtlán, Huajuapan, the Cuicatlán Cañada, and the southern Isthmus of Tehuantepec. Kent V. Flannery and Joyce Marcus have recently reconstructed the evolution of these civilizations in an excellent book, albeit one that espouses a very different perspective on Olmec relationships with Oaxaca than the one expressed here.[24]

The Valley of Oaxaca and the Mixteca Alta's Nochixtlán valley are the most relevant regions to the question of Olmec contacts with highland Oaxaca. The Valley of Oaxaca, the largest zone of arable land in the southern Mexican highlands and the hearth of Zapotec civilization, was the seat of Monte Albán, the great Classic-period Zapotec capital. Despite the generally arid environment, early mastery of irrigation, terracing, and dry farming techniques fostered population growth and cultural evolution. At least twenty small Early Formative Tierras Largas-phase (1400–1150 BC) hamlets have been identified. In the succeeding San José phase (1150–850 BC), San José Mogote emerged as the largest and most powerful community in the valley. By 850 BC the village covered 60–70 ha (148–173 acres) and contained almost half the estimated 1,000 people living in the entire valley. It was dominated by Structures 1 and 2, a 3.5-m (11.5-ft) high multi-stage platform faced with rough stone masonry. These two terraces may have supported the oldest public buildings erected in Oaxaca – the pole-and-thatch superstructures have long since disappeared, but two carved stone fragments depicting a feline and a raptorial bird were found with Structure 2. Selected San José Mogote households produced shell jewelry and other objects from raw materials imported from the Gulf of Mexico and Pacific coasts. Small mirrors crafted from magnetite and other local iron ores were widely traded throughout western Mesoamerica and two have been identified at San Lorenzo.

The arid, eroded slopes of the modern Mixteca Alta seem a most inhospitable place quite un-suited to be the hearth of the brilliant Mixtec civilization. However the well-watered valleys have supported substantial populations for millennia. In the Nochixtlán Valley, the most intensely studied part of the Mixteca Alta, the earliest known remains belong to the Red-on-Buff tradition Cruz A phase (1400–1200 BC). Excavations in Cruz B-phase (1200–900 BC) deposits at Etlatongo yielded a hollow, white-slipped Olmec-style Hollow Baby figurine that may have been manufactured by an itinerant craftsman from San Lorenzo.[25]

Gulf-coast Olmecs established long-term social and commercial relationships with people in Oaxaca that resulted in lively exchanges of exotic goods. Ceramics, Gulf-coast shells, and conch-shell trumpets, river turtle-shell drums, sting-ray spines and armadillo shells are potential imports from the

Gulf lowlands, while costume ornaments and iron ore mirrors manufactured at San José Mogote moved in the other direction. San Lorenzo and San José-phase ceramic assemblages share many pottery forms, decorative motifs, and Olmec-style icons. Actual trade wares included Xochiltepec White and Mina White vessels from San Lorenzo in Oaxaca and San José types Leandro Grey and Delfina Fine Grey at the Veracruz center.[26] The presence of Olmec were-jaguar and fire-serpent motifs on Oaxaca pottery has been explained in several ways. Marcus Winter and other Oaxaca specialists believe they were inspired by Olmecs who visited highland villages in search of magnetite objects and Pacific coast shells.[27] Flannery and Marcus, on the other hand, argue that the designs express a pan–Mesoamerican symbol system that emerged simultaneously in many places without owing anything to Olmec contacts.[28]

The Late Olmec horizon and Chalcatzingo

After 900 BC the Basin of Mexico and Oaxaca severed their ties with the Olmec world and began to evolve on their own tracks, a process that ultimately led to their respective Classic civilizations. However, new groups of Late-horizon Olmecs penetrated Morelos and adjacent lands. At San Miguel Amuco, Guerrero, a single Olmec-style stone sculpture bears mute testimony to what may have been ephemeral contacts.[29] At Chalcatzingo, Morelos, on the other hand, the evidence from sculpture, pottery, figurines, and ornaments point to intensive contacts with La Venta Olmecs.

Chalcatzingo was western Mesoamerica's most important Middle Formative center. Located at the base of Cerro Chalcatzingo and Cerro Delgado in the Amatzinac river valley, it occupied a critical node in commercial networks extending from west Mexico to the Gulf coast. In addition to its geographic advantage, the two spectacular igneous

122 San Miguel Amuco, Guerrero, Monument 1. Olmec stelae are quite rare, especially outside the heartland. Coarse sandstone. Ht 85 cm (33 in).

123 The abrupt cliffs looming over Chalcatzingo, Morelos, overlook the ancient community and the ritual theater at their base.

hills that rise abruptly behind Chalcatzingo were surely considered sacred   123
mountains by pre-Columbian peoples. Investigations by David C. Grove,
Jorge Angulo, and their colleagues have revealed the history of this important
center and its connections with the Olmec world.[30] The earliest occupants
erected two platform mounds on Terrace 1, a natural feature at the foot of
the Cerro Chalcatzingo during the Amate (1500–1100 BC) and Barranca
(1100–700 BC) phases. These platforms have not been explored in detail but
represent some of western Mesoamerica's oldest public architecture.

The Cantera phase (700–500 BC) was Chalcatzingo's "Golden Age,"
when its rulers established foreign contacts that extended from the Pacific
coast to La Venta and were able to commission Olmec-style bas-reliefs on
Cerro Chalcatzingo's rock faces. The Cantera-phase village covered 40 ha
(99 acres) and was divided into two distinct sections: a hillside ritual zone at
the south end of the community dotted with bas-relief carvings on the rock
faces, and a residential zone composed of artificial terraces that supported
public buildings and private dwellings, platform mounds, a sunken court,
and thirty stone monuments and bas-relief carvings.

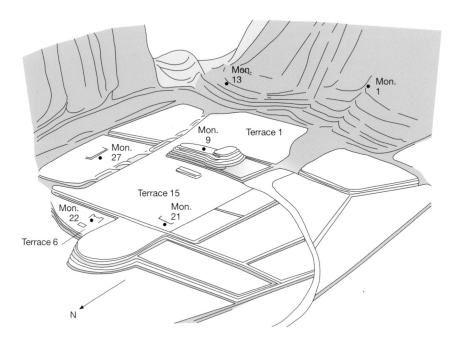

124 Chalcatzingo's inhabitants modified the natural terraces underlying their community and constructed the mound on Terrace 1.

124   Terrace 1, the focus of the earlier community at the foot of Cerro Chalcatzingo, continued to serve as the community's civic/ceremonial core. New elite residences, including perhaps the ruler's palace, were erected on Terrace 1 while the Barranca-phase platform mound at its north end was enlarged to 70 by 25 by 7 m (230 x 82 x 23 ft) high. A 100-m (330-ft) wide plaza or public meeting space separated the platform mound from the chief's residence. Monument 9, a thin, rectangular stone slab depicting an Earth Monster deity with an open cruciform mouth, and Monument 18, an Olmec-style seated figure, originally rested on top of the mound. Numerous well-stocked graves were placed within the platform. One included an Olmec-style standing greenstone figurine identical to those in Offering 4 at La Venta.

Terrace 1 dominated Chalcatzingo's physical and social landscape, but the lower terraces to the north also contained civic and ceremonial structures and stone sculptures. Terrace 6 supported a long cobblestone-faced platform mound where two in-situ basal stubs of stelae and a round stone "altar" were found. Terrace 25 had a large sunken, stone-lined patio similar to the one at Teopantecuanitlán. Chalcatzingo's patio lacks water channels or drains, instead it contains a large tabletop "throne" constructed of stone blocks and earth fill. Chalcatzingo's throne is similar to the monolithic thrones at La Venta and San Lorenzo but differs in two important ways. It is an ensemble or mosaic created from numerous individual carved-stone blocks, not a single block of stone, and the face depicts only the eyes of the Earth Monster, not the niche with its human occupant. The interior contained two human burials, and twenty-one additional human interments were placed beneath the court floor.

Chalcatzingo's glory is found in the thirty or so bas-relief carvings and stone monuments placed high on the hard-to-reach cliff faces above the site.[31] Sculptures of any sort are rare in western Mesoamerica and only Chalcatzingo, Teopantecuanitlán, and San Miguel Amuco, Guerrero, have yielded Late Olmec-horizon examples. Chalcatzingo's *corpus* far exceeds the other two combined, and its sculptures are so quintessentially Olmec in theme, motif, and execution that they must have been created by Gulf-coast Olmec sculptors commissioned by Chalcatzingo rulers.

Grove and Angulo have identified two distinct clusters of bas-relief carvings on the sides of Cerro Chalcatzingo and a third composed of freestanding sculptures within the village itself. Although each cluster has a distinct theme, they form an integrated functional assemblage. One cluster high on the mountainside includes Monument 1 (El Rey), and five smaller carvings in a line extending to the east. El Rey depicts a person seated inside a large niche or cave embellished with markings of a supernatural Earth Monster. He or she holds a rectangular box or ceremonial device adorned with a double scroll. Clouds and raindrops are portrayed above the cave and similar raindrops decorate the person's costume. Five smaller carvings depict small saurian creatures crouching on scrolls while looking up towards clouds and raindrops, three also show squash vines. Since no observer can see the entire set from a single vantage-point, they may have functioned as stations on a processional way leading to El Rey.

125

125 El Rey (Monument 1) is Chalcatzingo's best-known rock carving. It apparently functioned as the final destination on a ritual circuit dedicated to rain and water ceremonies. Ht 3.2 m (10.4 ft).

126 The four figures on Chalcatzingo Monument 2, known as the "Marching Olmecs," seem to depict a ritual in which three masked men dominate a seated man with exposed genitals and tied wrists. The scene has variously been interpreted as a fertility rite or a military conquest, depending on whether one views the paddle-shaped staffs as digging sticks or war clubs.

Rain and fertility are the apparent themes of this cluster, so it comes as no surprise that it occupies a natural rainwater runoff course down the slope.

 The second cluster includes six scenes carved on loose boulders and slabs on the talus slope at the foot of the Cerro. They all depict supernatural felines and other creatures that appear to attack or dominate four humans along what appears to form a second processional way. In this case, the humans are the focal point: three stand in what may be ritual postures while the fourth is seated in an inert, death-like pose.

 The final cluster of sculptures originally stood on the terraces in the habitation zone. These monuments emphasize rulers and rulership instead of the mythic or religious themes that pervade the cliff carvings. Stelae depict standing rulers, including a few possible females. Many were broken or mutilated where they stood, leaving several bases in place adjacent to the upper portions. Grove interprets their destruction as ritual acts following the death of the person depicted. Monument 9, the most spectacular of the group, is a large, thin slab embellished with a frontal depiction of an open-mouthed Earth Monster face. It was discovered by a local farmer sometime before 1968 and smuggled into the United States. The bottom of the mouth is worn through use and the opening is large enough to permit passing an offering or even a child from the back to the front as part of a ritual. The slab may originally have been positioned as a freestanding monument, part of the front wall of a temple or even a horizontal cover for a subterranean chamber. The monster's oval eyes contain crossed bands and there are vegetation motifs at the corners of the mouth, design elements that occur frequently at Chalcatzingo and that apparently symbolize the Earth Monster creature

pl. IX

126, pl. VIII

127

depicted on El Rey and Monument 13. The Earth Monster may have been Chalcatzingo's supreme supernatural patron and it is not surprising to find this image associated with monuments dedicated to rulers and rulership. Any astute leader would have eagerly advertised his or her special relationship with this important deity as a way to validate the right to the throne.

Grove believes that Chalcatzingo's entire sculptural *corpus* formed a larger pattern incorporating the three clusters into a coherent cosmological template reflecting the organizational principles behind the layout of the entire community.[32] According to this view, Chalcatzingo's builders integrated the sacred natural mountain they considered the home of rain and fertility deities with the human environment they created on the terraces below. They marked ritual processional routes on the mountain sides with mythic-religious carvings depicting themes related to rain and fertility while turning the natural terraces below into a constructed environment adorned with their portraits and those of their ancestors. This reinforced claims that Chalcatzingo's rulers had the power to intercede with the mountain-dwelling supernaturals that controlled rain, the most precious and least predictable element in this arid environment. As the fame of Chalcatzingo's ruler-priests grew, foreign pilgrims and merchants came to visit the sacred center at the foot of the steep, spectacular hills, adding to its sacred aura and the wealth of its leaders.

During this era of prosperity, Chalcatzingo established alliances with leaders at La Venta, Teopantecuanitlán, San Miguel Amuco, and other centers. Teopantecuanitlán predated the beginning of the Cantera phase by

127 The Earth Monster, shown in a frontal depiction on Monument 9, is frequently depicted at Chalcatzingo. The open mouth is large enough for a slender person to pass through. Ht 183 cm (72 in).

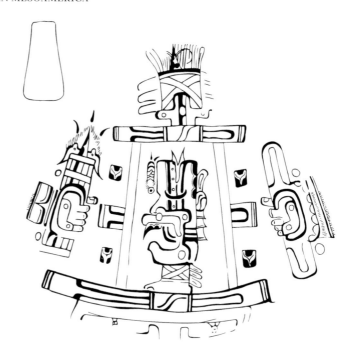

128 The very complex and poorly understood scene incised on the surface of this vase (see form top left) said to come from near Chalcatzingo, is dominated by an Olmec face shown in profile and other Olmec motifs. Ht 45 cm (17 in).

centuries and may have been the inspiration for Chalcatzingo's community layout. Both shared many architectural similarities, including carefully chosen settings on the landscape, artificial terraces, sunken courts, mound facades of carefully worked rectangular stone blocks, and Olmec-style sculpture. Teopantecuanitlán's North Platform and North Esplanade contain a few sculptures and architectural decorations that appear to post-date 700 BC, bringing its last occupation in line chronologically with the

128 Cantera phase. However, the Olmec component at Chalcatzingo is clear, especially in its sculpture, inspired – as was that of Teopantecuanitlán – by Gulf-coast Olmec traditions.

Olmec contacts with the outside world came to an end by 500 BC, as did Olmec civilization itself. The Late Formative period (500 BC–AD 200) was a time of vigorous growth in every part of Mesoamerica except for Olman, where what archaeologists call Epi-Olmec culture appeared in lower Papaloapan river drainage, a region that had been something of a cultural backwater in earlier days.

8 · Epi-Olmec Culture

By 400 BC La Venta and virtually all eastern Olman's riverine zone lay abandoned. Villages were deserted, artisans no longer created sculptures, jades, and pots in Olmec style and the trade networks that once connected Olmec capitals with the furthest reaches of Mesoamerica were silent. However, a vigorous new culture soon arose in the formerly marginal western Tuxtla mountains and Papaloapan lowlands. This Late and Terminal Formative period (300 BC–AD 200/250) Epi-Olmec culture bridged the gap between mature Olmec societies and later Classic Veracruz culture.

The term Epi-Olmec seems slightly defamatory, somehow implying a debased culture lying in the shadows of its glorious Olmec predecessors. Indeed this was the case in some senses but certainly not all. While the Epi-Olmec capital of Tres Zapotes was considerably smaller than San Lorenzo and La Venta and lacked their large public constructions, elaborate burials, complex iconographic programs, and exotic trade goods, its rulers did commission scores of stone monuments. They also made notable achievements in astronomy, writing, and calendrics, or at least were among the first to commit them to stone. Their achievements place them in the vanguard of ancient Native American intellectual culture and were a major legacy to later Mesoamerican civilizations.

The Tuxtla mountains are often considered the Epi-Olmec homeland, but in fact Tres Zapotes lies at the base of Cerro el Vigía overlooking the Papaloapan lowlands. Of course its realm probably encompassed much of the 4,500-sq. km (1,740-sq. mile) mountain massif. Relatively fertile soils, abundant moisture, and mild climate create an excellent environment for maize and other crops grown by the farmers who have lived here since at least 2500 BC. Other notable resources include basalt and excellent clay for pottery. The region is prone to natural hazards, particularly earthquakes and volcanic eruptions. Earthquakes knock down buildings, but normally do not exert long-term impacts on local residents unless they happen to be in the house when it collapses. Volcanic eruptions are a very different matter however – occasionally they blanket large portions of the region with deep layers of ash that render the land uncultivable for generations or even centuries. Despite these hazards, people have always returned to establish new societies in this rich environment.

Tres Zapotes: Olmec village and Epi-Olmec capital

Tres Zapotes is the best-known Epi-Olmec center and apparent capital of the region in the last centuries of the pre-Christian era.[1] Other known communities include La Joya and Bezuapan near Lake Catemaco, and La Mojarra, on the banks of the Acula river south of the gigantic Alvarado lagoon. Tres Zapotes is a concentration of earth mounds that line both sides of the Arroyo Hueyapan, a small stream that ultimately empties into the Papaloapan. Despite its modest size, the site has played a very important role in the history of Olmec studies, much greater perhaps than it ever did in Olmec times.

The chance discovery of Colossal Head 1 in the middle of the nineteenth century led Matthew W. Stirling to mount the first scientific investigations of Olmec culture at Tres Zapotes in 1938.[2] Unaware of the true nature of Olmec culture and sculpture, Stirling and his contemporaries misidentified the numerous Epi-Olmec monuments at the site as Olmec. Today we know that the 450-ha (1,112-acre) zone that archaeologists call Tres Zapotes encompasses several small, physically discrete ancient villages occupied more or less continuously for over 1,500 years. The Olmec-related portions of the site, tentatively dated by ceramics to 1200–1000 BC, lie buried beneath volcanic ash and debris from the larger Epi-Olmec and Classic-period occupations.[3]

At its height Tres Zapotes encompassed three clusters of modest-sized mounds surrounded by at least 100 small house mounds. It will be impossible to say whether all were occupied simultaneously or whether they replaced each other through time until archaeologists conduct extensive excavations at all three locales. The domestic areas and house mounds have not been studied in detail, but excavations at the nearby contemporary villages of Bezuapan and La Joya have yielded important insights into daily life in Epi-Olmec times.[4] Houses were constructed of wattle-and-daub with packed-earth wall footings, earth floors, and thatch roofs. The villagers stored maize in bell-shaped subterranean storage pits, ground it on basalt *manos* and *metates*, and consumed a wide array of locally available wild plants and animals. Each household manufactured pottery vessels for its own use and for exchange, spun (cotton?) thread that was woven into cloth, and manufactured tools from obsidian quarried at the Zaragoza and Oyameles sources 260 km (162 miles) to the west. Philip J. Arnold III's excavations into a Late Formative mound at La Joya uncovered several human burials accompanied by simple offerings. Remains of a ridged agricultural field at nearby Matacapan suggest that local farmers practiced intensive agriculture that involved hoeing soil around growing maize plants.[5] Bezuapan and La Joya were abandoned when ash from a volcanic eruption covered them and their agricultural fields.

Surveys of a 400-sq. km (155-sq. mile) region in the western Tuxtlas revealed lightly scattered Epi-Olmec populations residing in 1 small regional center, 8 villages, and 43 hamlets.[6] While none have yielded sculptures and other indicators of elite residents, El Picayo – a large, unexplored mound site near Santiago Tuxtla – may provide major archaeological surprises in the future. El Picayo appears to be a Late Formative site that may have surpassed even Tres Zapotes in size and importance. Furthermore, the piedmont and plain between the Tuxtla mountains and the town of Alvarado contain many large unexplored ancient centers. As Michael D. Coe observed forty years ago, "The frequency of such groups is so great that one may drive for 11 km along the road passing through Angel Cabada and Lerdo de Tejada and never be out of sight of mounds."[7] Today they still remain unexplored, waiting for some enterprising student to reveal their secrets and perhaps even unlock the mysterious origins of Mesoamerican writing and calendrics.

Epi-Olmec art

Epi-Olmec artisans created a broad range of decorated pottery, figurines, ornaments, and other objects, but today they are best known for their stone sculptures. More than forty monuments have appeared at Tres Zapotes and additional examples have been identified at Cerro el Vigía, Alvarado, and La Mojarra.[8] Epi-Olmec sculptures include stelae, flat "altars," rectangular boxes, tenoned busts, and other monument types that served as either free-standing monuments or architectural embellishments. They reflect a cosmopolitan blending of local and foreign stylistic elements. Stelae A and D recall La Venta sculptures believed to date to the latest occupation at that site, while Monuments C, F, and G represent a local post-Olmec style indigenous to south-central Veracruz. One or two sculptures even show influences from the Late Formative Izapan style of coastal Chiapas. Many sculptures that show humans seem to depict narratives or actions related to rulers and their supernatural patrons. Tres Zapotes sculptures appear to lack the rich detail and refinement characteristic of older Olmec monuments. In part this is a result of erosion and the rather coarse Cerro el Vigía basalt preferred by the sculptors, but even the best-preserved monuments failed to match the skill and artisanship of Olmec pieces.

Epi-Olmec intellectual achievements: writing, calendrics, and astronomy

Writing was a integral characteristic of Mesoamerican culture and more than a dozen distinct pre-Columbian writing systems have been identified. Classic Maya writing, the most complex and sophisticated system that existed, appears to have grown out of an Olmec and Epi-Olmec predecessor called the Isthmian script. The oldest known examples of Isthmian script recently appeared at San Andrés in Tabasco, near La Venta, as discussed in Chapter 4.[9] Early texts are extremely scarce and scattered at various places on the Isthmus of Tehuantepec (hence the name), and it is impossible to trace the development of Isthmian through time.

Nine probable Isthmian texts are known.[10] Since most of the texts are quite short or fragmentary, modern efforts at decipherment have focused on the three longest – those found on the Tuxtla Statuette, Tres Zapotes Stela C, and La Mojarra Stela 1. All three objects appeared in a small section of western Olman, leading some scholars to call the writing system Epi-Olmec or Tuxtla. Other inscriptions are found on stone stelae from Cerro de las Mesas and Alvarado, west of the Tuxtla mountains, and stone and pottery fragments from Chiapa de Corzo, Chiapas.

129 The Tuxtla Statuette was the first object with an Isthmian text to be discovered. This 16-cm (6.3-in) high piece of rounded greenstone depicts a priest wearing a bird-bill mask over his lower face and a bird cape. The bird has been mistakenly identified as a duck but is most likely a heron, one of the majestic denizens of the swampy lowland lagoons and backwaters that ring the Tuxtla mountains. The Statuette's most unusual feature is the 12-column text composed of 75 lightly incised glyphs, including the Long Count date 8.6.2.4.18 (AD 162). According to W. H. Holmes, the Smithsonian Institution archaeologist who reported the find, a farmer discovered the Statuette in 1902 while plowing his field at an unknown location in the Tuxtlas.[11] Within a year it was smuggled to New York, purportedly hidden in a shipment of the fine cigar tobacco leaf for which the region is famous. The Smithsonian Institution acquired it and today it is on public display at Dumbarton Oaks in Washington, DC.

Epigraphers were able to read the Long Count date from the beginning, but the other glyphs were unlike any known and thus undecipherable. Both Holmes and the Maya specialist Sylvanus G. Morley considered them Maya, but Holmes dated both the object and the text to the second century while Morley thought the text was inscribed at a much later date in an anachronistic style with references to earlier times.

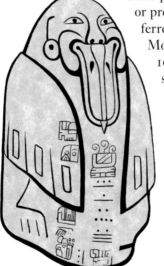

Other proposed attributions include Olmec, Zapotec, or proto-Mixe-Zoquean. Many archaeologists preferred to ignore the squat little enigma until La Mojarra Stela 1 with its long text appeared in 1988; epigraphers now realize that the texts share many glyphs and may even refer to the same events and individuals.

129 The Tuxtla Statuette provided the first indication of an Isthmian script rivaling that of the Maya in antiquity and complexity. Ht 15 cm (6 in).

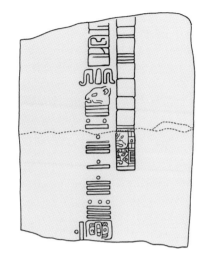

130 The front of Stela C at Tres Zapotes, Veracruz, probably depicts a ruler seated on a throne while the Long Count date on the back may refer to a solar eclipse. Ht 160 cm (57 in).

Tres Zapotes Stela C is Mesoamerica's oldest-known inscription to inte-   130
grate calendrics, astronomy, and writing. It is also one of Mesoamerica's most controversial stone sculptures and the history of its discovery could serve as the model for a mystery novel. Matthew W. Stirling encountered the lower fragment in 1939 when, as his widow Marion recounted sixty years later, he accidentally stubbed his toe on a corner sticking above the ground. Local residents discovered the missing upper section thirty years later and promptly placed it in the local jail so that state or federal authorities could not take it away as they had the lower portion years before. The locals also threatened to incarcerate and even kill archaeologist Francisco "Paco" Beverido when he tried to study the stone, but they finally relented, allowing him to take photographs in the dark cell but without benefit of a flash.[12] Today the lower section can be seen in Mexico City's National Museum of Anthropology while the upper portion occupies a place of pride in the small Tres Zapotes site museum.

One side of Stela C shows the profile face of a man on top of a complex mask that may represent a throne. The obverse contains a text composed of badly effaced glyphs and a well-preserved bar-and-dot inscription express-ing a date in the Mesoamerican Long Count calendar. As we saw in Chapter 4, Long Count dates recorded elapsed time since a mythic beginning date of 3114 BC and occur so frequently on Classic Maya sculpture that archaeolo-gists once credited the Maya with inventing the system. Today this seems very unlikely: no early inscriptions have ever appeared there, and as dis-cussed in Chapter 7, the region was very lightly populated until quite late in the Formative period. In fact, the earliest-known Long Count date (7.16.3.2.13 [8 December 36 BC]) occurs on the fragmentary Stela 2 at Chiapa de Corzo, Chiapas, and the eight earliest Long Count inscriptions known all occur outside the Maya homeland.

Marion Stirling correctly reconstructed Stela C's Long Count date as 7.16.6.16.18.6 Eznab, or 3 September 32 BC. Her reading was quite controversial because the initial numeral was missing, forcing her to reconstruct it on internal evidence.[13] The appearance of the upper half of the stone with a clear numeral 7 at the right place finally vindicated her and laid the controversy to rest. Matthew W. Stirling considered the mask and the inscription Olmec, but today we know that both post-date the demise of Olmec culture by centuries.

But what does Stela C say? The non-calendrical glyphs are illegible, owing to erosion or perhaps the fact that they were painted rather than carved. However, visual inspection suggests that the human head represents a local ruler and the date apparently commemorates something that occurred on 3 September 32 BC. But what might that event have been? Most archaeologists assume it marked a major occasion in the life of the ruler: perhaps his birth, death, accession to the throne, or the conquest of an enemy. Geographer Vincent Malmstrom, on the other hand, has offered an intriguing alternative explanation.[14] According to him, an annular solar eclipse that obscured 93 percent of the dawning sun in the Tuxtla mountains occurred on 30 August 32 BC. The evidence for this is based upon projecting known, fixed cycles of such events back into the unknown past – matters far beyond the limits of the present author's understanding. However, the result was that only a ring-like halo was visible as the solar disk rose out of the Gulf of Mexico. One can well imagine the incredible impact such an event might have had and the desire to record it if one had the means. Perhaps our nameless ruler even claimed responsibility for this divine act or perhaps Malmstrom has it all wrong. In any case, ideas of this sort keep Olmec studies lively and contentious.

Stela C is the oldest known sculptural text that integrates rulership, calendrics, and celestial events, themes that seem to recur later on La Mojarra Stela 1 and the Tuxtla Statuette. Like the Statuette and Stela C, the La Mojarra sculpture was an accidental find that became embroiled in considerable controversy. La Mojarra is a small village nestled in a bend of the Acula river. Artificial mounds and broken pottery testify to the human occupation of the high ground above the flood level for at least 2,000 years. Modern lore has it that a fisherman discovered the stone under his feet as he was casting his net in the shallow river.[15] Unfortunately, the truth is not quite so romantic; in reality, Stela 1 was never lost. It stood upright near the river's edge on the property of the Domínguez family, owners of this marginal pasture land since their Italian forebear carved a ranch out of the swampy wilderness in the 1870s while fathering more than fifty children.[16] The stela, known locally as "El Indio," never came to the attention of scholars, and

131

finally eroded into the river about fifty years ago. Although it was out of sight, it never disappeared from memory and in 1986 a marine engineering firm raised the large sculpture with some difficulty and delivered it to the new Museum of Anthropology then under construction in Xalapa, the state capital. For various reasons it was never put on display, but instead languished in the museum basement for a year or so. In 1988 a young student assigned to clean the surface discovered hundreds of lightly incised glyphs surrounding the much more deeply carved human figure. Some of the glyphs duplicated examples on the Tuxtla Statuette, and the text included two Long Count dates, 8.5.3.3.5 and 8.5.16.9.7 (21 May AD 143 and 13 July AD 157 respectively).

Stela 1 rocked the Mesoamerican world. What was the script? Could it be ancestral to Maya writing? Why was the sculpture "hidden from the public"? Was it authentically ancient? One museum director intimated that the text was a modern forgery designed to advance the careers of the perpetrators. As accurate copies of the text became available and scholars devoted their efforts to decipherment, the controversies over its authenticity died away. Today students of Isthmian writing agree that the text and Long Count dates are genuinely pre-Columbian.

Linguists Terrence Kaufman and John Justeson have devoted more than a decade to the decipherment of Stela 1 and other Isthmian texts. They have proposed a decipherment based on the premise that the script is grounded in the proto-Mixe-Zoquean language spoken by the Olmecs, or one closely related to it.[17] They believe Stela 1 records important events in the life of an Epi-Olmec ruler they call "Harvest Mountain Lord." Other scholars have challenged their decipherment on various grounds: some reject the premise that the spoken language was proto-Mixe-Zoquean, others maintain that many more texts are needed before enough patterns become

131 La Mojarra Stela 1, source of the longest-known Isthmian text, has sparked a fierce debate about the origins of Mesoamerican writing systems. Ht 234 cm (91 in).

apparent to have confidence in any decipherment.[18] And indeed, the search for additional texts has begun. Sergio Vásquez Zárate and the present author undertook a joint University of Alabama and University of Veracruz project at La Mojarra in 1995 using sophisticated sub-soil prospection techniques to locate additional monuments.[19] We found remnants of ceramic kilns but no stones, with or without texts; perhaps we needed the spirit of Matthew W. Stirling rather than a magnetometer. Fortunately, other investigators are continuing these efforts in other parts of the Epi-Olmec world and someday their efforts will pay off with additional monuments and texts.

After about AD 200/250, Epi-Olmec culture was replaced by what archaeologists call "Classic Veracruz" culture. New pottery and figurine styles appeared and new political centers replaced the older ones, but life probably did not change very much. Ordinary people continued to eat the same foods, live in similar houses, worship the same basic deities, and pay taxes to new or different rulers. An urbanized core of settlement grew around Cerro de las Mesas, the new capital of the region. Slightly later, Matacapan emerged as a regional center on the fertile volcanic soils near Lake Catemaco as part of a cultural development that had little if anything to do with the now-ancient Epi-Olmec cultures of the region.

La Mojarra continued to shelter a small population that constructed two or three modest mounds on the site. At some point they erected three kilns in the village plaza and used them to fire the locally used orange pottery. When they abandoned the kilns they ceremoniously filled them with carefully laid layers of stucco removed from the surface of a nearby building. La Mojarra's days of glory had passed, never to return.

Elsewhere in Mesoamerica Classic-period civilizations grew out of Late Formative-period foundations in the Maya region, Oaxaca, the Basin of Mexico and West Mexico. Each represented a great flowering of locally based culture history but every one owed a large debt to their Olmec and Epi-Olmec predecessors. That debt was the Olmec legacy, the reason we call the Olmecs the Mesoamerican Mother Culture.

The Olmec legacy

What was the Olmec contribution to the civilizations that followed? According to Mayanist David Freidel, "The Olmec left a rich legacy to their immediate intellectual and cultural descendants in Mesoamerica. They midwifed the successful birth of Mesoamerican civilization...."[20] Most Mesoamericanists (but certainly not all) agree with Freidel. His assertion is found in the catalogue for the Princeton Museum of Art's exhibition of Olmec art entitled *The Olmec World: Ritual and Rulership*. This exhibition was just one of several that highlighted Olmec achievements in ceramics and sculpture in recent years. However, the Olmec legacy extended far beyond the realms of art and the visual. Indeed the Olmecs either established or institutionalized many of the basic characteristics of Mesoamerican civilization.

The basic foundations of Mesoamerican culture were created in the Archaic period when nomadic foragers settled in permanent villages, domesticated food crops, began to erect buildings, and established the basic family and supra-familial social units that remained the building blocks of all later pre-Columbian societies. Most of the major underlying religious beliefs of later times also emerged in this period. In the second millennium BC people in the Soconusco and Olman began to elaborate these patterns. The Olmecs created entirely new social, political, religious, and artistic systems. These systems included complex settlement hierarchies, capital cities, politically integrated territories, rulership and the paraphernalia associated with it, large public works, and control over labor as the expression of asymmetrical power relationships. The Olmec legacy was especially notable in the realm of religion, and included town plans that expressed a shared vision of the cosmos, a sophisticated symbol system, the ball game, human sacrifice, and formal definition of supernaturals. The Olmecs passed this legacy on to later cultures but, just as no child is a clone of its mother, neither were the Mother Culture's descendants mere copies of the Olmecs. Each culture developed a unique identity through its own efforts.

Epilogue: News flashes from the Olmec World

Olmec culture ceased to exist 2,500 years ago but its story continues to unfold almost daily, with the news moving instantaneously across the world via e-mail and Internet postings. Although chance discoveries occur as they always have, carefully planned research plays a much more important role today than ever before. However, even careful research may not yield the desired results, as shown by our failure to discover stone monuments at La Mojarra. On the other hand, it often turns up things that are completely unexpected. Three such discoveries landed in my e-mail in-box in the past twelve months, each requiring me to rewrite sections of the manuscript and examine some of my long-held beliefs. First came the identification of the source of Olmec blue-green jadeite, located in the scrub thorn forests of Guatemala's Motagua river drainage, followed soon thereafter by a newly discovered Olmec tabletop throne in Veracruz. Finally, the discovery of true Olmec writing at San Andrés was published in *Science* magazine two weeks before I write these lines.

The Motagua river traverses Guatemala from the highlands to the Caribbean coast, cutting through metamorphic rock layers. These rocks were identified as the source of Classic Maya green jade in 1954, but the source(s) of Olmec blue-green jadeite remained a mystery until intensive field reconnaissance by geologists and archaeologists revealed raw jadeite rocks, chemically and visually identical to the elusive Olmec blue-green jade. Thus we can confidently eliminate Guerrero and Costa Rica as potential sources and also discard Miguel Covarrubias' theory that Olmec miners exhausted the supply of this highly prized stone: the scientists who surveyed the source report multi-ton boulders of the stuff lying on the ground surface. Future investigations may even uncover mines and workshops, producing important insights into the details of this craft.

While checking out the jadeite discovery in my university library, an e-mail from Christopher A. Pool alerted me to the accidental find of a large sculptured throne at El Marquesillo, Veracruz. El Marquesillo is a small village on the banks of the Río San Juan south of Laguna de los Cerros. Village officials reported finding a large carved stone on their farm and Mexican archaeologists exposed this Olmec tabletop throne in a controlled excavation. The photograph published in the 9 January, 2002 on-line edition of *El Liberal del Sur* (a newspaper I never even knew existed) shows a seated human figure similar to those found on thrones at La Venta and San Lorenzo. UNAM archaeologist Judith Zurita alerted her colleagues across the world via e-mail messages with attachments containing the article and photograph. We can be grateful that the local officials reported it to the proper authorities instead of selling it to an antiquities dealer, as has happened so often in the past. What might the presence of a ruler's throne at El Marquesillo mean? Was this apparently small site an unknown major Olmec center that will force us to rewrite the political history of Olmec culture? Or simply a sculpture abandoned along the road in antiquity while being transported to an unknown destination? Future investigations, said by the reporter to be in the offing, may resolve the issue. If so, the results will surely flash across the Internet before they appear in a professional archaeological journal.

The final proof that the Olmecs employed a writing system confirms the cherished beliefs of a few scholars and probably irritates many more. More important, however, are the questions it poses.

As I finish these lines, the dry season is coming on in Olman and at least a dozen archaeologists and students are preparing to start new investigations. What will they find? *¿Quién sabe?* I only hope this book will be too far into production to have to add new information.

Guide to Olmec Sites

General information

I must begin with the caveat that most Olmec archaeological sites are neither easy to reach nor as spectacular as later ruins. Furthermore, no major museum specializes only in Olmec materials and all those discussed below display remains of later cultures, allowing the visitor to appreciate the Olmecs as members of the great pre-Columbian cultural tradition. I assume that most readers will be foreign visitors who enter Mexico through Mexico City and therefore I have prepared an itinerary that originates in Mexico City. A driving tour in a personal or rental car or one of Mexico's many luxurious First Class motor coaches would go to Xalapa, then proceed through Olman from west to east, visiting Tres Zapotes, the San Lorenzo region, La Venta, and Villahermosa, in that sequence. People traveling by airplane might start either at Xalapa or Villahermosa.

"Must see" museums and sites

In order to truly grasp Olmec culture and art, one must visit the **National Museum of Anthropology** in Mexico City, the **Museo de Antropología** in Xalapa, Veracruz, and the **Parque La Venta** and **Carlos Pellicer Museum**, both in Villahermosa, Tabasco. A visit to La Venta site will provide an on-the-ground appreciation for Olmec architecture and town planning. The Gulf Coast Room at the National Museum of Anthropology contains Olmec sculpture and objects from numerous sites. The monuments include outstanding examples from San Lorenzo, La Venta and Tres Zapotes. The collection of jades is the largest and finest in existence and includes many from the offerings in La Venta's Complex A. Xalapa's Museo de Antropología contains magnificent stone monuments, pottery, and other objects, including a few Río Pesquero jades. The exhibits on later Veracruz cultures are the best in the world. Most of the La Venta sculptures have been relocated to an open-air museum alongside a lake in Villahermosa, the capital of Tabasco. Others are found inside the Carlos Pellicer Museum.

La Venta itself is located 124 km (78 miles) east of Villahermosa just off Mexico Highway 180, the main artery connecting Veracruz and Tabasco. Paths allow visitors to walk around the mounds and view modern replicas of stone monuments in their original locations. A small site museum provides basic information on La Venta and its history. Similar small site museums can be found at **Tres Zapotes** and in the town of Santiago Tuxtla, both on or near Highway 180 as it winds through the Tuxtla mountains, and in Tenochtitlán village near **San Lorenzo**.

Notes to the Text

Chapter 1 (pp. 11–28)
1 Coe 1968.
2 Niederberger 2000: 169.
3 Campbell and Kaufmann 1976; Wichmann 1995, 2002.
4 Melgar y Serrano 1871.
5 There are many. *See* Benson 1996.
6 Sahagún Book 10: 187.
7 Codex Mendoza 1992, vol. 4: 96–97.
8 Sahagún, Book 10: 187.
9 Bernal Diaz del Castillo 1956.
10 Pope, *et al.* 2001.
11 Rust and Leyden 1994.
12 Ortiz and Rodriguez 2000.
13 Coe and Diehl 1980, vol. 1: 137–159.
14 Symonds, Cyphers and Lunagómez 2002: 56.

Chapter 2 (pp. 29–59)
1 Sanders and Webster 1988.
2 Coe and Diehl 1980, chapter 4: 131–222.
3 Cyphers 1999: 155–181.
4 Symonds, *et al.* 2002.
5 Grove 1999.
6 Coe and Diehl 1980: 25–32.
7 Coe 1968.
8 Cyphers pers. comm. 2002.
9 Coe and Diehl 1980; Stirling 1955.
10 Cyphers 1999.
11 Cyphers 1999.
12 Coe and Diehl 1980, vol. 1: 293–374; Cyphers 1997.
13 Coe and Fernandez 1980.
14 Symonds, *et al.* 2002; Kruger 1996.
15 Ortiz and Rodríguez 2000.
16 Pool 2000.
17 Medellín Zenil 1960; Bove 1978.
18 Gillespie 2000.
19 Gómez Rueda 1996.
20 Medellín Zenil and A. Beltrán 1965.
21 Cobean 1996.
22 Ortiz Pérez and Cyphers 1997.

Chapter 3 (pp. 60–82)
1 Drucker, Heizer, and Squier 1959.
2 von Nagy, Pohl and Pope n.d.
3 González Lauck 1997.
4 González Lauck 1996; González Lauck and Solís 1996.
5 González Lauck 1988.
6 Reilly III 1999: 15.
7 Gallegos Gómara 1990.
8 Grove 1993.
9 Van Sertima 1976; Stirling 1943.
10 Heizer 1968.
11 González Lauck 1997.
12 Morrison, Clewlow, Jr. and Heizer 1970.

13 Reilly III 1999.
14 Drucker 1952; Drucker, Heizer, and Squier 1959.
15 Tedlock 1985.
16 Grove 1999.
17 Reilly III 1999.
18 Sisson 1970, Rust 1992, von Nagy 1997.
19 Rust 1992.
20 Pohl, Pope and von Nagy 2002.
21 Robb, Boxt, Bradford, Stokes, and González Lauck 2000.
22 Killion and Urcid n.d.; Symonds, Cyphers and Lunagómez 2002.
23 Gómez and Courtes 1987; von Nagy 1997.
24 Joralemon 1996: 236.
25 Blom and La Farge 1927, Benson and de la Fuente 1996.
26 Jiménez Salas 1990; Ortiz Pérez and Cyphers 1997.
27 Chase 1981.

Chapter 4 (pp. 83–107)
1 Rust 1992, Pope, *et al.* 2001; Raab, *et al.* 2000.
2 Cyphers 1999.
3 Pope, *et al.* 2001.
4 Coe, S. 1994.
5 Santley, Arnold, and Barrett 1997.
6 Coe and Diehl 1980.
7 Cobean, *et al.* 1971, 1990.
8 Benson and de la Fuente 1996: 222–23.
9 Cyphers 1999.
10 Gullberg, Heizer and Gullberg 1957; Carlson 1981.
11 Pires-Ferreira 1975.
12 Diehl 1989; Drucker 1981.
13 Coe 1989; Cyphers 1999.
14 Coe 1976.
15 Pohl, *et al.* 2002.
16 Franco 1985 (reissue of 1959).
17 Diehl 1987.
18 Joralemon 1976: 58–59.
19 Tedlock 1985.
20 Reilly 1999, 2002; Taube 2002; Schele 1996; Freidel, Schele, and Parker 1993.
21 Joralemon 1976, 1996.
22 Luckert 1976.
23 Joralemon 1976: 33.
24 Coe 1968.
25 Joralemon 1971, 1976.
26 Scott 1992.
27 Taube 1996, 2000.
28 Stirling 1955.
29 Furst 1968.
30 Benson and de la Fuente 1996; Guthrie 1995.

Chapter 5 (pp. 108–125)
1 Pasztory 1998: 28.
2 Covarrubias 1957: 54.

3 De la Fuente 1992: 123–24.
4 Westheimer 1974.
5 Clewlow, et al. 1967; de la Fuente 1973.
6 Melgar 1869; Van Sertima 1976; Diehl 2001.
7 Porter 1989.
8 Engelbach 1923: 22.
9 Medellín Zenil 1960.
10 Gillespie 1992.
11 Killion and Urcid 2001.
12 Velson and Clark 1975.
13 Princeton 1995; Benson and de la Fuente 1996.
14 Seitz, et al. 2001.
15 Furst 1995: 79.
16 Pasztory 2000.
17 Drucker 1952.
18 Carlson 1981.

Chapter 6 (pp. 126–151)
1 Caso 1942, 1965.
2 Covarrubias 1942, 1957.
3 Stirling 1940.
4 Thompson 1941; Wauchope 1950.
5 Diehl and Coe 1995; Clark and Pye 2000; Sharer and Grove 1989; Flannery and Marcus 1994, 2000.
6 Coe 1977; Lee 1989; Diehl and Coe 1995.
7 Clark and Pye 2000.
8 Clark and Pye 2000.
9 Blake 1991; Blake, et al. 1995; Clark 1991; Clark and Pye 2000.
10 Hill, Blake and Clark 1998.
11 Clark and Blake 1994.
12 Clark 1990.
13 Clark and Pye 2000.
14 Agrinier 1984.
15 Joyce and Henderson 2001.
16 Clark and Pye 2002.
17 Love 1999, 2002.
18 Joralemon 1996: 246.
19 Lee 1989.
20 Clark and Pye 2000.
21 Lowe 1981.
22 Graham 1979, 1989.
23 Shook and Heizer 1976.
24 Pye and Demarest 1991.
25 Sharer 1978.
26 Fash 1991.
27 Joyce and Henderson 2001.
28 Joyce 1992.
29 Baudez and Becquelin 1973.
30 Brady, Hasemann and Fogarty 1995.
31 Graham 1998.
32 Clark and Cheetham in press.
33 Smith 1982.
34 Freidel 1995.

Chapter 7 (pp. 152–180)
1 Grove 2000; Niederberger 1987, 1996.
2 Niederberger 2000.

3 Tolstoy and Paradis 1970; Niederberger 1987; Blanton 1972; Barba de Piña Chan 1956.
4 Niederberger 2000.
5 Tolstoy 1989; Tolstoy, et al. 1977.
6 Faulhaber 1965; Garcia Moll, et al. 1991; Joyce 2001.
7 Tolstoy 1989.
8 Piña Chan 1958; Coe 1965.
9 Niederberger 1987; Joralemon 2001.
10 Honan 2000.
11 Marcus 1998.
12 Coe 1965: 105.
13 Blomster 1998.
14 Vaillant and Vaillant 1934.
15 Grove 1974.
16 Brush 1965.
17 Paradis 1981; Henderson 1977.
18 Martínez Donjuán 1994.
19 Taube 1996.
20 Niederberger 1996.
21 Gay 1967.
22 Grove 1970.
23 Villela F. 1989.
24 Marcus and Flannery 1996; see Winter 1994 for an alternative reconstruction.
25 Blomster 1998.
26 Neff and Glascock n.d. (2002).
27 Winter 1994.
28 Marcus and Flannery 1996; Flannery and Marcus 1994, 2000.
29 Grove and Paradis 1971.
30 Grove 1984; Grove (ed.) 1987.
31 Grove and Angulo in Grove (ed.) 1987.
32 Grove 1999.

Chapter 8 (pp. 181–189)
1 Pool 2000.
2 Stirling 1939.
3 Pool 2000.
4 Pool 1997; Arnold III 2000.
5 Santley 1992.
6 Santley and Arnold III 1996.
7 Coe 1965: 679.
8 De la Fuente 1973; Winfield Capitaine 1988.
9 Pohl, Pope and von Nagy 2002.
10 Kaufmann and Justeson 2001.
11 Holmes 1907.
12 Beverido 1996.
13 Stirling 1940; Thompson 1941.
14 Malmstrom 1997.
15 Winfield Capitaine 1988.
16 Pers. comm. to Diehl from Domingo Dominguéz 1995.
17 Kaufmann and Justeson 1993; Justeson and Kaufmnn 2001.
18 Meuzin 1992; Lloyd Anderson pers. comm. to Diehl 2001; Coe 2002.
19 Diehl, et al. 1997.
20 Freidel 1995: 9.

Further Reading

The literature on the Olmecs is vast. Here I have emphasized the sources I have found most useful and most readily available. An exhaustive bibliography with more than 35,000 entries on all aspects of Mesoamerican archaeology, including Olmec studies, may be found at www.famsi.org/research/bibliography/htm, the website of the Foundation for the Advancement of Mesoamerican Studies, Inc. That website also contains reports of recent FAMSI-sponsored research projects on Olmec sites and materials at www.famsi.org/reports. www.mesoweb.org is another good on-line source of information. Printed sources of current information include the journals *Latin American Antiquity, Ancient Mesoamerica, Antiquity* and *Arqueologia Mexicana*. While no modern single volume synthesis of Olmec culture exists, four recent compilations contain many essays and articles that summarize recent research: *Los Olmecas en Mesoamérica*, John E. Clark (ed.); *The Olmec World: Ritual and Rulership*, Jill Guthrie (ed.); *Olmec Art of Ancient Mexico*, Elizabeth P. Benson and Beatriz de la Fuente (eds.); and *Olmec Art and Archaeology in Mesoamerica*, John E. Clark and Mary E. Pye (eds.).

AGRINIER, PIERRE. "The Early Olmec horizon at Mirador, Chiapas, Mexico," *Papers of the New World Archaeological Foundation* 48. Provo 1984.
— "Mirador-Plumajillo, Chiapas, y sus relaciones con cuatro sitios del horizonte olmeca en Veracruz, Chiapas, y la costa de Guatemala," *Arqueología* 2: 19–36. julio–diciembre 1989.
ANGULO V., JORGE. "The Chalcatzingo reliefs: an iconographic analysis," in *Ancient Chalcatzingo*, ed. D.C. Grove, 132–58. Austin 1987.
ARNOLD, PHILIP J. "Sociopolitical complexity and the Gulf Olmecs: A view from the Tuxtla mountains, Veracruz, Mexico," in *Olmec Art and Archaeology in Mesoamerica*, eds. J.E. Clark and M.E. Pye, 117–135. New Haven and London 2000.
BARNETT, WILLIAM K., AND JOHN W. HOOPES (eds.). *Emergence of Pottery: Technology and Innovation in Ancient Societies*. Washington 1995.
BAUADEZ, CLAUDE, AND PIERRE BECQUELIN *Archeologie de Los Naranjos, Honduras*. Mexico 1973.
BENSON, ELIZABETH P. (ed.). *Dumbarton Oaks Conference of the Olmec*. Washington 1968
— (ed.). *The Olmec and Their Neighbors: Essays in Memory of Matthew W. Stirling*. Washington 1981.
BENSON, ELIZABETH P. AND BEATRIZ DE LA FUENTE (eds.). *Olmec Art of Ancient Mexico*. Washington 1996.

BERDAN, FRANCES F., AND PATRICIA R. ANAWALT *The Codex Mendoza* (4 vols). Berkeley 1992.
BERNAL, IGNACIO. *The Olmec World*. Berkeley 1969.
BEVERIDO PEREAU, FRANCISCO *Estética Olmeca*. Xalapa 1996.
BLAKE, MICHAEL. "An Emerging Early Formative Chiefdom at Paso de la Amada, Chiapas, Mexico," in *The Formation of Complex Society in Southeastern Mesoamerica*, ed. W.R. Fowler, Jr., 27–46. Boca Raton 1991.
BLAKE, MICHAEL, BRIAN CHISHOLM, JOHN CLARK, BARBARA VOORHIES, AND MICHAEL LOVE. "Prehistoric subsistence in the Soconusco region," *Current Anthropology* 33: 83–94. 1992.
BLAKE, MICHAEL, JOHN E. CLARK, BARBARA VOORHIES, GEORGE MICHAELS, MICHAEL LOVE, MARY PYE, ARTHUR DEMAREST, AND BARBARA ARROYO. "Radiocarbon chronology for the Late Archaic and Formative periods on the Pacific coast of southeastern Mesoamerica," *Ancient Mesoamerica* Vol. 6, no.2: 161–83. 1995.
BLANTON, RICHARD E. "Prehistoric adaptation in the Ixtapalapa region, Mexico," *Science* Vol. 175: 1317–26. 1972.
BLOM, FRANS AND OLIVER LA FARGE. *Tribes and Temples: A Record of the Expedition to Middle America Conducted by the Tulane University of Louisiana in 1925* (2 vols.). New Orleans 1926.
BLOMSTER, JEFFREY P. "Context, cult, and Early Formative public ritual in the Mixteca Alta: analysis of a hollow-baby figurine from Etlatongo, Oaxaca," *Ancient Mesoamerica*, Vol.9, no.2: 309–26. 1998.
— "What and where is Olmec style? Regional perspectives on hollow figurines in Early Formative Mesoamerica," *Ancient Mesoamerica* Vol.13, no.2: 171–95.
BOVE, FREDERICK J. "Laguna de los Cerros: an Olmec central place," *Journal of New World Archaeology*, Vol.2, no.3. 1978.
BRADY, JAMES E. "A reassessment of the chronology and function of Gordon's Cave no.3, Copan, Honduras," *Ancient Mesoamerica* Vol.6, no.1: 29–38. 1995.
BRADY, JAMES E., GEORGE HASEMANN, AND JOHN FOGARTY. "Harvest of Skulls and Bones," *Archaeology* Vol. 48, no.3: 36–40. May/June 1995.
BRUSH, CHARLES. "Pox Pottery: earliest identified Mexican ceramic," *Science* Vol. 149, no.3680: 194–95. 1965.
CAMPBELL, LYLE R., AND TERRENCE S. KAUFMANN. "A linguistic look at the Olmecs," *American Antiquity*, Vol. 41, no.1: 80–89. 1976.

CARLSON, JOHN B. "Olmec iron-ore concave mirrors: the aesthetics of a lithic technology and the Lord of the Mirror (with an illustrated catalogue of mirrors)," in *The Olmec and Their Neighbors: Essays in Memory of Matthew W. Stirling*, ed. E.P. Benson, 117-47. Washington 1981.

CASO, ALFONSO. "Definición y extensión del complejo 'Olmeca'," in *Mayas y Olmecas: Segunda Reunión de Mesa Redonda Sobre Problemas Antropológicos de México y Centro América*, 43–46. Tuxtla Gutiérrez 1942.

— "¿Existío un imperio olmeca?," *Memoria de El Colegio Nacional* Vol.5, no.3: 11–60. 1956.

CEJA TENORIO, JORGE FAUSTO. "Paso de la Amada: an Early Preclassic site in the Soconusco, Chiapas, Mexico." *Papers of the New World Archaeological Foundation* no.49. Provo 1985.

CLARK, JOHN E. "Olmecas, olmequizmo y olmequización en Mesoamérica," *Arqueología* 3: 49–56. 1990.

— "The beginnings of Mesoamerica: apologia for the Soconusco Early Formative," in *The Formation of Complex Society in Southeastern Mesoamerica*, ed. W.R. Fowler, Jr., 13–26. Boca Raton 1991.

— (ed.) *Los Olmecas in Mesoamérica*. Mexico 1994.

— "Craft specialization and Olmec civilization," in *Craft Specialization and Social Evolution: In Memory of V. Gordon Childe*, ed. B. Wailes, 187–99. Philadelphia 1996.

— "The arts of government in Early Mesoamerica," *Annual Review of Anthropology* 26: 211–34. 1997.

CLARK, JOHN E., AND MICHAEL BLAKE. "The power of prestige: competitive generosity and the emergence of rank societies in lowland Mesoamerica," in *Factional Competition and Political Development in the New World*, eds. E. Brumfiel and J. Fox, 17–30. Cambridge 1994.

CLARK, JOHN E., AND DAVID CHEETHAM. "Mesoamerica's tribal foundations." Unpublished manuscript. 2003.

CLARK, JOHN E., AND DENNIS GOSSER. "Reinventing Mesoamerica's first pottery," in *The Emergence of Pottery: Technology and Innovation in Ancient Society*, eds. W. Barnett and J. Hoopes, 209–21. Washington 1995.

CLARK, JOHN E., AND MARY E. PYE (eds.). *Olmec Art and Archaeology in Mesoamerica*. New Haven and London 2000.

— "The Pacific coast and the Olmec question" in *Olmec Art and Archaeology in Mesoamerica*, eds. J.E. Clark and M.E. Pye, 217–51. New Haven and London 2000.

CLEWLOW, C. WILLIAM, RICHARD A. COWAN, JAMES F. O'CONNELL, AND CARLOS BENEMANN "Colossal Heads of the Olmec Culture," *Contributions of the University of California Archaeological Research Facility* no.4. 1967.

COBEAN, ROBERT. "La Oaxaqueña, Veracruz: un centro olmeca menor en su contexto regional," in *Arqueología Mesoamericana: Homenaje a William T. Sanders*, ed. A.G. Mastache, *et al.* 37–61. Mexico City: 1996.

COBEAN, ROBERT H., MICHAEL D. COE, EDWARD A. PERRY, JR., KARL K. TUREKIAN AND DINKAR P. KHARKAR. "Obsidian trade at San Lorenzo Tenochtitlán, Mexico,' *Science*, Vol.174: 666–71. 1971.

COBEAN, ROBERT H., JAMES R. VOGT, MICHAEL D. GLASSCOCK, AND TERRANCE L. STOCKER. "High precision trace-element characterization of major Mesoamerican obsidian sources and further analyses of artifacts from San Lorenzo Tenochtitlán, Mexico," *Latin American Antiquity*, Vol.2, no.1: 69–91. 1991.

COE, MICHAEL D. *The Jaguars' Children: Pre-Classic Central Mexico*. New York 1965.

— "Archaeological synthesis of southern Veracruz and Tabasco," in *Archaeology of Southern Mesoamerica*, Part 2, ed. G.R. Willey. *Handbook of Middle American Indians*, Vol.3, gen. ed. R. Wauchope, 679–715. Austin 1965.

— "The Olmec Style and its Distribution," in *Archaeology of Southern Mesoamerica*, Part 2, ed. G.R. Willey. *Handbook of Middle American Indians*, Vol.3, gen. ed. R. Wauchope, 739–75, Austin 1965.

— *America's First Civilization: Discovering the Olmec*. New York 1968.

— "Early steps in the evolution of Maya writing," in *Origins of Religious Art and Iconography in Preclassic Mesoamerica*, ed. H.B. Nicholson, 107–22. Los Angeles 1976.

— "Olmec and Maya: a study in relationships," in *The Origins of Maya Civilization*, ed. R.E.W. Adams, 183–96. Albuquerque 1977.

— "The Olmec heartland: evolution of ideology," in *Regional Perspectives on the Olmec*. ed. R.J. Sharer, and D.C. Grove, 68–82. Cambridge: ?

— March 19, 2002 "Deciphering Isthmian inscriptions," *The Times Literary Supplement* p.17. London 1989.

COE, MICHAEL D., AND RICHARD A. DIEHL *In the Land of the Olmec*, 2 vols. Austin 1980.

COE, MICHAEL D., AND LOUIS A. FERNANDEZ "Appendix 2: petrographic analysis of rock samples from San Lorenzo," in *In the Land of the Olmec* Vol.1, M.D. Coe and R.A. Diehl, 307–404. Austin 1980.

COE, SOPHIE D. *America's First Cuisines*. Austin 1994.

COVARRUBIAS, MIGUEL "Origen y Desarrollo del estilo artístico "Olmeca", in *Mayas y Olmecas: Segunda Reunión de Mesa Redonda Sobre Problemas Antropológicos de México y Centro América*, 46– 49. Tuxtla Gutiérrez 1942.

— *Mexico South: The Isthmus of Tehuantepec.* New York 1946.

— *Indian Art of Mexico and Central America.* New York 1957.

CYPHERS, ANN "From stone to symbols: Olmec art in social context at San Lorenzo Tenochtitlán," in *Social Patterns in Pre-Classic Mesoamerica*, ed. D.C. Grove and R.A. Joyce, 155–81. Washington 1999.

— (ed.) 1997 *Población, Subsistencia y Medio Ambiente en San Lorenzo Tenochtitlán.* Mexico City: ?

DE LA FUENTE, BEATRIZ *Escultura Monumental Olmeca.* Mexico City 1973.

— *Los Hombres de Piedra: Escultura Olmeca.* Mexico City 1984.

— *Cabezas Colosales Olmecas.* Mexico 1992.

— "Homocentrism in Olmec monumental art," in *Olmec Art in Ancient Mexico*, ed. E.P. Benson and B. de la Fuente, 41–49. Washington 1996.

DIAZ DEL CASTILLO, BERNAL. *The Discovery and Conquest of Mexico*, transl. A.P. Maudslay. New York 1956.

DIEHL, RICHARD A. "Olmec architecture: a comparison of San Lorenzo and La Venta," in *The Olmec and Their Neighbors: Essays in Memory of Matthew W. Stirling*, ed. E.P. Benson, 69–81. Washington 1981.

— "Olmec Religion," in *The Encyclopedia of Religion*, ed. Mircea Eliade, 65–68, Vol.11. New York 1987.

— "Olmec archaeology: what we know and what we wish we knew," in *Regional Perspectives on the Olmec*, eds. R.J. Sharer and D.C. Grove, 17–32. Cambridge 1989.

— "The Precolumbian cultures of the Gulf Coast," in *The Cambridge History of the Native Peoples of the Americas* Vol.2, *Mesoamerica* Part 2, eds. R.E.W. Adams and M. MacLeod, 156–96. Cambridge 2000.

— "Were the Olmecs African?," in *The Seventy Great Mysteries of the Ancient World*, ed. B. Fagan, 171–72, London and New York 2002.

DIEHL, RICHARD A., AND MICHAEL D. COE. "Olmec archaeology," in *The Olmec World: Ritual and Rulership*, ed. J. Guthrie, 11–25. Princeton 1995.

DIEHL, RICHARD A., ALFREDO VARGAS GONZÁLEZ, AND SERGIO VÁSQUEZ ZÁRATE. "Proyecto arqueológico La Mojarra," in *Memoria del Coloquio Arqueología del centro y sur de Veracruz*, eds. S.L. de Guevara González and S.V. Zárate, 197–210. Xalapa, Veracruz, Mexico 1997.

DRUCKER, PHILIP. "On the nature of Olmec polity," in *The Olmec and Their Neighbors: Essays in Memory of Matthew W. Stirling*, ed. E.P. Benson, 27–47. Washington 1981.

— "La Venta, Tabasco: a study in Olmec ceramics and art," *Bureau of American Ethnology Bulletin* no.153. Washington 1952.

DRUCKER, PHILIP, ROBERT F. HEIZER, AND ROBERT J.

SQUIER. "Excavations at La Venta, Tabasco, 1955," *Bureau of American Ethnology Bulletin* no.170. Washington, DC 1957.

ENGELBACH, REGINALD. *The problem of the Obelisks, from a Study of the Unfinished Obelisk at Aswan.* New York 1923.

FASH, WILLIAM L. *Scribes, Warriors and Kings: The City of Copan and the Ancient Maya.* London and New York 1991.

FLANNERY, KENT V., AND JOYCE MARCUS "Early Formative pottery of the Valley of Oaxaca, Mexico," *Memoirs of the Museum of Anthropology, University of Michigan* no.27. Ann Arbor 1994.

— "Formative Mexican chiefdoms and the myth of the 'Mother Culture'," *Journal of Anthropological Archaeology* Vol.19: 1–37. 2000.

FOWLER JR., WILLIAM (ed.). *Formation of Complex Society in Southeastern Mesoamerica.* Boca Raton, Fl. 1991.

FREIDEL, DAVID A. "Preparing the way," in *The Olmec World: Ritual and Rulership*, ed. J. Guthrie, 3–9. Princeton 1995.

FREIDEL, DAVID, LINDA SCHELE, AND JOY PARKER. *Maya Cosmos: Three Thousand Years on the Shaman's Path.* New York 1993.

FURST, PETER T. "The Olmec were-jaguar motif in the light of ethnographic reality," in *Dumbarton Oaks Conference on the Olmec*, ed. E.P. Benson, 143–78. Washington 1968.

— "Shamanism, transformation, and Olmec art," in *The Olmec World: Ritual and Rulership*, ed. J Guthrie. Princeton University 1995.

GALLEGOS GÓMARA, MIRIAM JUDITH. "Excavaciones en la Estructura D-7 en La Venta, Tabasco," *Arqueología* 3: 17–24. enero–junio 1990.

GARCÍA MOLL, ROBERTO, *et al. Catálogo de Entierros de San Luis Tlatilco, México,* Temporada IV. Mexico 1991.

GAY, CARLO T.E. "Oldest paintings in the New World," *Natural History* Vol.76, no.4: 28–35. 1967.

GILLESPIE, SUSAN D. "Llano del Jícaro: an Olmec monument workshop," *Ancient Mesoamerica* Vol.5: 231–42. 1994.

— "The Monuments of Laguna de los Cerros and its Hinterland," in *Olmec Art and Archaeology in Mesoamerica*, eds. J.E. Clark and M.E. Pye, 95–115. New Haven and London 2000.

GÓMEZ RUEDA, HERNANDO. "Las Limas, Veracruz, y otros asentamientos prehispánicos de la región olmeca," *Colección Científica* no.324. Mexico 1996.

GÓMEZ RUEDA, HECTOR, AND VALERIE COURTÉS. "Un pectoral olmeca de La Encrucijada, Tabasco: Observaciones sobre piezas menores olmecas," *Arqueología* 1: 73–88. 1987.

GONZÁLEZ LAUCK, REBECCA. "Proyecto Arqueológico La Venta," *Arqueología* 4: 121–65. 1988.

— "Acerca de pirámides de tierra y seres sobrenaturales: observaciones preliminares en torno al Edificio C-1, La Venta, Tabasco," *Arqueología* 17 (segunda época): 79–97. enero-junio 1997.

— "La Venta: an Olmec capital," in *Olmec Art of Ancient Mexico*, eds. E.P. Benson and B. de la Fuente, 73–81. Washington 1996.

GONZÁLEZ LAUCK, REBECCA, AND FELIPE SOLÍS OLGUÍN. "Olmec collections in the museums of Tabasco: a century of protecting a millennial civilization (1896–1996)," in *Olmec Art of Ancient Mexico*, eds. E.P. Benson and B. de la Fuente, 145–52. Washington 1996.

GRAHAM, JOHN. "Maya, Olmecs and Izapans at Abaj Takalik," *Actes du XLII Congres International des Americanistes* Vol.8: 179–88. 1979.

GRAHAM, JOHN. "Olmec diffusion: a sculptural view from Pacific Guatemala," in *Regional Perspectives on the Olmec*, eds. R.J. Sharer and D.C. Grove, 227–46. Cambridge 1989.

GRAHAM, MARK M. "Mesoamerican jade and Costa Rica," in *Jade in Ancient Costa Rica*, ed. J. Jones, 59–91. New York 1998.

GRIFFIN, GILLETT G. "Formative Guerrero and its jade," in *Precolumbian Jade: New Geological and Cultural Interpretations*, ed. F.W. Lange, 204–10. Salt Lake City 1993.

GROVE, DAVID C. "The Olmec paintings of Oxtotitlán Cave, Guerrero, Mexico," *Studies in Pre-Columbian Art and Archaeology* no.6. Washington 1970.

— "San Pablo Nexpa and the Early Formative archaeology of Morelos, Mexico," *Vanderbilt University Publications in Anthropology* 12. Nashville 1974.

— *Chalcatzingo: Excavations on the Olmec Frontier*. London 1984.

— (ed.). *Ancient Chalcatzingo*. Austin 1987.

— "'Olmec' horizons in Formative Period Mesoamerica: diffusion or social evolution?," in *Latin American Horizons*, ed. D.S. Rice, 83–111. Washington 1993.

— "Archaeological contexts of Olmec art outside of the Gulf Coast," in *Olmec Art of Ancient Mexico*, eds. E.P. Benson and B. de la Fuente, 105–17. Washington 1996.

— "Public monuments and sacred mountains: observations on three Formative Period landscapes," in *Social Patterns in Pre-Classic Mesoamerica*, ed. D.C. Grove and R.A. Joyce, 255–99. Washington 1999.

— "The Preclassic societies of the central highlands of Mesoamerica," in *The Cambridge History of the Native Peoples of the Americas* Vol.2, *Mesoamerica*, Part 1, eds. R.E.W. Adams and M.J. MacLeod, 122–55. Cambridge 2000.

GROVE, DAVID C. AND ROSEMARY A. JOYCE (eds.). *Social Patterns in Pre-Classic Mesoamerica*. Washington 1999.

GROVE, DAVID C., AND LOUISE I. PARADIS. "An Olmec stela from San Miguel Amuco, Guerrero," *American Antiquity* 36, 1: 95–102. 1971.

GUTHRIE, JILL. (ed.). *The Olmec World: Ritual and Rulership*. Princeton 1995.

GULLBERG, JONAS E. "Technical notes on concave mirrors," in P. Drucker, R.F. Heizer, and R.J. Squier "Excavations at La Venta, Tabasco, 1955," *Bureau of American Ethnology Bulletin*, no.170: 280–83. Washington, DC 1957.

HAMMOND, NORMAN. "The origins of Maya civilization – the beginnings of village life," in *Maya: Divine Kings of the Rain Forest*, ed. N. Grube, 34–47. Cologne 2000.

HATCH, MARION POPENOE. "An hypothesis on Olmec astronomy, with special reference to the La Venta site," in *Papers on Olmec and Maya Archaeology*, Contributions of the University of California Archaeological Research Facility 13:1–64. Berkeley 1971.

HEALY, PAUL. "The Cuyamel Caves: Preclassic sites in northeast Honduras," *American Antiquity* Vol.39, no.3: 435–47. 1974.

HEIZER, ROBERT F. "New observations on La Venta," in *Dumbarton Oaks Conference on the Olmec*, ed. E.P. Benson, 9–40. Washington 1968.

HEIZER, ROBERT F., AND JONAS E. GULLBERG. "Concave mirrors from the site of La Venta, Tabasco: their occurrence, mineralogy, optical description, and function," in *The Olmec and Their Neighbors: Essays in Memory of Matthew W. Stirling*, ed. E.P. Benson, 109–16. Washington 1981.

HENDERSON, JOHN S. "Atopula, Guerrero, and the Olmec horizons in Mesoamerica," *Yale University Publications in Anthropology* no.77. New Haven 1977.

HILL, WARREN D., MICHAEL BLAKE, AND JOHN E. CLARK. "Ball court design dates back 3,400 years," *Nature* 392: 878–79. 30 April 1998.

HOLMES, WILLIAM H. "On a Nephrite statuette from San Andres Tuxtla, Vera Cruz, Mexico," *American Anthropologist* 9: 691–701. 1907.

HONAN, WILLIAM H. "History of medical art gets Pre-Columbian chapter," *The New York Times*, p. D5. August 22, 2000.

JOESINK-MANDEVILLE, LEROY V. "Comayagua Valley," in *Pottery of Prehistoric Honduras: Regional Classification and Analysis*, ed. J.S. Henderson and M. Beaudry-Corbett, 235–47. Los Angeles 1993.

JIMÉNEZ SALAS, OSCAR H. "Geomorfología de la región de La Venta, Tabasco: un sistema fluvio-lagunar costero de cuaternario," *Arqueología* 3: 5–16. enero-junio 1990.

JONES, JULIE (ed.). *Jade in Ancient Costa Rica*. New York 1998.

JORALEMON, PETER DAVID. "A study in Olmec iconography," *Studies in Pre-Columbian Art and Archaeology* 7. Washington 1971.
— "The Olmec Dragon: a study in Olmec iconography," in *Origins of Religious Art and Iconography in Preclassic Mesoamerica*, ed. H.B. Nicholson, 27–71. Los Angeles 1976.
— "In search of the Olmec cosmos: reconstructing the world view of Mexico's first civilization," in *Olmec Art of Ancient Mexico*, ed. E.P. Benson and B. de la Fuente, 51–59. Washington 1996.
— "An incised bowl from Tlapacoya in the Barbier-Mueller collection," *Arts and Cultures* 2: no pagination. Museé Barbíer-Mueller, Geneva 2001.
JOYCE, ROSEMARY A. "Burying the dead at Tlatilco: social memory and social identities," in *Social Memory, Identity, and Death: Anthropological Perspectives on Mortuary Rituals*, ed. M.S. Chesson 12–26. Arlington, VA 2001.
JOYCE, ROSEMARY A. "Innovation, communication, and the archaeological record: a reassessment of Middle Formative Honduras," *Journal of the Steward Anthropological Society* Vol.20, nos 1 & 2: 235–56. 1992.
JOYCE, ROSEMARY A., AND JOHN S. HENDERSON "Beginnings of village life in Eastern Mesoamerica," *Latin American Antiquity* Vol.12, no.1: 5–24. 2001.
JUSTESON, JOHN S., AND TERRENCE KAUFMAN. "A decipherment of Epi-Olmec hieroglyphic writing," *Science* Vol.259: 1703–11. 19 March, 1993.
KAUFMANN, TERRENCE, AND JOHN JUSTESON *Epi-Olmec Hieroglyphic Writing and Texts*. Austin, Texas 2001.
KILLION, THOMAS W., AND JAVIER URCID. "The Olmec legacy: cultural continuity on Mexico's southern Gulf Coast," unpublished ms. 2002.
KRUGER, ROBERT P. *An Archaeological Survey in the Region of the Olmec, Veracruz, Mexico*. Unpublished Ph.D. dissertation, Pittsburgh n.d.
LANGE, FREDERICK (ed.). *Precolumbian Jade: New Geological and Cultural Interpretations*. Salt Lake City 1993.
LEE, JR., THOMAS A. "Chiapas and the Olmec," in *Regional Perspectives on the Olmec*, eds. R.J. Sharer and D.C. Grove, 198–226. Cambridge 1989.
LESURE, RICHARD G. "Early Formative platforms at Paso de la Amada, Chiapas, Mexico," *Latin American Antiquity* Vol.8, no.3: 217–35. September 1997.
— "Figurines and social identities in early sedentary societies of coastal Chiapas, Mexico, 1550–800 BC," in *Women in Prehistory: North America and Mesoamerica*, eds. C. Claassen and R.A. Joyce, 227–50. Philadelphia 1997.
LOVE, MICHAEL W. "Style and social complexity in Formative Mesoamerica," in *The Formation of*

Complex Society in Southeastern Mesoamerica, ed. W.R. Fowler, Jr., 47–76. Boca Raton 1991.
— "Ideology, material culture, and daily practice in Pre-Classic Mesoamerica: a Pacific Coast perspective," in *Social Patterns in Pre-Classic Mesoamerica*, eds. C. Grove and R.A. Joyce, 127–53. Washington, DC 1999.
LUCKERT, KARL W. *Olmec Religion: A Key to Middle America and Beyond*. Norman 1976.
MALMSTROM, VINCENT H. *Cycles of the Sun, Mysteries of the Moon: The Calendar in Mesoamerican Civilization*. Austin, Texas 1997.
MARCUS, JOYCE "Women's ritual in Formative Oaxaca: figurine-making, divination, death and the ancestors," *Memoirs of the Museum of Anthropology, University of Michigan* no.33. Ann Arbor 1998.
MARCUS, JOYCE, AND KENT V. FLANNERY *Zapotec Civilization: How Urban Society Evolved in Mexico's Oaxaca Valley*. London 1996.
MARTÍNEZ DONJUÁN, GUADALUPE. "Los olmecas en el estado de Guerrero," in *Los Olmecas en Mesoamérica*, ed. John E. Clark, 143–63. Mexico 1994.
MEDELLÍN ZENIL, ALFONSO. "Monolitos inéditos olmecas," *La Palabra y el Hombre* Vol.16: 75–97. 1960.
— "La Escultura de las Limas," *Boletín del Instituto Nacional de Antropología e Historia* no.21: 5–8. 1965.
MELGAR Y SERRANO, JOSÉ MARÍA. "Antigüedades Mexicanas," *Boletín de la Sociedad Mexicana de Geografía y Estadística*, época 2, vol.1: 292–97. 1869.
MELUZÍN, SYLVIA "The Tuxtla script: steps toward decipherment based on La Mojarra Stela 1," *Latin American Antiquity* 3: 283–97. 1992.
MORRISON, FRANK, C. W. CLEWLOW, JR., AND ROBERT F. HEIZER. "Magnetometer survey of the La Venta pyramid, 1969," in *Contributions to the University of California Archaeological Research Facility*, no.8: 2–20. June, 1970.
NEFF, HECTOR, AND MICHAEL D. GLASCOCK. "Instrumental neutron activation analysis of Olmec pottery," unpublished ms. n.d.
NIEDERBERGER, CHRISTINE. "Zohapilco: cinco milenios de ocupación humana en un sitio Lacustre de la Cuenca de México," *Colección Científica* 30. Mexico 1976.
— *Paleopaysages et Archeologie Pre-Urbaine du Bassin de Mexico* (2 vols.). Mexico 1987.
— "The Basin of Mexico: a multimillennial development toward cultural complexity," in *Olmec Art of Ancient Mexico*, eds. E.P. Benson and B. de la Fuente, 83–93. Washington 1996.
— "Olmec horizon Guerrero," in *Olmec Art of Ancient Mexico*, eds. E.P. Benson and B. de la Fuente, 95–103. Washington 1996.
— "Ranked societies, iconographic complexity, and economic wealth in the Basin of Mexico toward

1200 BC," in *Olmec Art and Archaeology in Mesoamerica*, eds. J.E. Clark and M.E. Pye, 161–91. New York and London 2000.

ORTIZ PÉREZ, MARIO ARTURO, AND ANN CYPHERS "La geomorfología y las evidencias arqueológicas en la región de San Lorenzo Tenochtitlán, Veracruz," in *Población, Subsistencia y Medio Ambiente en San Lorenzo Tenochtitlán*, ed. A. Cyphers, 31–53. Mexico City 1997.

ORTIZ, PONCIANO, AND MARÍA DEL CARMEN RODRÍGUEZ "The sacred hill of Manatí: a preliminary discussion of the site's ritual paraphernalia," in *Olmec Art and Archaeology in Mesoamerica*, eds. J.E. Clark and M.E. Pye, 75–93. New York and London 2000.

PARADIS, LOUISE ISEUT. "Guerrero and the Olmec," in *The Olmec and Their Neighbors: Essays in Memory of Matthew W. Stirling*, ed. E.P. Benson, 195–208. Washington 1981.

PASZTORY, ESTHER. *Pre-Columbian Art*. Cambridge 1998.

— "The portrait and the mask: invention and translation," in *Olmec Art and Archaeology in Mesoamerica*, eds. J.E. Clark and M.E. Pye, 265–75. New Haven and London 2000.

PIÑA CHAN, ROMÁN. *Tlatilco* (2 vols.). Mexico 2000.

— *The Olmec: Mother Culture of Mesoamerica* (ed. Laura Laurencich Minelli). New York 1989.

PIÑA CHAN, ROMÁN, AND VALENTIN LÓPEZ. "Excavaciones in Atlihuayán, Morelos," *Tlatoani* 1: 1. 1952.

PIÑA CHAN, ROMÁN, AND LUIS COVARRUBIAS. *El Pueblo del Jaguar*. Mexico 1964.

PÉREZ SUÁREZ, TOMÁS. "The Maya and their Olmec neighbors," in *Maya*, eds. P. Schmidt, M. de la Garza and E. Nalda, 73–83. New York 1998.

POHL, MARY E.D., KEVIN O. POPE, AND CHRISTOPHER VON NAGY. "Olmec origins of Mesoamerican writing," *Science* 298: 1984–87. 6 December 2002.

POHORILENKO, ANATOLE. "The Olmec style and Costa Rican archaeology," in *The Olmec and Their Neighbors*, ed. E.P. Benson, 309–27. Washington 1981.

POHORILENKO, ANATOLE. "Portable carvings in the Olmec style," in *Olmec Art of Ancient Mexico*, eds. E.P. Benson and B. de la Fuente, 119–31. Washington 1996.

POOL, CHRISTOPHER A. "The spatial structure of Formative houselots at Bezuapan," in *Olmec to Aztec: Settlement Patterns in the Ancient Gulf Lowlands*, eds. B.L. Stark and P.J. Arnold III, 40–67. Tucson 1997.

— "From Olmec to Epi-Olmec at Tres Zapotes, Veracruz, Mexico," in *Olmec Art and Archaeology in Mesoamerica*, eds. J.E. Clark and M.E. Pye, 137–53. New Haven and London 2000.

POPE, KEVIN O., *et al.* "Origin and environmental setting of ancient agriculture in the lowlands of Mesoamerica," *Science* Vol.292: 1370–73. May 1, 2001.

PORTER, JAMES B. "Olmec colossal heads as recarved thrones: "mutilation," revolution, and recarving," *RES* 17/18: 23–29. 1989.

PORTER, MURIEL NOE. *Tlatilco and the Pre-Classic Cultures of the New World*. New York 1953.

PYE, MARY E., AND JOHN E. CLARK. "Introducing Olmec archaeology," in *Olmec Art and Archaeology in Mesoamerica*, eds. J.E. Clark and M.E. Pye, 9–17. New York and London 2000.

PYE, MARY E., AND ARTHUR A. DEMAREST. "The evolution of complex societies in southeastern Mesoamerica: new evidence from El Mezak, Guatemala," in *The Formation of Complex Society in Southeastern Mesoamerica*, ed. W.R. Fowler, Jr., 77–100. Boca Raton 1991.

RAAB, L. MARK, MATTHEW A. BOXT, KATHERINE BRADFORD, BRIAN STOKES, AND REBECCA B. GONZÁLEZ LAUCK. "Testing at Isla Alor in the La Venta Olmec hinterland," *Journal of Field Archaeology* Vol.27, no.3: 257–70. Fall 2000.

REILLY, III, F. KENT. "Art, ritual and rulership in the Olmec world," in *The Olmec World: Ritual and Rulership*, ed. J. Guthrie, 27–46. Princeton 1995.

— "Mountains of creation and underworld portals: the ritual function of Olmec architecture at La Venta, Tabasco," in *Mesoamerican Architecture as a Cultural Symbol*, ed. J.K. Kowalski, 14–39. Oxford 1999.

— "The landscape of creation: architecture, tomb, and monument placement at the Olmec site of La Venta," in *Heart of Creation: The Mesoamerican World and the Legacy of Linda Schele*, ed. A. Stone, 34–65. Tuscaloosa, Al 2002.

RODRÍGUEZ, MARÍA DEL CARMEN, AND PONCIANO ORTIZ. "A massive offering of axes at La Merced, Hidalgotitlán, Veracruz, Mexico," in *Olmec Art and Archaeology in Mesoamerica*, ed. J.E. Clark and M.E. Pye, 155–67. New York and London 2000.

ROMANO, ARTURO "Tlatilco," *Boletín del INAH* época 1, no.30: 28–42. 1967.

RUST, WILLIAM. "New ceremonial and settlement evidence at La Venta and its relation to Preclassic Maya cultures," in *New Theories on the Ancient Maya*, eds. E.C. Danien and R.J. Sharer. Philadelphia 1992.

RUST, WILLIAM, AND ROBERT J. SHARER "Olmec settlement data from La Venta, Tabasco, Mexico," *Science* Vol.242: 102–04. 7 October 1988.

RUST, WILLIAM F., AND BARBARA F. LEYDEN. "Evidence of maize use at Early and Middle Preclassic La Venta Olmec sites," in *Corn and Culture in the Prehistoric New World*, ed. S.

Johannessen and C. Hastorf, 181–201. Boulder, Colorado 1994.

SAHAGÚN, BERNARDINO DE *The Florentine Codex: General History of the Things of New Spain*, ed. and transl. C.E. Dibble and A.J.O. Anderson, Book 10. Santa Fe, New Mexico 1961.

SANDERS, WILLIAM T., AND DAVID WEBSTER. "The Mesoamerican urban tradition," *American Anthropologist* Vol.90, no.3: 521–46. September, 1988.

SANTLEY, ROBERT S. "A consideration of the Olmec phenomenon in the Tuxtlas: Early Formative settlement pattern land use and refuse disposal at Matacapan, Veracruz, Mexico," in *Gardens of Prehistory: The Archaeology of Settlement Agriculture in Greater Mesoamerica*, ed. T.W. Killion, 150–83. Tuscaloosa, Alabama 1992.

SANTLEY, ROBERT S., AND PHILIP J. ARNOLD III. "Prehispanic settlement patterns in the Tuxtla mountains, southern Veracruz, Mexico," *Journal of Field Archaeology*, 23: 225–59. 1996.

SANTLEY, ROBERT, PHILIP J. ARNOLD III, AND THOMAS P. BARRETT. "Formative period settlement patterns in the Tuxtla mountains," in *Olmec to Aztec: Settlement Patterns in the Ancient Gulf Lowlands*, eds. B.L. Stark and P.J. Arnold III, 174–205. Tucson 1997.

SCHELE, LINDA. "The Olmec mountain and Tree of Creation in Mesoamerican cosmology," in *The Olmec World: Ritual and Rulership*, ed. J Guthrie, 105–17. Princeton 1996.

SCHMIDT SCHOENBERG, PAUL. *Arqueología de Xochipala, Guerrero*. Mexico 1990.

SCOTT, SUE. "Teotihuacan Mazapan figurines and the Xipe Totec statue: a link between the Basin of Mexico and the Valley of Oaxaca," *Vanderbilt University Publications in Anthropology* Vol.44. Nashville 1993.

SEITZ, ROBERT J., G. E. HARLOW, V. B. SISSON, AND KARL E. TAUBE. "'Olmec Blue' and Formative jade sources: new discoveries in Guatemala," *Antiquity* 75: 687–88. 2001.

SHARER, ROBERT (ed.). *The Prehistory of Chalchuapa, El Salvador* (3 vols.). Philadelphia 1978.

SHARER, ROBERT J., AND DAVID C. GROVE (eds.). *Regional Perspectives on the Olmec*. Cambridge 1989.

SHOOK, EDWIN M. AND ROBERT F. HEIZER "An Olmec sculpture from the south (Pacific) coast of Guatemala," *Journal of New Word Archaeology* Vol.1, no.3, 1–8. 1976.

SISSON, EDWARD B. "Settlement patterns and land use in the northwestern Chontalpa, Tabasco, Mexico: a progress report," *Cerámica de Cultura Maya* Vol.6: 41–54. 1970.

SMITH. A. LEDYARD. "Major architecture and caches," in Peabody Museum Memoirs Vol.15, no.1,

Excavations at Seibal, Department of Peten, Guatemala. Cambridge 1982.

SOUSTELLE, JACQUES. *The Olmecs: The Oldest Civilization in Mexico*. Garden City 1984.

STARK, BARBARA L. AND PHILLIP J. ARNOLD III (eds.). *Olmec to Aztec: Settlement Patterns in the Ancient Gulf Lowlands*. Tucson 1997.

STIRLING, MATTHEW W. "Discovering the New World's oldest dated work of Man," *National Geographic Magazine* 76: 183–218. 1939.

— "An initial series from Tres Zapotes, Vera Cruz, Mexico," *National Geographic Society, Contributed Technical Papers, Mexican Archaeology Series*, 1: 1. 1940.

— "Expedition unearths buried masterpieces of carved jade," *National Geographic Magazine* 80: 278–302. 1941.

— "Stone monuments of southern Mexico," *Smithsonian Institution Bureau of American Ethnology Bulletin* 138. Washington 1943.

— "On the trail of La Venta man," *National Geographic Magazine* 91: 137–72. 1947.

— "Stone monuments of the Rio Chiquito, Veracruz, Mexico," *Smithsonian Institution Bureau of American Ethnology Bulletin* 157. Washington 1955.

STUART, GEORGE E. "The carved stela from La Mojarra, Veracruz, Mexico," *Science* Vol.259: 1700–01. 19 March 1993.

SYMONDS, STACY, ANN CYPHERS, AND ROBERTO LUNAGÓMEZ *Asentamiento Prehispánico en San Lorenzo Tenochtitlán*. Mexico City 2002.

TAUBE, KARL. *Olmec Art at Dumbarton Oaks*. Washington 2003.

— "The Olmec Maize God: the face of corn in Formative Mesoamerica," *RES* Vol.29/30: 39–82. Spring/Autumn 1996.

— "The Rainmakers: the Olmec and their contribution to Mesoamerican belief and ritual," in *The Olmec World: Ritual and Rulership*, ed. J. Guthrie, 83–103. Princeton 1996.

— "Lightning celts and corn fetishes: the Formative Olmec and the development of maize symbolism in Mesoamerica and the American southwest," in *Olmec Art and Archaeology in Mesoamerica*, eds. J.E. Clark and M.E. Pye, 297–337. Washington 2000.

TEDLOCK, DENNIS (transl.). *Popol Vuh: The Definitive Edition of the Mayan Book of the Dawn of Life and the Glories of Gods and Kings*. New York 1985.

THOMPSON, J. ERIC S. "Dating of certain inscriptions of non-Maya origins," in *Carnegie Institution of Washington: Theoretical Approaches to Problems* Vol.1. Washington, DC 1941.

TOLSTOY, PAUL. "Western Mesoamerica and the Olmec," in *Regional Perspectives on the Olmec*, eds. R.J. Sharer and D.C. Grove, 275–302. Cambridge 1989.

— "Coapexco and Tlatilco: sites with Olmec materials in the Basin of Mexico," in *Regional Perspectives on the Olmec*, eds. R.J. Sharer and D.C. Grove, 85–121. Cambridge 1989.

TOLSTOY, PAUL, AND LOUISE PARADIS "Early and Middle Preclassic culture in the Basin of Mexico," *Science* 167: 344–51. 1970.

TOLSTOY, PAUL, SUSAN K. FISH, MARTIN W. BOKSENBAUM, KATHRYN BLAIR VAUGHN, AND C. EARLE SMITH, JR. "Early sedentary communities in the Basin of Mexico: a summary of recent investigations," *Journal of Field Archaeology* 4: 92–106. 1977.

VAILLANT, SUSANNAH B., AND GEORGE C. VAILLANT. "Excavations at Gualupita," *Anthropological Papers of the American Museum of Natural History* 35: 1. New York 1934.

VAN SERTIMA, IVAN. *They Came before Columbus: The African Presence in Ancient America*. New York 1976.

VELSON, JOSEPH F., AND THOMAS C. CLARK. "Transport of stone monuments to the La Venta and San Lorenzo sites," *Contributions of the University of California Archaeological Research Facility* no.24: 1–39. 1975.

VILLELA F., SAMUEL L. "Nuevo testimonio rupestre olmeca en el oriente de Guerrero," *Arqueología* 2: 19–36. julio-diciembre 1989.

VON NAGY, CHRISTOPHER "The geoarchaeology of settlement in the Grijalva Delta," in *Olmec to Aztec: Settlement Patterns in the Ancient Gulf Lowlands*, eds.

B.L. Stark and P.J. Arnold III, 253–77. Tucson 1997.

VON NAGY, CHRISTOPHER, MARY D. POHL, AND KEVIN O. POPE. "Ceramic chronology of the La Venta Olmec polity: the view from San Andrés, Tabasco," Society for American Archaeology annual meeting, unpublished ms. 2002.

VOORHIES, BARBARA (ed.). *Ancient Trade and Tribute: Economies of the Soconusco Region of Mesoamerica.*, Salt Lake City 1989.

WAUCHOPE, ROBERT. "A tentative sequence of Pre-Classic ceramics in Middle America," in *Tulane University: Middle American Records* Vol.1, 211–50. New Orleans 1950.

WESTHEIMER, DAVID. *The Olmec Head*. New York 1974.

WICKE, CHARLES W. *Olmec: An Early Art Style of Precolumbian Mexico*. Tucson 1971.

WICHMANN, SORIN. *The Relationship Among the Mixe-Zoquean Languages of Mexico*. Salt Lake City 1995.

— "A conservative look at diffusion involving Mixe-Zoquean languages," in *Archaeology and Language II: Archaeological Data and Linguistic Hypotheses*, eds. R Blench and M. Spriggs, 297–323. London 2002.

WINFIELD CAPITAINE, FERNANDO. "La Estela 1 de La Mojarra, Veracruz, Mexico," *Research Reports on Ancient Maya Writing* 16. Washington 1998.

WINTER, MARCUS. "Los Altos de Oaxaca y los olmecas," in *Los Olmecas en Mesoamerica*, ed. J.E. Clark, 119–41. Mexico 1994.

Sources of Illustrations

Colour plates
I Kenneth Garrett; II Kenneth Garrett; III Felipe Dávalos; IV Felipe Dávalos; V Kenneth Garrett; VI National Geographic/Richard H. Stewart; VII Colin McEwan; VIII Kenneth Garrett; IX Kenneth Garrett; X Felipe Dávalos/ Dumbarton Oaks Pre-Columbian Collection, Washington, DC; XI Justin Kerr; XII Dallas Museum of Art (gift of Mrs Eugene McDermott, The Roberta Coke Camp Fund and the Art Museum League Fund); XIII Citibank/Mexico; XIV Kenneth Garrett; XV Jorge Pérez de Lara; XVI Justin Kerr; XVII Dumbarton Oaks, Pre-Columbian Collection, Washington, DC; XVIII Justin Kerr; XIX Justin Kerr; XX Kenneth Garrett

In-text illustrations
(l left; m middle; r right)
American Museum of Natural History 80, 115, 118; Francisco Beverido 4; T. Carmona 60 l; Citibank/

Mexico 13, 21, 24–26, 31, 48, 73, 75r, 88, 104, 106, 108, 114, 116, 123; Michael D. Coe 7, 16, 19, 46, 103, 120; Felipe Dávalos 17, 18, 65–66, 68, 71 (l, mr, r), 78, 121; Richard A. Diehl 5, 23, 45; Dumbarton Oaks, Pre-Columbian Collection, Washington, DC 42, 69, 83–84, 87; Kenneth Garrett 6, 9, 22, 67, 119; Justin Kerr 82, 85, 113; David Lentz 8; Metropolitan Museum of Art 112, 117; Middle American Research Institute, Tulane University 100; Ayax Moreno 60 r; National Gallery of Art, Washington, DC 39, 44, 92; National Geographic/Richard H. Stewart 3; Jorge Pérez de Lara 35, 37, 70; Ponciano Ortíz 10; Photo © Great Temple Project, Mexico City frontispiece; Doug Shinholster 14, 27, 29, 30, 33–34, 36, 38, 40–41, 43, 47, 49–59, 61–64, 71 ml, 72, 74, 75l, 76–77, 79, 81, 86, 89–91, 93–99, 105, 107, 109–11, 122, 125–131; University of Alabama Cartography Lab 1, 2, 11, 12, 15, 20, 28, 32, 101–02, 124

Index